Applied Artificial Intelligence and Machine Learning Techniques for Engineering Applications

This book presents various machine learning applications in the field of engineering with a focus on deep learning-based machine learning approaches. It examines the relationship between three different multidisciplinary engineering branches: biomedical engineering, signal processing, and computer science.

Applied Artificial Intelligence and Machine Learning Techniques for Engineering Applications explores recent advancements in the use of AI/ML in practical engineering applications by inviting top experts to share the outcomes of their most recent work. Among the topics explored are detection, measurement, and monitoring of signals (biosensors and biomedical devices) and the use of diagnostic interpretations of bioelectric data using signal-processing techniques. The authors also address several machine learning tasks, such as classification (supervised learning) and clustering (unsupervised learning), in the context of engineering. Finally, the book also describes the development of new biomaterials for use in the body.

The book will be a great help to researchers and academics working in the fields of biomedical signaling and/or human-machine interface.

Materials, Devices, and Circuits: Design and Reliability

Series Editor: Shubham Tayal, K. K. Paliwal, Amit Kumar Jainy

This series is designed to illustrate the many new and exciting challenges in the expansive and interdisciplinary field of materials science, device engineering, reliability, device-circuit co-design and their applications. The scope of this series is broad, with reference works and textbooks offering insight into all aspects of materials development, device fabrication, circuit analysis and their reliability. The titles in this series deliver authoritative information to professionals, researchers, and students across material and device engineering as well as other scientific disciplines. Each volume offers a comprehensive approach covering fundamentals, technologies, their evolution advancements and applications and includes real-world examples where appropriate.

Applied Artificial Intelligence and Machine Learning Techniques for Engineering Applications
Edited by Ravichander Janapati, Usha Desai, Steven Fernandes, Rakesh Sengupta, and Shubham Tayal

Advancing VLSI through Machine Learning
Edited by Abhishek Narayan Tripathi, Jagana Bihari Padhy, Indrasen Singh, Shubham Tayal, and Ghanshyam Singh

Tunneling Field Effect Transistors
Design, Modeling and Applications
Edited by T.S. Arun Samuel, Young Suh Song, Shubham Tayal, P. Vimala, and Shiromani Balmukund Rahi

Quantum-Dot Cellular Automata Circuits for Nanocomputing Applications
Edited by Trailokya Sasamal, Hari Mohan Gaur, Ashutosh Kumar Singh, and Xiaoqing Wen

Device Circuit Co-Design Issues in FETs
Edited by Shubham Tayal, Billel Smaani, Shiromani Balmukund Rahi, Samir Labiod, and Zeinab Ramezani

Human-Machine Interface Technology Advancements and Applications
Edited by Ravichander Janapati, Usha Desai, Shrirang Ambaji Kulkarni, and Shubham Tayal

Negative Capacitance Field Effect Transistors: Physics, Design, Modeling and Applications
Edited by Young Suh Song, Shubham Tayal, Shiromani Balmukund Rahi, and Abhishek Kumar Upadhyay

For more information about this series, please visit: https://www.routledge.com/Materials-Devices-and-Circuits/book-series/MDCDR

Applied Artificial Intelligence and Machine Learning Techniques for Engineering Applications

Edited by
Ravichander Janapati, Usha Desai,
Steven Fernandes, Rakesh Sengupta, and
Shubham Tayal

CRC Press
Taylor & Francis Group
Boca Raton London New York

CRC Press is an imprint of the
Taylor & Francis Group, an **informa** business

Designed cover image: Shutterstock

First edition published 2026
by CRC Press
2385 NW Executive Center Drive, Suite 320, Boca Raton FL 33431

and by CRC Press
4 Park Square, Milton Park, Abingdon, Oxon, OX14 4RN

CRC Press is an imprint of Taylor & Francis Group, LLC

ISBN: 978-1-032-75324-9 (hbk)
ISBN: 978-1-032-75325-6 (pbk)
ISBN: 978-1-003-47344-2 (ebk)

DOI: 10.1201/9781003473442

Typeset in Times
by Apex CoVantage, LLC

Contents

About the Editors

Dr. Ravichander Janapati is presently working as an associate professor in the Department of ECE, SR University, Warangal. He is a senior member of IEEE and graduated in electronics and communication engineering from JNTU Hyderabad. He received his PhD in the adhoc wireless sensor networks field and MTech in digital electronics and communication systems from the Jawaharlal Nehru Technical University, Anantapur. His research areas are wireless sensor networks and brain computer interface.

Dr. Usha Desai is presently working as a professor and dean (Research & Development) for S.E.A College of Engineering & Technology, Bengaluru, India. She received her PhD in biomedical signal processing from REVA University, Bengaluru, and MTech and BE from Visvesvaraya Technological University (VTU), Belagavi, Karnataka, India. She received the DST International Travel Grant to present her research paper at 39th IEEE EMBS International Annual Conference held at Jeju Island, South Korea. She has organized the International Conference on Innovative Research Development (ICIRD-2024) at Shinawatra University, Bangkok, Thailand. She served as an organizer and session chair at the reputed IEEE international conferences. Also, she has presented papers in many reputed conferences and authored more than 50 research publications. She has authored five books on biomedical healthcare. She has six patents. She is presently a senior member of IEEE and life member of ISTE.

Dr. Steven Fernandes began his postdoctoral research at the University of Alabama-Birmingham after receiving his PhD in electronics and communication engineering from Karunya Institute of Technology and Science and his masters in microelectronics from Manipal Institute of Technology. There he worked on NIH-funded projects. He also conducted postdoctoral research at the University of Central Florida. This research included working on DARPA, NSF, and RBC funded projects. Steven's current area of research is focused on using artificial intelligence techniques to extract useful patterns from big data. This includes robust computer vision applications using deep learning and computer-aided diagnosis using medical image processing.

Dr. Rakesh Sengupta is a cognitive scientist specializing in vision, attention, and working memory. While working on his dissertation, Rakesh spent two years as a visiting fellow at Center for Mind/Brain Sciences (CiMec) at the University of Trento, Italy. He completed his PhD from the Center for Neural and Cognitive Science, University of Hyderabad, in 2015. His current research involves building a visual working memory module for selective tuning based cognitive architecture, as well as building computational models of the human motor system using computational, theoretical, behavioral, and neuroimaging methods.

Dr. Shubham Tayal is a layout design engineer at Synopsys India Pvt. Ltd., Hyderabad, India. He has more than eight years of academic/research experience of teaching at the UG and PG level. He has received his PhD in microelectronics & VLSI design from National Institute of Technology, Kurukshetra; MTech (VLSI design) from YMCA University of Science and Technology, Faridabad; and BTech (electronics and communication engineering) from MDU, Rohtak. His research interests include simulation and modelling of multigate semiconductor devices, device-circuit co-design in digital/analog domain, machine learning, and IOT.

Contributors

Ashiru Aliyu Zainulabidin
Department of Biochemistry
School of Sciences and Humanities
SR University, Warangal
Telangana, India

Ashoka Hadagali
Department of Biotechnology
B.M.S. College of Engineering
Bengaluru, India

Babu D Ramesh
School of Business
SR University, Warangal
Telangana, India

Behra Saswati
Department of Computer Science and Engineering
S.E.A. College of Engineering & Technology
Bengaluru, Karnataka, India

Bhattarcharya Eishani
School of Computer Science and Engineering
Vellore Institute of Technology
Bhopal, Madhya Pradesh, India

Cevallos Manuel E
Medical Education Department, School of Medicine
Creighton University
Phoenix, AZ, USA

Cook Carina
Computer Science & Informatics
College of Arts and Sciences
Creighton University
Omaha, NE, USA

Dani Mahendra
School of Computer Science and Engineering
Vellore Institute of Technology
Bhopal, Madhya Pradesh, India

Das Debanjan
Centre of Excellence in Affordable Healthcare
Indian Institute of Technology (IIT)
Kharagpur, India

Desai Usha
Department of Computer Science Engineering (IoT-Cybersecurity with Blockchain Technology)
South East Asian College of Engineering & Technology
Bengaluru, India

Deshpande Shubhada
University of Mumbai
Maharashtra, India

Devi Manju
Department of Electronics & Communication Engineering
The Oxford College of Engineering
Bengaluru, India

Eldo Jessica
Department of Computer Science and Engineering
Christ University, Kengeri Campus
Bangalore, India

Eswaran Sivaraman
Department of Electrical and Computer Engineering
Curtin University Malaysia
Miri, Sarawak, Malaysia

Fernandes Steven L
Computer Science & Informatics
College of Arts and Sciences
Creighton University
Omaha, NE, USA

G S Nijaguna
Department of Information
Science Engineering
S.E.A. College of Engineering &
Technology
Bengaluru, Karnataka, India

Gaud Chirra Anudeep
Computer Science and Engineering,
Symbiosis Institute of Technology
Pune
and
Symbiosis International (Deemed
University)
Pune, India

Hazarika Ruhul Amin
Department of Information Technology
Manipal Institute of Technology
Bengaluru
and
Manipal Academy of Higher Education
Manipal, India

Joshi Saee
School of Computer Science and
Engineering
Vellore Institute of Technology
Bhopal, Madhya Pradesh, India

K Manjunath
Department of Agriculture Engineering
S.E.A. College of Engineering &
Technology
Bengaluru Karnataka, India

Krudwig Cole J
Computer Science & Informatics
College of Arts and Sciences
Creighton University
Omaha, NE, USA

Kumar Susheel K
Department of Information Technology
Manipal Institute of Technology
Bengaluru
Manipal Academy of Higher Education
Manipal, India

M T Thasleema
Department of Computer Science
Central University of Kerala
Kasargod, Kerala, India

Maji Arnab Kumar
Department of Information
Technology
North Eastern Hill University
Shillong, Meghalaya, India

Marry Ann
Department of Computer Science and
Engineering
Christ University, Kengeri Campus
Bangalore, India

Mathur Sanjeev Kumar
ITS School of Management
Ghaziabad, Uttar Pradesh, India

Naik Nithesh
Department of Mechanical and
Industrial Engineering
Manipal Institute of Technology
Manipal Academy of
Higher Education
Manipal, Karnataka, India

Natarajan Jayapandian
Department of Computer Science and
Engineering
Christ University, Kengeri Campus
Bangalore, India

Nath Keshab
Department of Computer Science and
Engineering
Bhattadev University
Bajali, Assam, India

Nowlen Frances M
Medical Education Department
School of Medicine
Creighton University
Phoenix, AZ, USA

P R Krishna Kumar
Department of Computer Science and Engineering
S.E.A College of Engineering & Technology
Bengaluru, Karnataka, India

Reddy Bhavanam Gireesh
Computer Science and Engineering
Symbiosis Institute of Technology
Pune
and
Symbiosis International (Deemed University)
Pune, India

Roy Kumar Sekhar
Department of Computer Science and Engineering
Manipal Institute of Technology
Bengaluru
Manipal Academy of Higher Education
Manipal, India

S Pradeep
Department of Biotechnology
B.M.S. College of Engineering
Bengaluru, India

Sardar Tanvir H
Dept of Computer Science and Engineering
GITAM School of Technology
GITAM University
Bengaluru, India

Saxena Akash
School of Engineering and Technology
Central University of Haryana
India

Sengupta Rakesh
Department of Cognitive Science
School of Sciences and Humanities
SR University, Warangal
Telangana, India

Singh Nirmit Pratap
School of Computer Science and Engineering
Vellore Institute of Technology
Bhopal, Madhya Pradesh, India

Sinha Aparna
Department of Electrical Engineering
Indian Institute of Technology (IIT)
Roorkee, India

Sk Mahmudul Hassan
Department of Information Technology
Manipal Institute of Technology
Bengaluru
and
Manipal Academy of Higher Education
Manipal, India

Sufyan Aminu Jibril
Department of Biochemistry
School of Sciences and Humanities
SR University, Warangal
Telangana, India

Sujith Annie
Department of Computer Science and Engineering
Jyothy Institute of Technology
Bengaluru, India

Thirunavukkarasu Muthu Kumar
Department of Biotechnology
School of Sciences and Humanities
SR University
Warangal Telangana, India

Tojo Laya
Department of Electronics & Communication Engineering
The Oxford College of Engineering
Bengaluru, India

V Shibina
Department of Computer Science
Central University of Kerala
Kasargod, Kerala, India

Yasmin Huda
Department of Computer Science and Engineering
Christ University, Kengeri Campus
Bangalore, India

Zade Nilima
Computer Science and Engineering, Symbiosis Institute of Technology Pune
Symbiosis International (Deemed University)
Pune, India

1 AI in Communication
A Chatbot to Practice a Clinical Interview in Spanish (BOTES)

Manuel E Cevallos, Steven L Fernandes, Carina Cook, Cole J Krudwig, and Frances M Nowlen

1.1 INTRODUCTION

Communication, a complex and multifaceted process, is the cornerstone of human existence and knowledge transmission. It involves exchanging information, experiences, emotions, and ideas; fostering mutual understanding; and incorporating cultural context. More than that, the thread weaves the fabric of our social bonds, connecting us and promoting personal growth. Communication is not just a part of human conduct; it is a necessity for the survival of society. Its importance is evident in both personal and professional domains. Effective communication is not just a skill; it's a key to success in medical, business, and interpersonal relationships, motivating us to improve our communication skills constantly [1].

1.1.1 AI in Health Care

The options for artificial intelligence (AI) in health care show a positive trend [2]. Chatbots with communication capabilities can answer emails and questions, help schedule, and perform other public relations functions in customer service related to insurance and the front desk. That interaction can also be done in any language. In administration, AI can help to analyze data, prepare reports, and summarize meetings.

Machine learning (ML) can be used as a predictive model to analyze data, develop algorithms for patient triage or diagnosis (precision models), and analyze images for radiological image interpretation and histological image diagnostics. The development of surgical robots for automated procedures such as suturing is an example of ML's capabilities.

Moreover, natural language processing can interpret and classify clinical charts, research analysis and publications, patient interactions, and discharge form interactions. It can also translate prescriptions to the patient's primary language or clarify concepts in the maternal language.

DOI: 10.1201/9781003473442-1

1.1.2 AI in Healthcare Communication

AI is revolutionizing healthcare communication. The easy access, low cost, and substantial improvements in the last decades are causing AI to be considered as part of the design of the current and future healthcare system. However, four primary considerations need to be considered before the implementation of AI in health care: the integration with some existing healthcare systems, the accuracy and reliability of AI (it needs frequent "training" and updates), the human "touch factor," and HIPPA compliance (personal data protection.) The ethical considerations in the AI model need to be seriously investigated and addressed before adopting the tool [2, 3].

AI in healthcare communication can enhance patient care, streamline processes, and improve outcomes. Here is a comprehensive list of benefits:

1. AI-assisted medical education: It can improve communication skills in training for healthcare professionals, interact with patients to discuss discharge forms and assess them, and give personalized interactions.
2. AI-virtual health assistant and AI-assisted patient monitoring: Interaction with the patient can help remind the patient of times for prescription and health tracking, interact with elderly patients, avoiding isolation and connecting directly with health services for scheduling or emergencies [4, 5].
3. AI-enhanced telemedicine: It is an essential solution for remote patients or those with transport limitations, for example. It can incorporate images and analyze symptoms. Also, it can be vital since it can translate the language in real-time for patient interaction [3].
4. AI-powered chatbots: A chatbot can be accessed 24/7, helping with essential information and offering guidance in health. It can be used as part of the triage.
5. Natural language processing: It can enhance voice recognition, understanding, and interpretation of human language, which is a skill that complements medical transcription, medical coding, and chatbots.
6. Sentiment analysis: It can be related to evaluating emotional voice conversations, which helps improve patient communication. It can also assess the characteristics of patient feedback and interpret anxiety and depression [6].
7. AI-enhanced patient communication: It facilitates finding information on the web and personal health portal, delivers personal messages to healthcare providers, and keeps track of appointments and prescription reminders.
8. Language translation: Associated with the chatbots and NLP is the strong bond that reduces the language barrier.

1.1.3 The Clinical or Medical Interview

The clinical or medical interview is a systematic and standardized questionnaire that physicians use to collect patient data, such as chief complaints and characteristics, personal and familial medical history, and social components [7]. It is also when the physician establishes rapport with the patient by fostering trust, a central feature of the physician–patient relationship. This trust is built by behaviors in the clinical interview—an interview with clear objectives and solid questions where time is respected, patients' doubts and questions can be clarified, the patient is shown empathy and compassion, and a holistic perception of the evaluation is conducted [8–10].

Medical students from the first year are exposed to this questionnaire to become familiar with the questions, the wording of questions, the sequence of questions grouped in blocks, pauses and reinforcement in the conversation, and other skills to develop rapport and facilitate an exceptional engagement with the patient.

Individuals with limited English proficiency (LEP) face significant disparities in health care, such as reduced understanding of medical diagnoses, lower adherence to medication and lifestyle recommendations, increased medication complications, and decreased satisfaction with care compared to English-speaking individuals [11]. Multiple factors, such as migration, lack of adequate medical training, insufficient number of certified medical interpreters, and others, are associated with the health disparity [12]. For example, when the migration factor is included as a determinant of health, Maldonado et al. cited in their article: "Mexican immigrants are 18% more likely to have limited access to care, and undocumented immigrants are 45% more likely to be uninsured, compared to US citizens" [13].

Providing language-concordant care, where patients and their physicians communicate in the same language, can help overcome these language barriers [14]. In 2023, Mustafa et al. highlighted six identified themes related to a language barrier in the doctor–patient relationship: frustration, lack of rapport, trust issues, patient dissatisfaction, compliance issues, and threat to patient safety [15].

1.1.4 Population Demographics

The Hispanic population in Phoenix, Arizona, is 2.27% higher than the U.S. national average [16–19]. Also, 30.6% of Phoenix residents reported speaking Spanish at home [20]. However, only 6% of physicians identify as Hispanic, and only 2% of non-Hispanic physicians speak Spanish in the United States [21]. This imbalance is a solid language barrier in the clinical interview process. It produces anxiety and frustration for students, physicians, and patients about inclusive patient safety (because they cannot clearly understand recommendations and prescriptions) [22].

Understanding the demographics of Phoenix, Arizona, the Spanish Clinical Skills Club at Creighton University is a club for health students interested in learning and practicing medical interviews in Spanish. It has medical students of different years and physician assistant students and accepts all levels of Spanish-speaking members. Their mission is to decrease the language barrier gap.

Generative artificial intelligence is a powerful new tool that can be adapted to medical education. A type of generative AI is the chatbot, a computer program that engages in conversation with users. For example, Baglivo et al. described the efficacy of an AI chatbot in answering questions related to vaccination and providing educational support [23]. AI chatbots can also be used to teach languages [24–27].

1.2 PURPOSE

We developed a chatbot in Spanish (BOTES) using generative artificial intelligence that plays the role of the patient so that the students can practice the interview in

FIGURE 1.1 BOTES app.

Spanish. The application aimed to enhance clinical interview skills in Spanish, foster inclusive health care, and serve as an accessible 24/7 tool for individual daily practice (Figure 1.1).

1.3 MATERIAL AND METHODS

The protocol had two phases: Part A was the design of the beta application of BOTES, a chatbot AI for clinical skills in Spanish. The objective was to build an application that could be loaded with a specific clinical case in Spanish, where the chatbot would play the role of the patient and the student would be the interviewer. The application could be used on a desktop, iPhone, or Android smartphone. Part B was a satisfaction survey that included feedback on BOTES, intending to modify and update the current beta version.

1.3.1 Part A

The BOTES app leverages state-of-the-art technologies, including GPT-4 [27], to create personalized chatbots to facilitate Spanish clinical conversations. By enriching the chatbot's knowledge base with extensive support for the Spanish language, the app enhances cross-cultural and global knowledge integration (Figure 1.2). The implementation includes a retriever module that searches a comprehensive knowledge base containing clinical data and conversational snippets, feeding this information into a generation module powered by GPT-4 to synthesize accurate and contextually relevant responses. The robust backend infrastructure, supported by Firebase [28], stores and synchronizes the Spanish clinical case database, allowing administrators to

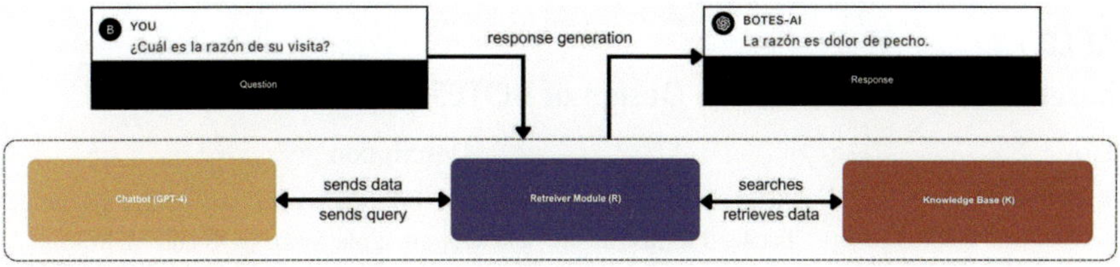

FIGURE 1.2 Block diagram of the proposed BOTES app working model.

perform automatic updates and ensuring that all users have access to the most current information. The mobile app frontend is accessible on both iOS and Android platforms and incorporates a speech-to-text capability that accurately emulates clinical case conversations and provides verbal responses. The development process involved training the BOTES application with clinical conversation data, including patient introductions, main complaints, and clinical histories, leveraging GPT-4's capabilities to support medical clinical conversations in Spanish and significantly enhance practical communication skills. The secure storage of the Spanish clinical case database is maintained by Firebase, and extensive testing on both iOS and Android platforms guarantees robust performance across diverse medical settings. The design and construction of the BOTES app had the following phases presented in Table 1.1.

1.3.2 Part B

A chatbot was designed to accelerate the frequency of practice medical interviews. BOTES was delivered to 13 first-year Spanish Clinical Skills Club medical students at Creighton University, Phoenix campus. All of them were invited to participate in a voluntary and anonymous online survey conducted using the Qualtrics software. The survey explored satisfaction, advantages, and disadvantages and requested feedback for future updates. The Institutional Review Board at Creighton University approved protocol #2004602–01.

Additionally, users were surveyed with follow-up questions after using the app and their responses were analyzed using the DistilBERT model ¼, which outputs the average sentiment score for each question asked where the score is between 0.0 and 1.0 with 1.0 being the most positive. The model is explained in further detail next.

Input:

- Set of comments C with features $\left\{Q_i, F_{ij}\right\}$ where Q_i is the i-th question and $F_{i,j}$ is the j-th feedback for question Q_i
- Pre-trained sentiment analysis model M (DistilBERT model: "'distilbert-base-uncased-finetuned-sst-2-english'")

Output:

- Average sentiment scores for each question

TABLE 1.1
Phases and Definitions in the Design of BOTES App

Phase	Description
1. Define Components	Specify large language model (GPT-4), knowledge base (K), Firebase backend infrastructure, and supported platforms (iOS and Android).
2. Enrich Knowledge Base	Enhance the knowledge base (K) with extensive support for the Spanish language to enable cross-cultural and global knowledge integration.
3. Develop Retriever Module	Create a retriever module (R) that searches the knowledge base (K) for relevant data (D) based on the user query (q).
4. Develop Generation Module	Implement a generation module (G) that uses retrieved data (D) to generate accurate and contextually relevant responses (r) using GPT-4.
5. Setup Firebase Backend	Establish Firebase backend to store and synchronize the Spanish clinical case database (S).
6. Enable Automatic Updates	Allow administrators to perform automatic updates on the clinical case database (S) to ensure users have the most current information.
7. Develop Mobile App Interface	Build a mobile app interface that is accessible on both iOS and Android platforms.
8. Integrate Speech-to-Text Feature	Incorporate a speech-to-text capability to emulate clinical case conversations and provide verbal responses.
9. Train BOTES Application	Use clinical conversation data to train the BOTES application, focusing on patient introductions, main complaints, and clinical histories.
10. Test and Deploy Application	Conduct extensive testing on iOS and Android platforms to ensure robust performance and secure storage of the clinical case database in Firebase.

Steps:

1. Define the set of questions:

   $$Q = \{Q_1, Q_2, \ldots, Q_n\}$$

   Initializes the set of questions from the survey.
2. Define the set of feedback comments:

   $$F = \{F_{i,j} \mid i \in [1, m_i]\}$$

   Initializes the set of feedback comments where $F_{i,j}$ is the j-th feedback for the i-th question.
3. Flatten comments and associate them with questions:

   $$flattened\_comments = \cup_{i=0}^{n} \{Q_1 \mid j \in [1, m_i]\}$$

   $$questions = \cup_{i=0}^{n} \{F_{ij} \mid j \in [1, m_i]\}$$

   Flattens the nested structure of feedback comments into a single list and creates a corresponding list of questions.
4. Perform sentiment analysis on flattened_comments using M:

   $$sentiments = M(flattened\_comments)$$

Applies the pre-trained sentiment analysis model M to the flattened comments. The output is a list of sentiment predictions for each comment, including a sentiment label (e.g., 'POSITIVE', 'NEGATIVE') and a confidence score.

5. Extract sentiment labels sentiment_labels and scores sentiment_scores:

$$sentiment\_labels = \{sentiment['label'] \mid sentiment \in sentiments\}$$

$$sentiment\_scores = \{sentiment['score'] \mid sentiment \in sentiments\}$$

Extracts the sentiment labels and confidence scores from the sentiment analysis results.

6. Create DataFrame sentiment_df with columns Question, Comment, Sentiment, and Score:

$$sentiment\_df = Question: questions, Comment: flattened\_comments, \\ Sentiment: sentiment\_labels, Score: sentiment\_scores$$

Constructs a DataFrame with the feedback comments, their associated questions, sentiment labels, and sentiment scores.

7. Calculate average sentiment scores for each question:

$$average\_sentiment\_score = mean(group\,by\,Question)$$

Groups the DataFrame by 'Question' and calculates the average sentiment score for each question.

8. Return average_sentiment_scores:

$$return\,average\_sentiment\_scores$$

Returns the average sentiment score for each question.

1.4 RESULTS

The participation rate in the satisfaction survey was 31% in this beta-test application. The overall grade was 75% satisfaction. Four characteristics of the application were evaluated using a scale of 1 to 5, where one was the lowest and five was the highest: (a) improving memorization, (b) students' confidence, (c) reducing stress in the learning process, and (d) helping to practice the questions more frequently. The average results for each area were 5, 4.67, 4.33, and 4.67, respectively (Figure 1.3).

The positive comments were the opportunity to practice conducting interviews in Spanish at any time, the possibility to practice medical Spanish comprehension, and the possibility to modify the clinical case according to the topic to evaluate (Figure 1.4). 100% of participants were willing to use BOTES in the future.

We have developed a sentiment analysis system that utilizes natural language processing techniques to assess and visualize sentiment in textual data. The process begins with consolidating feedback comments associated with specific questions into a single list. The *distilbert-base-uncased-finetuned-sst-2-english* pre-trained sentiment analysis model from the transformer's library evaluates these comments, generating sentiment labels (e.g., Positive, Negative) and sentiment scores. A sentiment score is a numerical value representing the confidence level of the assigned

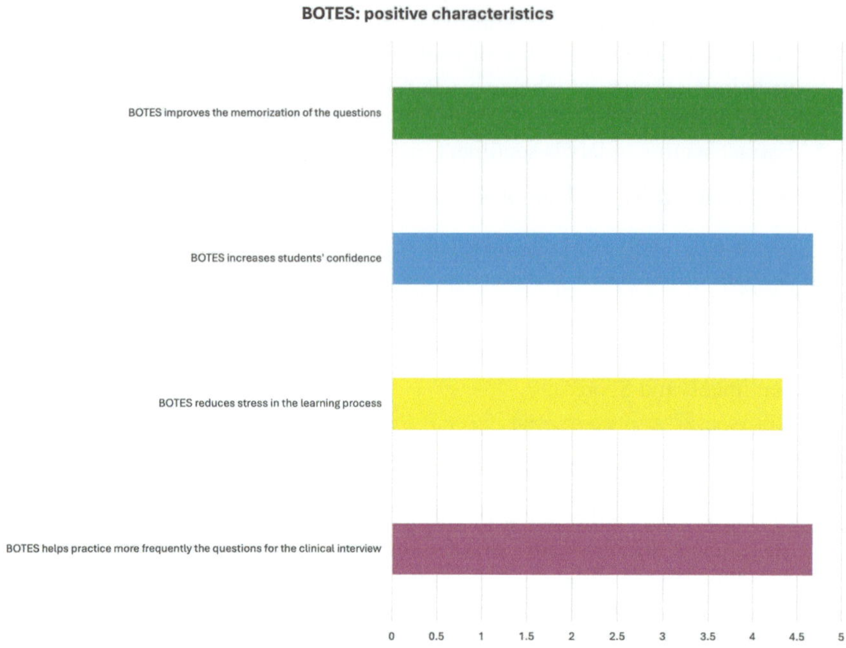

FIGURE 1.3 Average results for positive characteristics using BOTES.

sentiment, indicating the probability that a comment expresses a particular sentiment. Our sentiment analysis system aims to quantitatively measure and compare the sentiment expressed in feedback comments across different questions. Sentiment scores provide a standardized way to assess the emotional tone of textual data, facilitating the identification of trends and patterns in user feedback. These scores are systematically organized into a DataFrame, including the original questions, comments, sentiment labels, and scores. To calculate the mean sentiment score for each question, we group the DataFrame by the question column and compute the mean of the sentiment scores within each group using the *group by* method followed by the *mean* function in pandas. This results in a mean sentiment score reflecting the average sentiment confidence for each question. These scores are visualized using Figure 1.5, providing a clear comparison of average sentiments across different questions, thereby enabling a comprehensive analysis of user feedback.

These sentiment scores indicate users' overall strong positive feelings about the app. The average sentiment score from the feedback to questions was 0.959.

User feedback described some modifications that will be incorporated in an updated version. Those comments included the addition of pre-loaded clinical scenarios that the user could elect to practice with, such as a patient presenting with chest pain or pneumonia symptoms. Another suggestion was to streamline the setup process before initiating the clinical interview simulation.

A significant limitation of BOTES was its difficulties in capturing sounds in Spanish for students with little experience in the Spanish language.

Hello, my name is Manuel, and I am a medical. The doctor told me to take a clinical history. What is your name? *-My name is George Washington, nice to meet you.*	What is the reason or motive for your visit today? *-The reason is chest pain.*
What would you prefer me to call you? *-You can call me George, thanks.* What is your birthdate? *-I was born on December 11, 1978.*	When did chest pain begin? *-The pain began a month ago, but it is not constant.* Have you noticed something that worsens or increases the pain? *-The pain increases when I climb stairs or walk a long distance.*
What is your sex at birth? *-My birth sex is male.*	Is there anything that would decrease the pain? *-Pain decreased when I stopped the physical activity.*
How do you prefer to be sexually identified? *-I identify myself as a man.*	Can, you describe the pain on a scale from one to ten? One is minimal pain, and ten is the more pain than you have ever experienced. *-The pain has an intensity of seven when this is present.*

FIGURE 1.4 Typical sample of BOTES training for medical Spanish understanding. An example of a clinical interview in Spanish between a bot and a medical student. (a) In green is the Spanish clinical interview; (b) In the table, the same conversation is translated into English.

Users suggested a few enhancements, including extending the duration for which the app listens to spoken input, providing more comprehensive clinical scenarios, and making interface improvements, such as enlarging the spacebar by removing the "@" symbol and differentiating message colors for better clarity. These suggestions indicate a desire for a more user-friendly and comprehensive tool, demonstrating that the BOTES app has significant potential to be an asset for medical students and professionals seeking to improve their clinical Spanish skills. The high ratings and positive user feedback confirm the app's efficacy in enhancing practical communication skills, establishing it as an essential tool in medical education and training.

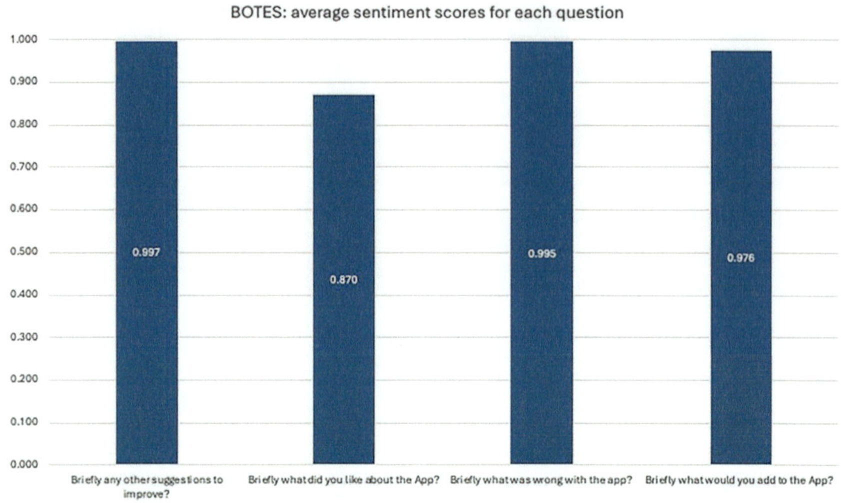

FIGURE 1.5 Sentiment analysis results gathered from feedback to questions.

1.5 CONCLUSION

The chatbot in Spanish (BOTES) can facilitate the memorization and practice of the clinical interview in preparation for an interview with the Hispanic and Spanish-speaking, limited English proficient populations to address disparities caused by Spanish-to-English language barriers. This tool can help the student practice a clinical interview in Spanish, leading to a faster, more accurate interview and improving the relationship with a Spanish speaker in clinical settings. Also, having a routine, quick process to ask clinical questions will provide confidence in the interviewer, giving them extra time in the interview to be more compassionate and have a holistic approach to the patient. The flow of the questions will turn the interview into a conversational experience for the patient instead of just a checkbox for each question.

It is essential to highlight that the BOTES application aims to facilitate learning and increase practice. It does not intend to replace the human interview.

Limitations: The primary limitation was using Spanish speakers from different countries to test the model. The accents, speed of communication, and vocabulary used in other Hispanic countries are different, which produced some errors in interpreting the conversation for the bot. To avoid that substantial variable, it was decided to standardize the bot with Mexican Spanish, the most used language in U.S. classrooms.

The next step is to adopt the feedback and upgrade the application to use it as a complementary tool in clinical interviews in Spanish. Since the chatbot can interpret different languages, the basic BOTES app can be upgraded to work in various languages to facilitate learning interviews in foreign languages, decreasing the language barrier in other cultures.

1.5.1 Statements and Declarations

This work was supported by the 2023–2024 Center for Faculty Excellence Grant awarded from Creighton University: Clinical Skills Interview Chatbot in Spanish from Creighton University.

Author Manuel E Cevallos has received the award.

1.5.2 Ethics Approval

The Institutional Review Board at Creighton University approved the questionnaire and methodology for this study, protocol #2004602–01.

REFERENCES

[1] Tariq, Z. N. (2023). Life of communication process: A critical and philosophical approach study of communication process. *Qlantic Journal of Social Sciences and Humanities*, *4*(4), 297–309. https://doi.org/10.55737/qjssh.498899116

[2] Davenport, T., & Kalakota, R. (2019). The potential for artificial intelligence in healthcare. *Future Healthcare Journal*, *6*(2), 94–98. https://doi.org/10.7861/futurehosp.6-2-94

[3] Jiang, F., Jiang, Y., Zhi, H., Dong, Y., Li, H., Ma, S., Wang, Y., Dong, Q., Shen, H., & Wang, Y. (2017). Artificial intelligence in healthcare: Past, present and future. *Stroke and Vascular Neurology*, *2*(4), 230–243. https://doi.org/10.1136/svn-2017–000101

[4] Boyle, P. (2023, August 8). *How AI is helping doctors communicate with patients*. Association of American Medical Colleges. https://www.aamc.org/news/how-ai-helping-doctors-communicate-patients

[5] Malamas, N., Papangelou, K., & Symeonidis, A. L. (2022). Upon improving the performance of localized healthcare virtual assistants. *Healthcare (Basel, Switzerland)*, *10*(1), 99. https://doi.org/10.3390/healthcare10010099

[6] Gallegos, C., Kausler, R., Alderden, J., Davis, M., & Wang, L. (2024). Can artificial intelligence chatbots improve mental health?: A scoping review. *Computers, Informatics, Nursing: CIN*. Advance online publication. https://doi.org/10.1097/CIN.0000000000001155

[7] Lichstein, P. R. (1990). Chapter 3: The medical interview. In H. K. Walker, W. D. Hall, & J. W. Hurst (Eds.), *Clinical methods: The history, physical, and laboratory examinations* (3rd ed.). Boston: Butterworths. https://www.ncbi.nlm.nih.gov/books/NBK349/

[8] Pearson, S. D., & Raeke, L. H. (2000). Patients' trust in physicians: Many theories, few measures, and little data. *Journal of General Internal Medicine*, *15*(7), 509–513. https://doi.org/10.1046/j.1525–1497.2000.11002.x

[9] Adekunle, T. A., Knowles, J. M., Hantzmon, S. V., DasGupta, M. N., Pollak, K. I., & Gaither, S. E. (2023). A qualitative analysis of trust and distrust within patient-clinician interactions. *PEC Innovation*, *3*, 100187. https://doi.org/10.1016/j.pecinn.2023.100187

[10] Greene, J., & Wolfson, D. (2023). Physician perspectives on building trust with patients. *The Hastings Center Report*, *53*(Suppl 2), S86–S90. https://doi.org/10.1002/hast.1528

[11] Greek, A. A., Kieckhefer, G. M., Kim, H., Joesch, J. M., & Baydar, N. (2006). Family perceptions of the usual source of care among children with asthma by race/ethnicity, language, and family income. *Journal of Asthma*, *43*(1), 61–69. https://doi.org/10.1080/02770900500448639

[12] Mecham, J. C., Salazar, M. M., Perez, R. M., Castaneda, U., Stamps, B. G., Chavez, A. S., & Kling, J. M. (2022). Exploring the factors that influence ethical Spanish use among

medical students and solutions for improvement. *Teaching and Learning in Medicine*, *34*(5), 522–529. https://doi.org/10.1080/10401334.2021.1949996

[13] Maldonado, A., Martinez, D. E., Villavicencio, E. A., Crocker, R., & Garcia, D. O. (2024). Salud sin Fronteras: Identifying determinants of frequency of healthcare use among Mexican immigrants in Southern Arizona. *Journal of Racial Ethnic Health Disparities*. Advance online publication. https://doi.org/10.1007/s40615-024-02024-x

[14] Garcia, M. E., Williams, M., Mutha, S., Diamond, L. C., Jih, J., Handley, M. A., Pathak, S., & Karliner, L. S. (2023). Language-concordant care: A qualitative study examining implementation of physician non-english language proficiency assessment. *Journal of General Internal Medicine*, *38*(14), 3099–3106. https://doi.org/10.1007/s11606-023-08354-6

[15] Mustafa, R., Mahboob, U., Khan, R. A., & Anjum, A. (2023). Impact of language barriers in doctor-patient relationship: A qualitative study. *Pakistan Journal of Medical Sciences*, *39*(1), 41–45. https://doi.org/10.12669/pjms.39.1.5805

[16] Hispanic or Latino in U.S. (2020). *U.S. Census Bureau*. https://www.census.gov/search-results.html?q=hispanic+or+latino+in+the+US&page=1&stateGeo=none&searchtype=web&cssp=SERP&_charset_=UTF-8

[17] Frey, W. (2018, March 14). *The US will become a 'minority white' in 2045*. Brookings. https://www.brookings.edu/blog/the-avenue/2018/03/14/the-us-will-become-minority-white-in-2045-census-projects/

[18] U.S. Census Bureau. (2020). *The total population in Arizona*. https://www.census.gov/search-results.html?q=arizona+population&page=1&stateGeo=none&searchtype=web&cssp=SERP&_charset_=UTF-8

[19] Quick Facts, U.S. Census Bureau. (2020). *Hispanic or Latino in Arizona*. https://www.census.gov/quickfacts/fact/table/phoenixcityarizona/RHI725221#qf-headnote-b

[20] U.S. Census Bureau. (2020). *The total population in Phoenix, Arizona*. https://data.census.gov/profile/Phoenix_city,_Arizona?g=160XX00US0455000

[21] Balch, B. (2023, July 18). *The United States needs more Spanish-speaking physicians*. The Association of American Medical Colleges (AAMC). https://www.aamc.org/news/united-states-needs-more-spanish-speaking-physicians#:~:text=Yet%2C%20only%206%25%20of%20physicians,Spanish%2Dspeaking%2C%20Anaya%20says

[22] Al Shamsi, H., Almutairi, A. G., Al Mashrafi, S., & Al Kalbani, T. (2020). Implications of language barriers for healthcare: A systematic review. *Oman Medical Journal*, *35*(2), e122. https://doi.org/10.5001/omj.2020.40

[23] Baglivo, F., De Angelis, L., Casigliani, V., Arzilli, G., Privitera, G. P., & Rizzo, C. (2023). Exploring the possible use of AI chatbots in public health education: Feasibility study. *JMIR Medical Education*, *9*, e51421. https://doi.org/10.2196/51421

[24] Nghi, T. T., Phuc, T. H., & Thang, N. T. (2019). Applying AI chatbot for teaching a foreign language: An empirical research. *International Journal of Scientific and Technology Research*, *8*(12), 897–902.

[25] Kohnke, L. (2023). A pedagogical chatbot: A supplemental language learning tool. *Higher Education for the Future*, *54*(3), 133–141. https://doi.org/10.1177/2347631120983481

[26] Kumar, P. P., Sindhu, P., Jahnavi, A., Charan, B. P., & Prashanth, S. (2023). University Chatbot System using natural language processing. In *Human-machine interface technology advancements and applications* (pp. 301–312). CRC Press.

[27] Achiam, J., Adler, S., Agarwal, S., Ahmad, L., Akkaya, I., Aleman, F. L., Almeida, D., Altenschmidt, J., Altman, S., Anadkat, S., Avila, R., Babuschkin, I., Balaji, S., Balcom, V., Baltescu, P., Bao, H., Bavarian, M., Belgum, J., Bello, I., . . . Zoph, B. (2023). GPT-4 technical report. *ArXiv*. /abs/2303.08774

[28] Google for Developers. (2023). *Firebase documentation*. https://firebase.google.com/docs

2 AI-Driven Diagnostic Assistance for the Gastrointestinal Tract Diseases

Bhavanam Gireesh Reddy, Nilima Zade, Shubhada Deshpande, Chirra Anudeep Gaud, Saswati Behra, and Nithesh Naik

2.1 INTRODUCTION

Gastrointestinal diseases pose a severe threat to people worldwide, resulting in millions of cases and significant economic and social costs. From simple conditions such as gastrointestinal infections and gastrointestinal ulcers to more complicated diseases like gastric cancer diseases, early signs and related symptoms may be overlooked, leading to delayed diagnosis and complications for patients. Preventive management and prompt diagnosis are recognized as major independent factors in the treatment of these diseases, ultimately enhancing the quality of patient care. The disease prognosis and prediction can be assisted through the integration of medical imaging and artificial intelligence (AI). The current availability of large quantities of clinical imaging data has enabled researchers and clinicians to leverage machine learning (ML) technologies to create new models capable of successfully predicting the existence and nature of stomach diseases. Another commonly applied method involves training artificial intelligence models that classify the endoscopic images of the gastrointestinal tract. Over 8,000 real clinical images have been gathered into a sizable collection known as the Kvasir v2 dataset. This dataset encompasses nearly all diseases that are commonly seen in clinical practice involving the gastrointestinal tract, maladies including erosions, ulcers, polyps, and malignant disease.

The present study focuses on the opportunities and problems that come with using AI to assist in the diagnosis of gastrointestinal diseases using the Kvasir v2 dataset. Techniques for model training and model evaluation processes are explored in the study. People may have similar symptoms for different diseases and obtain different diagnoses from different institutions, which is why there is frequently a discrepancy. The use of computer-aided diagnostics facilitates quicker and more deliberate decision-making for practitioners [1]. Through the application of cutting-edge ML algorithms, this effort seeks to close these gaps in the early identification and mitigation

DOI: 10.1201/9781003473442-2

of delays in gastrointestinal health disorders. The study implements CNNs and transfer learning approaches for feature extraction, recognizing and categorizing various gastrointestinal diseases in the stomach region using endoscopic images. The practical values of AI models are established by highlighting their models' performance and demonstrating how AI can enhance patients' survival through individualized treatment plans, prompt diagnosis, and intervention. This research is expected to improve current approaches and plans for managing gastrointestinal disorders, having a significant impact on public health programs worldwide.

Detection not only contributes to enhanced timely treatment but also promotes the establishment of preventive measures. The lack of accuracy in the predictive model has been addressed through the inclusion of regularization and dropout techniques in the training and testing phases. These techniques aid in better determination of the exact disease manifested in the images. AI-driven computer-aided assistance results in effectively diagnosing stomach diseases, enriching the healthcare sector and extending the prospects of superior disease management.

The rest of the chapter is organized as follows. Section 2.2 refers to the published work of renowned researchers. Section 2.3 lays down the methods and procedures adopted in this work. Section 2.4 discusses the results, and Section 2.5 concludes with future possible direction of work.

2.2 LITERATURE REVIEW

The authors in [2] presented a systematic review of 12 distinct models to predict gastric cancer. It is observed that strong discriminative models have used clinical findings along with microscopic images. It is recommended that independent datasets be utilized in conjunction with the splitting dataset technique for validation. Making use of The Cancer Genome Atlas referred as TCGA dataset, the authors in [3] presented the MultiDeepCox-SC model for detecting stomach cancer. Using the CPH, or Cox proportional hazards model, the MultiDeepCox-SC takes into account the DeepCox-SC risk score, age, and expression of 10 genes. Histopathological pictures were used to train the DeepCox-SC model. Then, using the Cox regression technique, the model's output—the DeepCox-SC risk score—was merged with clinical information (age) and gene expression (10 genes). The number of samples was y, 442 whole-slide histopathology images. The accuracy achieved is 83.3%. The training phase of the proposed method is based on selected patches using cellularity and Cell Profiler software that affect the performance. High-power microscopic images with more patches are needed to improve the performance. The authors [4] proposed the XGBoost model to predict stomach disease using individual patient data from 25,942 and 1431 patients as a dataset for prediction. Each participant must have a data label (case: $y = 1$, control: $y = 0$). They identified 89 patients as part of the case group ($y = 1$) who had stomach cancer discovered within 122 months. The accuracy attained is 77.7%, and AOC is 89.9%. They observed that the dataset taken lacks in number, so to improve the accuracy, a large dataset for training and to predict more accurately needs to be taken. The authors in [5] presented a systematic analysis of 11 distinct machine learning models to predict diseases using public healthcare datasets. It was observed that the strongest model is k-nearest neighbor (KNN) and has an accuracy of 93.5%. The data splitting is done randomly, and even some models are dependent on the parameters, and the value of k varies for different models, which affects the accuracy. Selecting appropriate parameters helps to increase the accuracy. The authors in [6] proposed the GC risk (gastric cancer risk) model to predict gastric cancer using 450 people's hospital data. The achieved accuracy of positive prediction is 83.6%. The training is done on the selected parameters like body mass index (BMI), history of cancer, etc., and mainly focused on the polygenic risk score (PRS) and single-nucleotide polymorphism (SNP) for prediction of gastric cancer, which affects the accuracy. The dataset used is also small, and to predict more accurately, it needs to take a large dataset. The authors in [7] presented the systematic analysis of six different machine learning models to predict gastric cancer using 2029 individual data points from a gastric cancer database at Ayatollah Taleghani Hospital in Iran. XGBoost is concluded to be the best model among all the six different machine learning models in that it acquires an accuracy of 83.4% for selected features and 65.2% for all the features. The training time model is trained on the selected features by using a relief algorithm. However, the model needs to be validated on the larger dataset for better prediction and results. The authors in [8] presented the systematic analysis of ML models and deep learning-based models to predict gastric cancer using combined datasets of different images. For feature selection, they used transfer learning techniques and used the dragonfly algorithm as an optimizer. Proposed algorithms are generalized normalized (GN)-Bayes, C-k-nearest neighbour (C-KNN), LD (linear discriminant), and ResNet50. The achieved accuracy is promising by these models when compared to previous studies but increased the computational cost and concatenation. The authors in [9] proposed the neural networks spss-v.18 using 430 patient data as a dataset of a Baghban clinic to predict gastric cancer. The acquired right prediction is 92%. The training phase of the proposed method is based on the selected features, and they haven't considered the family history as a feature for the prediction. This affects the prediction accuracy because cancer may occur from the family history too. The selection of the right features for prediction increases the performance and correct prediction percentage. The authors in [10] presented the systematic analysis of different machine learning models using 133 patients' data. Among the six different machine learning models, random forest is concluded to be the best model for disease prediction. The acquired accuracy is 80.8%. The number of features is high, and the dataset is less. So, due to that, it may undergo overfitting. Reducing the number of features to only those that are necessary for the prediction will improve performance and accuracy. The authors in [11] proposed the artificial intelligence model "MIL-gastro cancer" model to predict gastric cancer using 1200 individual patient data. The achieved accuracy is 92%. During the training phase, the model uses 10- and 5-times magnified images, which has an impact on accuracy. Additionally, large-scale manual pixel-leveling is required, which takes a lot of time. For better accuracy, data augmentation and pixel-leveling can be done with the help of code. The study in [12] gives an overview of the most current studies that have segmented polyps using deep learning models and techniques. The study in [13] presents a statistical examination of deep learning models using polyp datasets and performance indicators. In this study, Kvasir-SEG, an open-access dataset of colonoscopy images for polyp detection, localization, and segmentation, was used as a benchmark to evaluate the accuracy and speed of many contemporary state-of-the-art approaches. The study in [14] provides the findings of comparative analysis of polyp detection techniques, outlines subsequent research to variations among approaches, and offers evaluation datasets and performance metrics definitions so that different approaches can be compared.

2.3 METHODOLOGY

2.3.1 Data Description and Data Preprocessing

The Kvasir v2 dataset has been downloaded from Kaggle website [15]. The images within the Kvasir v2 dataset have proven useful for categorical data of gastrointestinal diseases. It is a collection of new, high-quality endoscopic images from clinical environments. This dataset encompasses a diverse range of gastrointestinal pathologies, including benign (B) pathologies like erosions, ulcers, and polyps as well as malignant (M) pathologies like tumors and cancer, among others like gastritis, esophagitis, and Barrett's esophagus. The samples are categorized into eight groups, each of which offers a variety of gastrointestinal disorders and their distinguishing features. Due to its rich features and various input image types from endoscopy and colonoscopy, the proposed dataset can be utilized for building and testing AI-based predictive models to improve diagnostic accuracy and classification. The open-access nature of the dataset is an additional incentive for choosing this richly equipped dataset for research. The data has been divided into 80% for training data and 20% for validation data. The best of modern-day machine learning algorithms, including CNNs and the transfer learning model ResNet50, have been focused on this research. In addition InceptionV3, Xception, Visual Geometry Group 19 (VGG19), and long short-term memory (LSTM) have been used for experimentation and comparison.

Table 2.1 indicates the training and testing datasets after splitting the data. As the data is imbalanced, no image was selected for the training for the cancer type, but the model, after implementation, correctly identifies the class.

TABLE 2.1
Testing and Training Dataset Considered in the Proposed Study

No.	Classes	Training Data Images	Testing Data Images
1	Normal	993	86
2	Erosions B	983	101
3	Polyp B	975	88
4	Ulcer B	997	107
5	Gastritis B/M	1000	88
6	Hiatal Hernia B/M	967	105
7	Dysplasia B/M	392	112
8	Cancer M	0	112

2.3.2 Model Training and Architecture

InceptionV3, Xception, VGG19, LSTM, and ResNet50 are implemented on the data. This deep learning model is known for its robust performance. The training data for the model is 80% of the data, with the remaining data divided into validation and test data. The information is preprocessed, features are extracted, and the technique used is transfer learning model. The model is optimized with Adam optimizer and extracts the required features from the image. Max pulling and flattening layers are applied, converting the images to single dimension images. This representation is passed through convolution layers. The model comprises 32 layers, ultimately producing the final output. During the training process, the validation accuracy, validation loss, and model accuracy for each epoch are obtained. The model is trained for 100 epochs. Overfitting can occur due to large datasets or other factors. To address this, dropout functions are employed, which drop some layers during training, and L2 regularization is used to prevent overfitting. These techniques help to improve accuracy. Figure 2.1 shows the eight disease data groups considered. Figure 2.2 shows the workflow of the model architecture, and Figure 2.3 shows the architecture configuration of developed deep learning methodology. Figure 2.4 gives the details of implementation of deep learning models.

The validation data is used to assess the model, and the model's applicability is assessed by the accuracy given by the graph obtained using validation data.

An advanced deep learning set of rules is offered by the mathematical model represented as Equation 2.1. To address the vanishing gradient problem encountered during the training of very deep neurons, residual blocks are utilized, making it easier to examine residual functions rather than directly attempting to learn preference map interpolation.

$$y = F(x) + {}^{W2}\!\!\Big/_{sigma\left(W1+b1\right)} + b2 \quad (2.1)$$

Here's a breakdown of the elements:

- x: Input to the block.
- W1 and W2: Learnable weight parameters.
- b1 and b2: Bias terms.
- sigma: SoftMax Activation function.
- F(x): Represents the residual mapping that the block aims to learn.
- H(x) = W_2\sigma (W_1x + b_1) + b_2: Denotes the learned residual mapping.
- y: Output of the block.

The algorithm steps are

Input:

- Let X denote the input.
  Initial Convolution and Pooling:

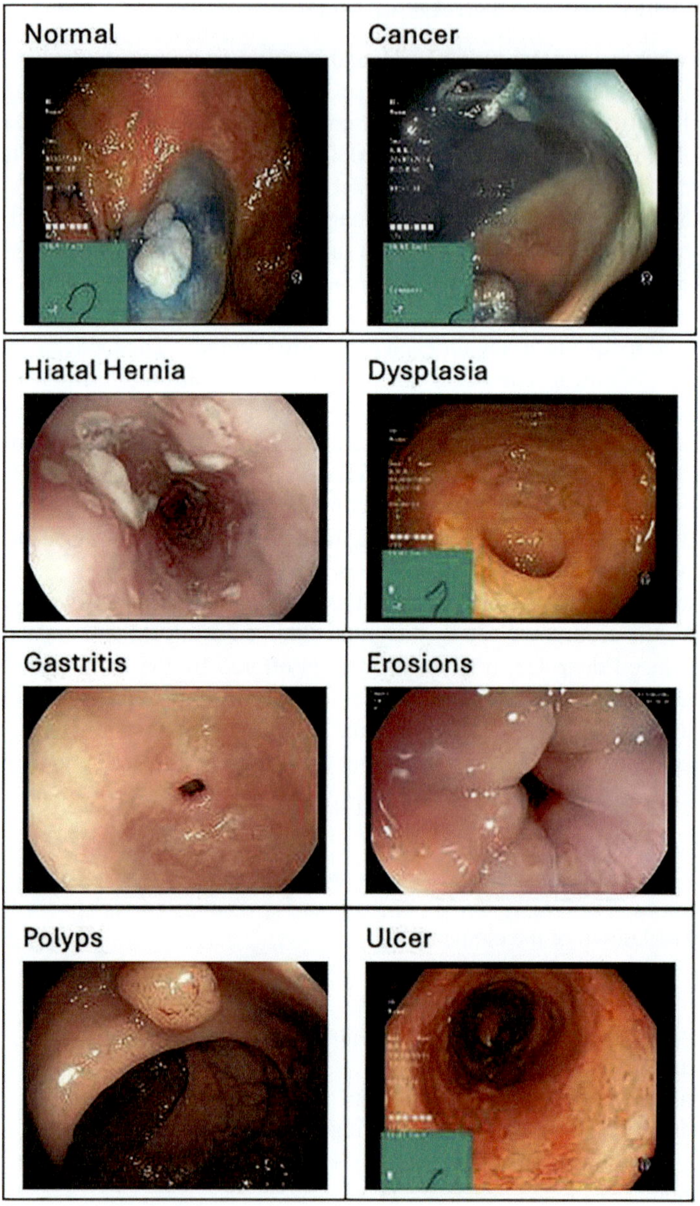

FIGURE 2.1 Images of disease categories from the Kvasir v2 dataset.

- Input undergoes an initial convolutional layer followed by max pooling:
  C1 = Conv (X. W1) + b1
  P1 = Max Pooling (C1)
  W1 = weights of initial convolution layer
  b1 = bias term
  Residual Blocks:

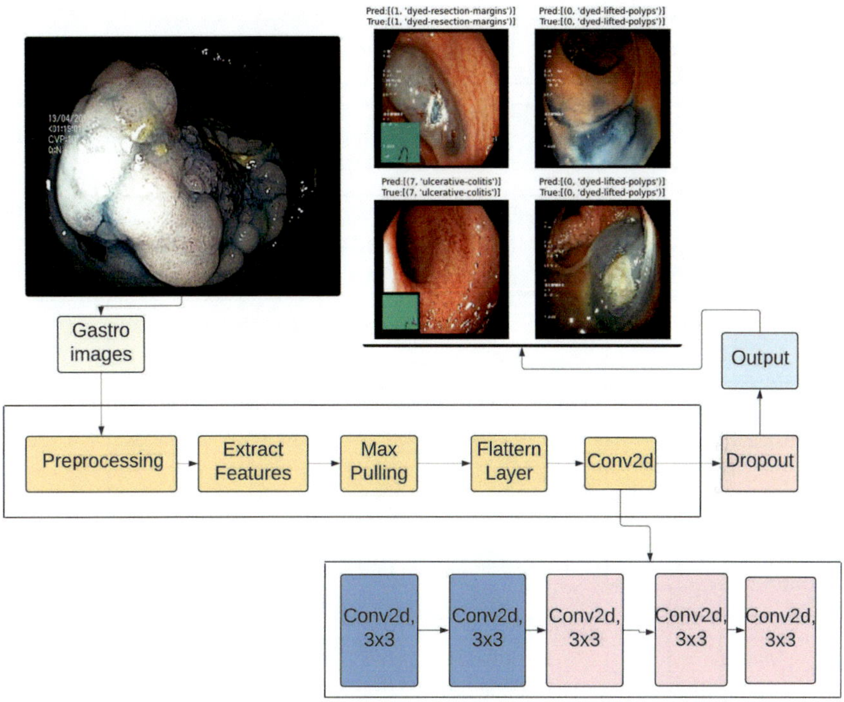

FIGURE 2.2 Workflow of the model architecture.

- ResNet50 is composed of several residual blocks, each containing multiple convolution layers:
  R = Residual Block (Pi-1, {Wij}Ni j = 1) (4)
  Pi-1 = Output of the previous pooling or residual block
  Wij = weights of the convolution layer within block i
  Ni = number of convolution layers in block i
  Final Layer:
- Global Average Pooling (GAP):
  G = GAP(Rfinal)
- Final Connected Layers:
  FC1 = G.WFC1 + bFC1
  FC2 = ReLU(FC1.WFC2 + bFC2)
  WFC1, WFC2 are weight matrices, bFC1, bFC2 are bias vectors.
- SoftMax Activation Function:
  y^ = Softmax(FC2)
  Softmax(z)i = ezi/sigmaCj=1ezj
  C = Number of Classes
  L2 Regularization:
- L2 regularization can be applied to the weights
  Regularized Loss =
  Categorical_Crossentropy (^y, ytrue) + λ·||WFC1||22 + λ·||WFC2||22
- λ is the regularization parameter.

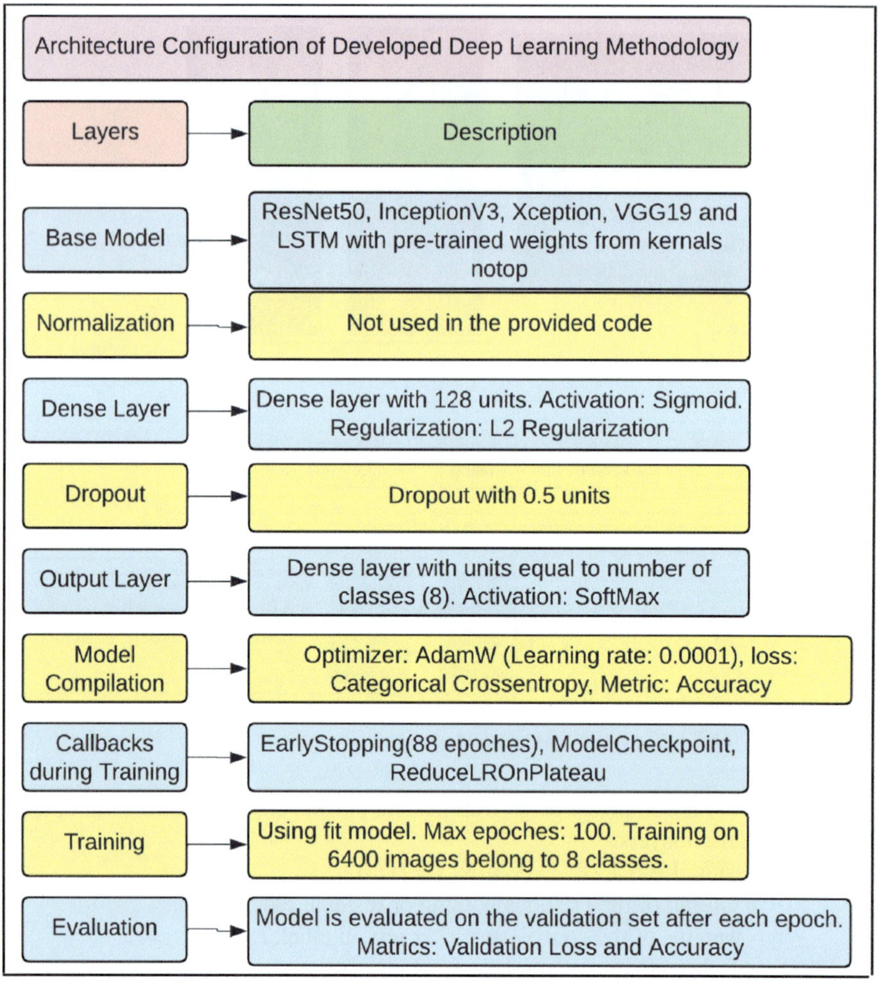

FIGURE 2.3 Architecture configuration of developed deep learning methodology.

To assess the effectiveness of the model, a confusion matrix is implemented in machine learning. The matrix contrasts a collection of data's actual case count with the predicted case count produced by the model as shown in Figure 2.4. The accuracy is obtained as in Equation 2.2.

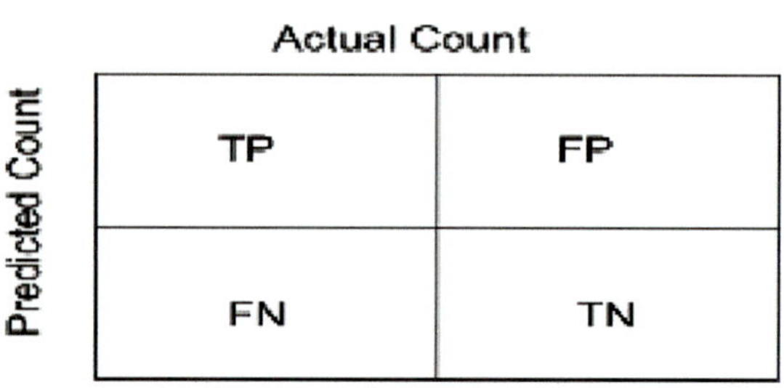

Implementation	ResNet 50	InceptionV3	Xception	VGG19	LSTM
Convolution Layers	Several ConvolutionLayers(50) with different filter sizes (32, 224, 224, 3) "Sigmoid" / SoftMax activation Function.	Several Convolution Layers(48) with different filter size(32, 299, 299, 3) "Sigmoid" / Softmax Activation Function	Several Convolution Layers(71) with different filter size(32, 299, 299, 3) "Sigmoid" / Softmax Activation Function.	Several Convolution Layers(16) and (3)fully connected Layers with different filter size(64, 224, 224, 3) "Sigmoid" / Softmax Activation Function.	LSTM is recurrent neural network type and has different layers of Convolution Layers(32) with different filter size(64, 224, 224, 3) "Tanh" / Softmax Activation.
Max Pooling Layers	1	NA	NA	NA	2
Dropout Layers	0.5	0.5	0.5	NA	0.5
Flatten Layers	1	NA	NA	1	1
Dense Layers	Fully connected with 128 units			NA	256
Loss Function	Category Cross entropy				
Batch Size	32			64	
Optimizer	AdamW				
Validation On split %	20% with accuracy as Evolution Metric				
Steps per epoch	200 steps per epoch (100 epochs)			100 steps per epoch(100 epochs)	

FIGURE 2.4 Implementation detail of deep learning models.

$$Accuracy = {(TP+TN)} \Big/ {(TP+TN+FP+FN)} \tag{2.2}$$

Here is the breakdown of the elements: True Positive: TP, True Negative: TN False Positive: FP, False Negative: FN.

2.4 RESULT AND DISCUSSION

Promising results from the stomach disease prediction using the Kvasir v2 dataset demonstrate deep learning's potential algorithms in aiding the early detection and classification of stomach diseases based on endoscopic images. The key findings of this research, along with a discussion of their clinical implications and areas for further investigation, are presented here. Figure 2.5 gives the gap between validation and training errors. The training error is calculated as the distinction between the model's predictions and the real figures from the data it was trained on. Validation error, on the other hand, is determined by comparing the model's predictions to the actual values of a distinct dataset that wasn't utilized for training. Ideally, training error and validation error would be similar. However, in the image, the training error (blue line) is observed to be higher than the validation error (red line) throughout most of the epochs. This discrepancy implies that the training data are being

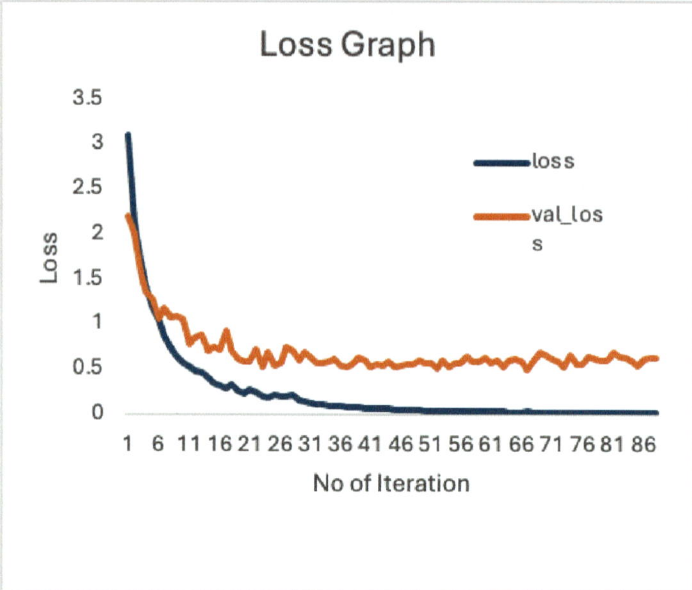

FIGURE 2.5 Gap between validation and training errors.

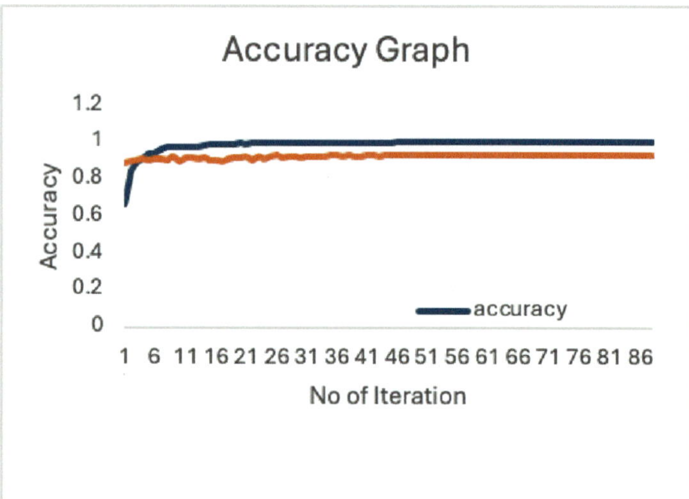

FIGURE 2.6 Comparison between training accuracy and validation accuracy.

overfitted by the model. Overfitting is a modelling issue that can be addressed by employing regularization techniques. L2 regularization was utilized to mitigate the overfitting problem. Figure 2.6 depicts the performance of a model designed to predict stomach diseases. The graph contains two lines that show the accuracy of the training and validation accuracy. Training accuracy indicates the model's predicted execution on the data it was trained with, while validation accuracy measures its performance on a separate, unseen dataset. Ideally, these lines should be closely aligned. Several scenarios can be interpreted from the graph. Similar training and validation accuracy suggest that the model is generalizable and capable of making accurate predictions on new data, representing a positive outcome.

Training accuracy exceeding validation accuracy might indicate overfitting. This suggests that during training, the model operates effectively with training data but struggles with unseen data. Addressing this issue might require adjustments to the model or the inclusion of more training data. Figure 2.7 shows the confusion matrix for the training stage, and Figure 2.8 shows the testing stage's confusion matrix. The model generally performs well, with high accuracy across most categories. However, it shows some difficulty in distinguishing subtle erosion from normal tissue and might confuse polyps with dysplasia. Gastritis is consistently identified, while hiatal hernia occasionally gets mistakes for polyps. The model correctly identifies cancer with only

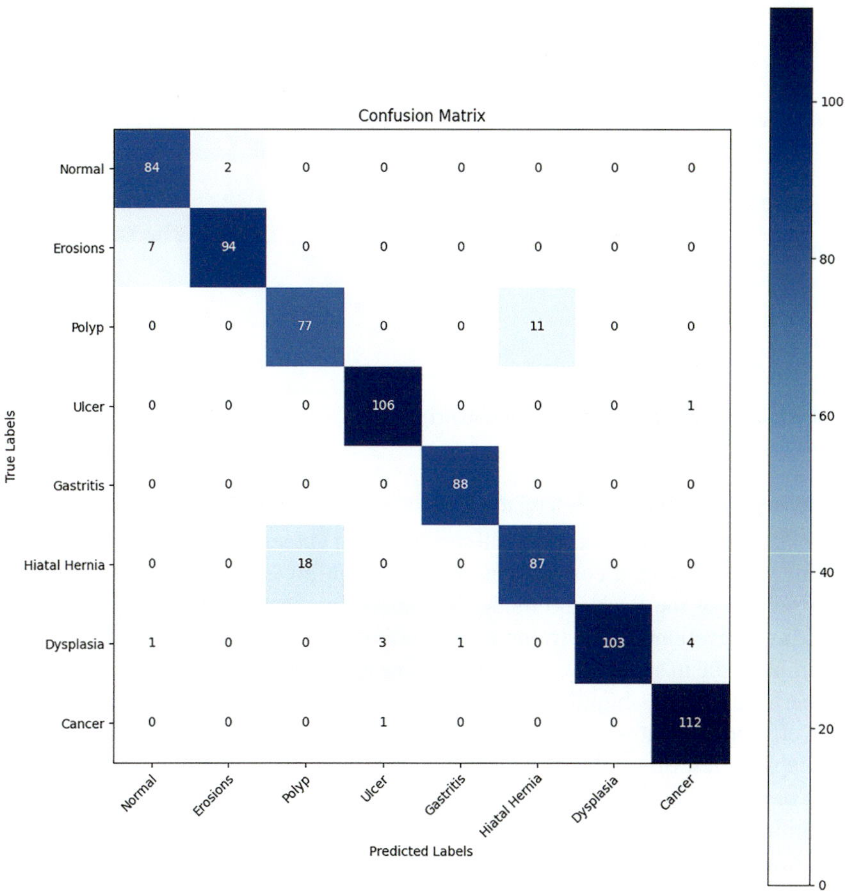

FIGURE 2.7 Training phase confusion matrix.

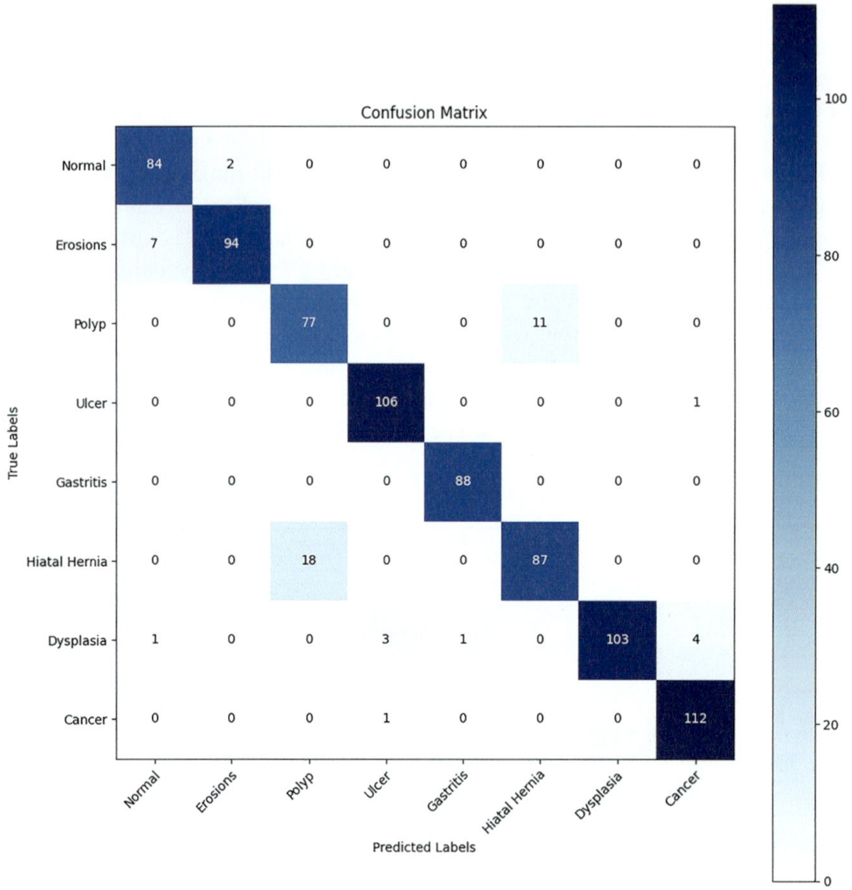

FIGURE 2.8 Testing phase confusion matrix.

one misclassification. This is a relatively good outcome considering there is a potential lack of training data for cancer but still shows a slight vulnerability for misclassification.

Table 2.2 presents a comparison of various optimizers and their impact on the performance of the ResNet50 model for classifying gastrointestinal diseases using SoftMax activation during training. The effectiveness of the chosen optimizer in minimizing mean squared error is found to be a significant determinant of the model's performance. As highlighted in Table 2.2, Adam and AdamW emerged as the most efficient algorithms, achieving a score of 94%, demonstrating their optimization capabilities. Similarly, the stochastic gradient descent (SGD) method yielded a score of 91%, while RMSprop achieved a score of 88%. In contrast, Nadam obtained a significantly lower score of 60.4%. Based on these results and the table's description, Nadam is deemed unsuitable as an optimizer for disease prediction. Table 2.3 presents the proposed work's comparison with the published work considering the dataset used and the accuracy achieved with the model used. With the proposed model the accuracy achieved is 98.6%.

TABLE 2.2
Comparative Study of Optimizer Used

Activation Function	Optimizers	Accuracy (%)
SoftMax	AdamW	94
	Adam	94
	RMSProp	88
	SGD	91
	Nadam	60.4

TABLE 2.3
Comparison with Published Results for Gastrointestinal Tract Diseases Detection

Reff No	Dataset	Model	Precision	Recall	F1	Accuracy
[11]	175 digital pictures of 91 GC patients	CNN	–	–	–	92
[14]	ETIS-LaribPolypDB	CNN	0.69	0.495	0.125	–
[14]	CVC-ClinicDB	CNN	0.10	0.49	0.165	–
Our study	**ETIS-LaribPolypDB**	**ResNet50**	**0.79**	**0.65**	**0.69**	**82**
Our study	**CVC-ClinicDB**	**ResNet50**	**0.7**	**0.65**	**0.6**	**85**

TABLE 2.4
Comparison with Published Results

Reff no	Dataset	Model	Precision	Recall	F1	Accuracy
[13]	Kvasir-SEG	ResNet34	0.8435	0.8496	0.8206	94.93
Our study	**Kvasir-SEG**	**ResnNet50**	**0.71**	**0.79**	**0.64**	**92**
	Kvasir Dataset (polyp)		**0.895**	**0.875**	**0.885**	**98.6**

Table 2.3 shows the results given in studies [10, 13]. In [13] working with CNN models and data comprises of polyp images. For comparison purpose datasets 175 digital pictures of 91 GC patients, ETIS-LaribPolypDB, CVC-ClinicDB (polyp) are considered. Our results obtained using ResNet50 model show a distinct advancement for datasets ETIS-Larib PolypDB with accuracy obtained as 82%, and for datasets CVC-ClinicDB with accuracy obtained as 85%. Also precision, recall, and F1 score has improved remarkably, indicating the enhanced robustness of the model.

Table 2.4 compares the results given in published study [12] working with ResNet34 model and dataset Kvasir-SEG (polyp) with our results working with

TABLE 2.5
Performance of ResNet34 and ResNet50 Model on the Kvasir Dataset

Model	Precision	Recall	F1	Accuracy
ResNet34	0.69	0.62	0.71	90.5
ResnNet50	**0.95**	**0.94**	**0.94**	**94**

ResNet50 model and both datasets Kvasir-SEG (polyp) and Kvasir dataset (polyp). With dataset Kvasir dataset (polyp) with accuracy obtained as 98.6%. What could be the reason ResNet34 gives better accuracy with Kvasir-SEG than Kvasir datasets? The Kvasir-SEG and Kvasir datasets are both related to medical image analysis, specifically for gastrointestinal endoscopy. However, they serve different purposes and contain different types of data. Kvasir-SEG is more specialized for segmentation tasks, whereas the Kvasir dataset serves broader detection and classification needs. Kvasir-SEG is used for training and evaluating machine learning models for image segmentation rather than classification. It helps models learn how to outline the boundaries of polyps in endoscopic images. ResNet34's skip connections allow it to retain both high- and low-level features, which is particularly beneficial for segmentation tasks where precise boundary detection is needed. This capability aligns well with Kvasir-SEG's task of finding polyp edges. ResNet50 shows a distinct advantage.

Table 2.5 gives our model performance of ResNet34 and ResNet50. Also, precision, recall, and F1 score have improved remarkably, indicating the enhanced robustness of the model. The Kvasir dataset covers a wider range of gastrointestinal diseases and anatomical locations, which increases the complexity of the task. The diversity of classes, diseases, and regions makes it harder for the model to learn all the variations effectively, and ResNet34 might struggle with the variability in image content. For classification, the model needs to learn more abstract, high-level features. Given the diverse nature of the Kvasir dataset, ResNet34 may not perform as well as a more specialized or deeper model suited for multi-class classification tasks in complex medical imaging datasets. Our results obtained using the ResNet34 and ResNet50 model for Kvasir dataset show that ResNet50 performs better with accuracy obtained as 94.6%. ResNet50 has an upper hand. Proposed methodology for gastrointestinal tract diseases detection system the source code is available in GitHub repository [16].

Table 2.6 shows the results obtained for the different classes of images considered with the proposed ResNet50 model. The accuracy surpasses the 97% mark, touching even 100%. Precision, recall, and F1 score are also topmost in line. Proposed algorithms source code is available in GitHub repository [16].

2.5 CONCLUSION

In this study, the CNN model ResNet50 was trained on the Kvasir v2 dataset utilizing various optimizers. The results obtained from comparing the performance of these optimizers demonstrated that Adam and AdamW are the most efficient, achieving

TABLE 2.6
Category-Wise Performance Analysis of ResNet50 Model on the Kvasir Dataset

Class	Precision	Recall	F1	Accuracy
Normal	0.913	0.923	0.918	99.7
Erosions	0.922	0.979	0.95	97.2
Polyp	0.895	0.875	0.885	98.6
Ulcer	0.972	1	0.986	100
Gastritis	0.967	1	0.983	100
Hiatal Hernia	0.956	0.829	0.888	98
Dysplasia	0.963	0.92	0.941	99.4
Cancer	1	0.991	0.995	100

an accuracy of 94%. These optimizers were found to predict 14% more accurately than other optimizers. Comparison with the published work indicates robustness and enhanced performance of the proposed model ResNet50 when compared with different datasets and different CNN algorithms. The model performs more accurately with an overall accuracy of 98.6%. The model is trained and tested on Kvasir v2 dataset, a set of general open-source images from different regions of the gastrointestinal tract, with annotations such as labels for diseases like polyps, ulcers, and more, and Kvasir-SEG a subset of the Kvasir dataset that is specifically focused on segmentation tasks providing images with pixel-wise segmentation masks, which indicate the exact boundaries of polyps or other abnormal regions within the gastrointestinal tract. The performance of the model ResNet50 is also tested for the Kvasir-SEG and Kvasir v2 dataset. The model performs more accurately with an overall accuracy of 94%. The category wise performance of the model shows the prediction accuracy surpassing 97% for the different classes considered and reaching 100% for three of them. For the most painful gastritis and ulcer as well as the most fearful cancer it is 100%. These results allow us to conclude that the development of a novel, efficient diagnostic tool and a well-generalized benchmarking technique for supporting gastrointestinal tract professionals has been accomplished.

Future directions for this study include improving accuracy through the implementation of data argumentation methods and combining multiple models to evaluate their performance. The development of an application that assists individuals in predicting the diseases proactively is also envisioned. This application would allow medical practitioners to input their activities and medical report images, enabling the model to generate predictions. The application of deepening models in the medical field offers significant potential for improved predictions.

This study contributes to the field by providing insights into early disease prediction, potentially aiding doctors in identifying diseases before they worsen. By leveraging patient conditions and past medical reports, the model can provide basic medication recommendations, enabling doctors to make more informed decisions and deliver improved treatment.

2.5.1 Acknowledgment

We are thankful to the authorities of the Symbiosis Institute of Technology for supporting research.

2.5.2 Funding Source

The work is supported by research support fund of Symbiosis international university.

No conflict of interest.

Hereby all authors declare no conflict of interest.

2.5.3 Ethical Statement

Not applicable because the chapter does not involve research on animals or human subjects under the Bioethics Act; it has not induced or influenced the psychological or social behavior of the respondents.

REFERENCES

[1] Zade, N., K. Gupta, S. Mutha, O. Mengshetti, G. Joshi, and R. K. Iyer. "Technical Analysis of Stock Market Trends Using LSTM for Price Prognosis." *2023 7th International Symposium on Multidisciplinary Studies and Innovative Technologies (ISMSIT)*, Ankara, Turkiye, 2023, pp. 1–5, https://doi.org/10.1109/ISMSIT58785.2023.10304934.

[2] Gu, Jianhua, Ru Chen, Shao-Ming Wang, Minjuan Li, Zhiyuan Fan, Xinqing Li, Jiachen Zhou, Kexin Sun, and Wenqiang Wei. "Prediction Models for Gastric Cancer Risk in the General Population: A Systematic Review." *Cancer Prevention Research* 15, no. 5 (2022): 309–18.

[3] Wei, Ting, Xin Yuan, Ruitian Gao, Luke Johnston, Jie Zhou, Yifan Wang, Weiming Kong, Y. Xie, Y. Zhang, D. Xu, and Z. Yu. "Survival Prediction of Stomach Cancer Using Expression Data and Deep Learning Models With Histopathological Images." *Cancer Science* 114, no. 2 (2023): 690–701.

[4] Taninaga, Junichi, Yu Nishiyama, Kazutoshi Fujibayashi, Toshiaki Gunji, Noriko Sasabe, Kimiko Iijima, and Toshio Naito. "Prediction of Future Gastric Cancer Risk Using a Machine Learning Algorithm and Comprehensive Medical Check-Up Data: A Case-Control Study." *Scientific Reports* 9, no. 1 (2019): 12384.

[5] Keniya, Rinkal, Aman Khakharia, Vruddhi Shah, Vrushabh Gada, Ruchi Manjalkar, Tirth Thaker, Mahesh Warang, and Ninad Mehendale. "Disease Prediction From Various Symptoms Using Machine Learning." Available at: SSRN 3661426 (2020).

[6] Park, Boyoung, Sarah Yang, Jeonghee Lee, Il Ju Choi, Young-Il Kim, and Jeongseon Kim. "Gastric Cancer Risk Prediction Using an Epidemiological Risk Assessment Model and Polygenic Risk Score." *Cancers* 13, no. 4 (2021): 876.

[7] Afrash, Mohammad Reza, Mohsen Shafiee, and Hadi Kazemi-Arpanahi. "Establishing Machine Learning Models to Predict the Early Risk of Gastric Cancer Based on Lifestyle Factors." *BMC Gastroenterology* 23, no. 1 (2023): 6.

[8] Mohammad, Farah, and Muna Al-Razgan. "Deep Feature Fusion and Optimization-Based Approach for Stomach Disease Classification." *Sensors* 22, no. 7 (2022): 2801.

[9] Charati, Jamshid Yazdani, Ghasem Janbabaei, Nadia Alipour, Soraya Mohammadi, Somayeh Ghorbani Gholiabad, and Afsaneh Fendereski. "Survival Prediction of Gastric

Cancer Patients by Artificial Neural Network Model." *Gastroenterology and Hepatology From Bed to Bench* 11, no. 2 (2018): 110.

[10] Ferjani, Marouane. (2020). *Disease prediction using machine learning*. https://doi.org/10.13140/RG.2.2.18279.47521.

[11] Huang, Binglu, Shan Tian, Na Zhan, Jingjing Ma, Zhiwei Huang, Chukang Zhang, Hao Zhang, F. Ming, F. Liao, M. Ji, and J. Zhang. "Accurate Diagnosis and Prognosis Prediction of Gastric Cancer Using Deep Learning on Digital Pathological Images: A Retrospective Multicentre Study." *EBioMedicine* 73 (2021).

[12] Gupta, Mayuri, and Ashish Mishra. "A Systematic Review of Deep Learning Based Image Segmentation to Detect Polyp." *Artificial Intelligence Review* 57, no. 1 (2024): 7.

[13] Jha, Debesh, Sharib Ali, Nikhil Kumar Tomar, Håvard D. Johansen, Dag Johansen, Jens Rittscher, Michael A. Riegler, and Pål Halvorsen. "Real-Time Polyp Detection, Localization and Segmentation in Colonoscopy Using Deep Learning." *IEEE Access* 9 (2021): 40496–510.

[14] Bernal, Jorge, Nima Tajkbaksh, Francisco Javier Sanchez, Bogdan J. Matuszewski, Hao Chen, Lequan Yu, Quentin Angermann, O. Romain, B. Rustad, I. Balasingham, and K. Pogorelov. "Comparative Validation of Polyp Detection Methods in Video Colonoscopy: Results From the MICCAI 2015 Endoscopic Vision Challenge." *IEEE Transactions on Medical Imaging* 36, no. 6 (2017): 1231–49. https://doi.org/10.1109/TMI.2017.2664042.

[15] https://www.kaggle.com/datasets/plhalvorsen/kvasir-v2-a-gastrointestinal-tract-dataset. Accessed January 2024.

[16] https://github.com/Bhavanam-Gireesh-Reddy/Stomach-Disease-Prediction.

3 Data-Driven Techniques for Fault Diagnosis and Predictive Maintenance

Aparna Sinha and Debanjan Das

3.1 INTRODUCTION

In the new era of Industry 4.0, industries need to evolve and adapt to the use of new technologies to make them self-aware and self-sustainable. The maintenance and health diagnosis of industrial machines, equipment, and systems play a crucial role in ensuring safety, reliability, and production efficiency across several industries. A fault is an abnormal condition that may prevent the industrial equipment from performing its required function. This leads to non-permitted deviation of one or more characteristic properties of the system from their acceptable conditions [Gao et al., 2015]. The machine's health may degrade due to prolonged usage, aging, harsh working conditions, etc., causing unscheduled downtime and accidents and impacting the yield and manufacturing cost of the industry [Webert et al., 2022]. It is to be noted that the maintenance cost accounts for nearly 15% to 60% of the manufacturing cost in the industry [Shukla et al., 2022]. Traditional health monitoring techniques involve manual inspection at scheduled intervals, which depends on the operator's experience and is prone to human error. Another primitive strategy is corrective maintenance or 'run-to-failure' in which the maintenance is done after the failure occurs [Nunes et al., 2023], leading to unexpected production halt and decreasing the life expectancy of the equipment concerned. In order to mitigate the financial losses incurred due to unexpected production stops, a proactive approach known as predictive maintenance (PdM) has evolved, which predicts a failure before its occurrence. This results in less downtime in safety-critical operations, longer asset life, and improved yield and efficiency of the industry. This chapter aims to develop a fault diagnosis framework for the overall PdM of the industrial systems and the associated machines and equipment.

In general, the existing fault diagnosis techniques can be broadly classified as model-based and data-driven. The model-based methods involve complex mathematical modeling [Topan et al., 2016], but they require vast knowledge of the internal workings of the concerned machine and are difficult to implement for real-time applications. These challenges can be mitigated using data-driven artificial intelligence (AI) and machine learning (ML) methods in conjunction with the Internet of Things (IoT). The IoT plays a pivotal role in predictive maintenance by enabling real-time and remote monitoring, data collection, and analysis, which are critical for

DOI: 10.1201/9781003473442-3

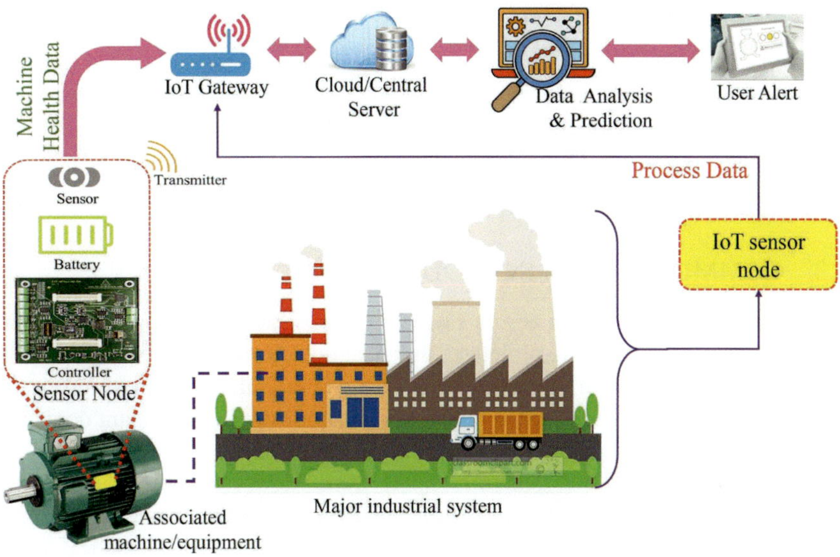

FIGURE 3.1 End-to-end predictive maintenance solution for Safe, Smart and Sustainable Industry 4.0.

anticipating equipment failures and optimizing maintenance schedules and costs. Additionally, IoT technology is highly scalable, making it suitable for monitoring thousands of assets across large industrial operations. The industrial IoT or IIoT [Yang et al., 2022] helps to improve the reliability, security, robustness, and timeliness of industrial systems. Figure 3.1 shows one such real-life industrial scenario where the IoT platform is utilized for efficient PdM.

3.2 DATA CATEGORIES FOR PREDICTIVE MAINTENANCE

In industry, predictive maintenance relies on two categories of data—process data and the associated machine health data, and each of them provides unique insights into the condition of the system or machine. As shown in Figure 3.1, both these data are acquired through the IoT platform. Now, let us first discuss these two data categories in detail.

3.2.1 Process Data

Process data refers to information related to the real-time operation or functioning of a system. This includes various system process metrics, such as temperature, pressure, flow rates, speed, concentration, voltage, current, etc. These process data are often acquired via a distributed control system (DCS), such as a supervisory control and data acquisition (SCADA) system, or using the IoT platform. Process data helps monitor the system's performance during operation. By analyzing these metrics, industrial operators can detect abnormal behaviors or deviations from normal operating ranges, which may indicate potential issues before they escalate into failures.

3.2.2 Machine Health Data

Health data provides information about the condition or integrity of the machine/equipment. It reflects the physical or structural health of the equipment. The health data are often collected through sensors and include metrics such as vibration, acoustic, ultrasound, etc. The equipment lifespan and rate of failure can be predicted by analyzing the health data.

3.3 COMMON FAULTS IN INDUSTRIES

In industries, faults can occur across a wide range of sectors, affecting systems, subsystems, and machines due to prolonged usage, aging, overheating, leakage, unfavorable working environment, poor insulation, etc. These faults have an adverse effect on the operations and yield, cause safety issues, and result in significant downtime. Some common industrial faults are discussed in this section.

Large industrial systems generally suffer from various faulty phenomena that accumulate gradually over time and ultimately lead to catastrophic accidents, unexpected downtime, and significant loss of yield. One such critical industrial system is the boiler, which is widely used in various industries such as power plants and petrochemical, textile, building and construction, and paper and pulp industries, etc. These boilers often suffers from different faults like corrosion [Nugraha et al., 2023], slagging [Xu et al., 2021], fouling [Shohet et al., 2019], clinkering [Sinha et al., 2023b], etc. The early detection and prediction of such faults in the industrial system using the different process data is essential.

Apart from the major industrial systems, there are several associated machines and auxiliary equipment that help in controlling the various operations of these systems. These include pumps, motors, valves, fans, conveyor belts, etc., and various mechanical and electrical faults may arise in these machines. The pumps are prone to cavitation faults [Liu et al., 2023], seal damage and corrosion [Ahmad et al., 2020], which can be detected using health data such as vibration and acoustic emission signals. Another important industrial machine is the motor, and it suffers from different stator [Sinha and Das, 2023b], rotor [Xu et al., 2022], and bearing [Sinha et al., 2023a] faults. Valves play an important role in regulating, directing, or controlling the flow of fluids in industrial systems, and they suffer from failures such as leakage, clearance, cracks, and notches [Jafari et al., 2014]. The industrial fans and blowers undergo dust accumulation, blade damage, misalignment, etc. [Ciaburro et al., 2023; Dhamande et al., 2023], which may also be detected by intelligent analysis of health data such as vibration and acoustic.

The continuous health data acquisition for machine health diagnosis is carried out by mounting sensor nodes, which contain sensors, batteries, microcontroller, and trans-receiver. Among these components, the microcontroller and trans-receiver are less prone to faults compared to the sensors and batteries. For a sustainable solution, the node architecture must be capable of self-health monitoring of these electronic components. Rechargeable Li-ion batteries are commonly used due to their higher energy density, lower self-discharge, and prolonged lifetime compared to other battery types [Liu et al., 2022]. However, they also degrade over time with an increase in charge-discharge cycles. Since the battery provides power to the entire sensor node, its timely health prediction is essential [Sinha et al., 2022]. Another vital component of the node, the sensors, suffers from various faults such as drift, bias, complete failure, and precision degradation [Sinha and Das, 2023c]. The presence of these faults may mask or indicate faults in the associated machines; hence, automatic sensor fault detection becomes very important [Sinha and Das, 2023d]. In real-life industrial scenarios, faults may occur simultaneously in both the sensors and the associated machines. In such situations, sensor fault isolation and correction are required for successful health monitoring of the industrial machines [Sinha and Das, 2023a].

3.4 PREDICTIVE MAINTENANCE: THE GOOD AND THE BAD

Traditionally, the industry operators perform preventive maintenance (PM) on a scheduled basis, regardless of the machine's condition and necessity for maintenance. This often leads to higher maintenance costs and inefficient use of resources. On the other hand, reactive maintenance (RM) is performed only after a failure occurs, causing unexpected downtime and higher repair costs. The challenges posed by these under-maintenance and over-maintenance methods can be overcome by predictive maintenance. It is a proactive maintenance strategy that uses data-driven methods to predict when industrial machines or systems may fail and allows early maintenance to be performed to prevent failures. The following subsections discuss the advantages and disadvantages of PdM.

3.4.1 Advantages of Predictive Maintenance

Some important advantages of PdM are listed as follows:

- **Reduced Downtime:** PdM reduces unexpected machine failures by identifying potential issues before complete breakdown. This ensures that maintenance is scheduled during planned downtime, thereby minimizing unplanned operational halts.
- **Cost Efficiency:** PdM averts major equipment failures and optimizes maintenance schedules, thereby minimizing costly emergency repairs and overtime labor.
- **Extended Equipment Lifespan:** Early detection of faults prevents excessive damage to machines, allowing them to operate more efficiently for a longer period.
- **Improved Safety:** Early identification of potential hazards and machine failures reduces the risk of accidents and injuries caused by malfunctioning machinery, ensuring a safer work environment.
- **Data-Driven Insights:** PdM analyses data collected via sensors and IoT to monitor equipment performance in real-time, providing valuable insights into machine health and efficiency and assisting in informed decision-making.
- **Asset Management:** PdM optimizes resource usage by conducting maintenance only when necessary, thus helping with efficient asset management.
- **Increased Reliability:** PdM strategy ensures well-maintained and monitored equipment, which improves reliability and reduces the frequency and severity of production interruptions, thereby increasing the yield.

- **Energy Efficiency:** PdM increases energy efficiency by keeping machines in optimal working condition, avoiding excess energy consumption by faulty machines.
- **Environmental Benefits:** PdM helps to maintain machines in optimal working conditions, prevents unexpected breakdowns, improves energy efficiency, and reduces waste, emissions, and adverse impact on the environment. Thus, the industries can meet sustainability goals with reduced energy consumption.

For a better understanding, the advantages of PdM over the traditional PM and RM strategies have been summarized in Table 3.1. Despite its many advantages, PdM comes with its own set of challenges, which are discussed in the next subsection.

3.4.2 Disadvantages of Predictive Maintenance

The key disadvantages of PdM are discussed as follows:

- **High Initial Costs:** A significant initial investment is required in technology, including sensors, data acquisition tools, and predictive analytics software to set up a PdM system. Small and medium-sized businesses with limited budgets may struggle to manage the high initial costs.
- **Technical Expertise:** Another challenge in PdM implementation is the requirement of specialized knowledge in data analytics, machine learning, and condition-monitoring technologies. Industries will need to hire or train personnel with expertise in these areas, leading to additional expenses.
- **Compatibility Issues:** PdM is not suitable for all types of equipment (e.g., low-criticality or simple machines), making traditional maintenance strategies more justifiable for such assets. Another challenge may arise in integrating

TABLE 3.1
Performance Comparison of PdM with PM and RM Strategies

Criteria	PdM	PM	RM
Maintenance Timing	Real-time condition based	At pre-scheduled intervals	Post failure
Health Monitoring	Real-time, data-driven	Usage or time-based	None
Downtime	Minimal, planned	Moderate, planned	High, unplanned
Cost Efficiency	High	Moderate	Low
Equipment Lifespan	Maximum extended	Extended	Reduced
Safety	High	Moderate	Low
Asset Management	Optimized	Inefficient	Inefficient
Reliability	High	Moderate	Low
Energy Efficiency	High	Moderate	Low
Environmental Impact	Low	Moderate	High

PdM systems with existing systems like enterprise resource planning (ERP), computerized maintenance management systems (CMMS), or supervisory control and data acquisition (SCADA), requiring significant customization.

- **False Alarms:** PdM systems can sometimes generate false positives (predicting a failure that does not happen) or false negatives (failing to predict an impending failure). Such prediction errors can lead to unnecessary or missed maintenance, respectively.
- **Cybersecurity Risks:** PdM systems using IoT devices and cloud-based platforms are often vulnerable to cyberattacks, causing data breaches, disruption of operations, and compromised asset security.
- **Cultural Resistance:** Shifting from traditional maintenance strategies to PdM requires a cultural change within the organization. Employees and management may resist adopting new technologies or processes, especially if they are comfortable with current practices.

For industries considering PdM implementation, it is important to weigh these disadvantages against the potential long-term benefits, taking into account factors like the type of equipment, available resources, and readiness for technological adoption.

3.5 THE PREDICTIVE MAINTENANCE BLUEPRINT

Predictive maintenance involves a systematic approach to condition monitoring, starting from real-time data acquisition to detection and prediction of machine failures. The key steps of predictive maintenance workflow in industries are shown in Figure 3.2. The detailed breakdown of the steps involved in PdM has been explained in the following subsections.

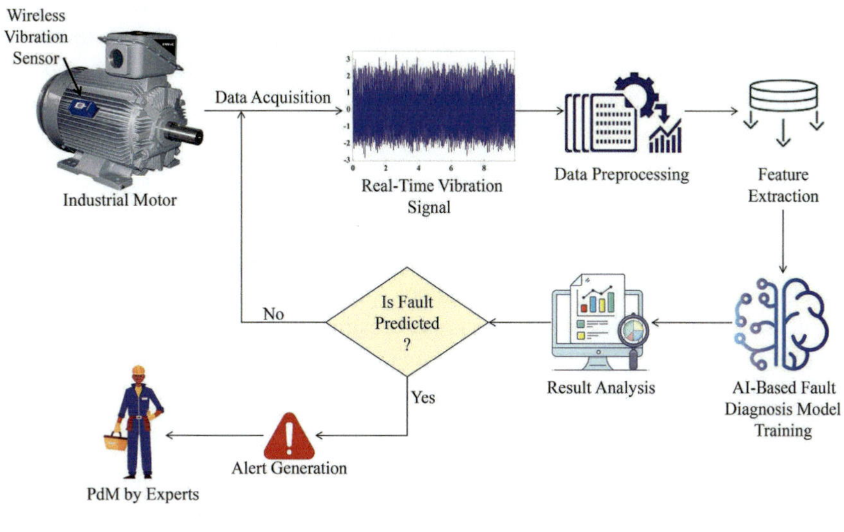

FIGURE 3.2 Generalized workflow for implementing predictive maintenance in industries.

3.5.1 Data Acquisition

Data acquisition forms the foundation of the PdM strategy, as it provides the raw information required for effective fault diagnosis and prediction. Some of the common sensors used for data collection for PdM are as follows:

(i) Vibration Sensors: These sensors measure the vibrations in rotating machinery. Abnormality in vibrations may indicate wear, misalignment, or any other faults.
(ii) Acoustic Sensors: These sensors help in detecting sound waves generated by machines. Abnormal acoustic data can indicate a wide variety of faults, such as leaks, cracks, etc.
(iii) Temperature Sensors: These sensors are often employed to detect overheating, which is a sign of mechanical or electrical issues. They are also used to maintain an optimum environment in critical applications such as warehouse management.
(iv) Ultrasound Sensors: The ultrasound sensors capture high-frequency sounds to detect leaks, electrical discharges, material fatigue in structures, or bearing lubrication issues.
(v) Flow Sensors: These sensors measure the flow rate in fluid systems to detect the presence of any irregularities or blockages.
(vi) Proximity Sensors: These sensors can identify alignment problems by measuring the distance or positioning of moving parts.
(vii) Current/Voltage Sensors: These sensors monitor the health of electrical machines to detect faults such as spikes, short circuits, etc.

In certain industrial applications, data acquisition systems (DAQ) are utilized to collect sensor data and convert it into digital form for further analysis. They contain signal conditioners to prepare raw sensor signals for processing by filtering or amplification. DAQ systems also include analog-to-digital converters (ADC) to convert the analog sensor signals into digital data so that they can be analyzed by computers. The effectiveness of the different sensors heavily relies on how and where they are installed. Incorrect sensor mounting can lead to false readings, missed faults, and inaccurate diagnosis.

3.5.1.1 Sensor Mounting

To ensure that the collected data (e.g., vibration, temperature, sound, etc.) accurately reflects the true condition of the machines, proper sensor mounting is essential. Correct sensor positioning ensures consistent reading and helps minimize noise from external factors. This enables a reliable trend analysis and fault diagnosis scheme for critical industrial machines and systems. Some common sensor mounting techniques are discussed here.

(i) Direct/Contact Mounting: The sensor is directly attached to the machine under testing, such that the sensor is in constant contact with the machinery and obtains real-time data. However, they are not securely fastened and may cause data loss due to sensor movement. This type of mounting is often done for mounting vibration sensors on motor or pump casings.

(ii) Magnetic Mounting: In this process, the sensors are mounted using magnets, enabling quick attachment and removal. This is generally used in temporary or portable applications. This type of mounting is also used to mount certain vibration sensors on electrical machines. It does not provide as firm a contact as permanent mounting and is not suitable for non-metallic surfaces.

(iii) Stud Mounting: This is a permanent sensor mounting method in which the sensor is bolted or screwed into place using a threaded stud. This mounting often finds use in attaching vibration sensors on a rotating machine. The attachment is secure with minimum sensor movement, but the installation can be time-consuming and may require certain equipment modifications.

(iv) Adhesive Mounting: It is a semi-permanent sensor installation where the sensors are mounted directly on the machine surface using strong industrial adhesives or epoxy. This type of mounting is done to attach lightweight accelerometers or thermometers on non-metallic surfaces. However, it is unsuitable for heavy sensors or high-vibration environments, which may lead to the weakening of the adhesive with time, affecting the reliability of the data collected.

Figure 3.3 depicts the pictorial representation of these sensor installation techniques. Apart from this, the suitable method (online/offline) for data collection must also be determined, taking the necessity and available resources into consideration, as discussed in the next subsection.

3.5.1.2 Online and Offline Data Collection

Real-time health monitoring can be performed by continuous collection and analysis of data. For example, enterprise systems like SCADA collect and transmit process data. Another example includes online data collection in remote areas via IoT-enabled sensors, which can send data wirelessly to cloud storage. In some applications, data processing and analysis occur locally at the sensor node before transmission. This is known as *edge computing*, and it reduces latency, transmission power, and bandwidth usage.

Apart from online data collection, health monitoring data is sometimes collected periodically or manually. The operators use portable sensory devices for manual data logging at specific intervals. Dataloggers are often utilized in areas without

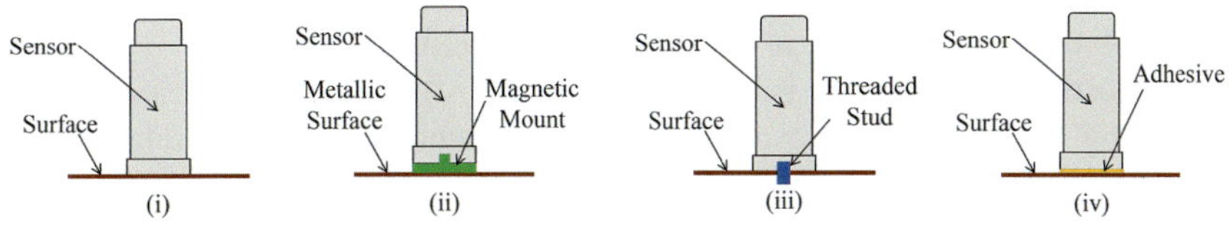

FIGURE 3.3 Some popular sensor mounting techniques: (i) direct, (ii) magnetic, (iii) stud, and (iv) adhesive mounting.

constant network connectivity to collect and store sensor data at regular intervals for later analysis. Before using the collected raw data for model training and analysis, proper cleaning and preprocessing must be done to make it suitable for statistical analysis, which is explained in the following subsection.

3.5.1.3 Data Preprocessing

One of the most important steps in the PdM blueprint is data preprocessing, which transforms raw sensor data into a clean, structured, and useful format by handling noise, missing values, and inconsistencies. The key steps involved in data preprocessing for PdM are as follows:

- In PdM, sensors can fail, communication errors may occur, or data may be lost, resulting in missing values. Missing data can be handled by imputation, forward/backward fill, interpolation, or dropping the missing records.
- Sensor data often contains noise, outliers, or inconsistencies that can affect model performance. Data cleaning using smoothing, low-pass filters, or statistical methods (e.g., Z-scores, interquartile range) helps remove irrelevant or erroneous data.
- The data can be rescaled by normalization or standardization to make it suitable for the statistical models.

Apart from these preprocessing steps, the PdM strategy also faces the challenge of data imbalance, which has been explained in detail in the next subsection.

3.5.1.4 Data Imbalance Issue

In real-life scenarios, industrial machines mostly operate in healthy conditions, and faulty instances are few and far between. Hence, the normal operation data is significantly more compared to the faulty data. This often gives rise to the data imbalance issue, where the trained AI models may become biased toward the majority class (normal operation) and fail to correctly predict rare but critical failure events. Thus, the trained models will be ineffective at detecting faults, despite having high accuracy. In order to address the data imbalance issue, the following methods may be applied:

- Oversampling faulty class data by interpolation can help balance the dataset. SMOTE (synthetic minority oversampling technique) is a widely used algorithm that generates synthetic data samples to mitigate the imbalance issue.
- Unsupervised learning algorithms (such as autoencoders) can be used for fault detection as they can be trained using healthy data only.
- Boosting algorithms (e.g., AdaBoost, XGBoost) ensure the efficient handling of data imbalance problem by giving more weight to misclassified instances, particularly from the minority class.
- Generative adversarial networks (GANs) can also be used to create realistic synthetic failure data based on the patterns in the original dataset, thereby balancing the dataset.

- Cross-validation with stratified sampling will ensure that the training and test splits are balanced and the trained model is evaluated on data from both healthy and faulty classes.

After the collected data is preprocessed, it becomes suitable for further training and analysis. Based on the application and resource availability, the model training can be performed in the edge device or in the local/cloud server. The introduction of IoT has paved the way for wireless data communication between sensor nodes and servers. This has been briefly explained in the next subsection.

3.5.1.5 Data Communication

The data collected by sensors are transmitted wirelessly to centralized databases or cloud storage via IoT gateways, using different protocols as mentioned next:

- Wi-Fi/Bluetooth/Zigbee for short-range wireless communication.
- Cellular networks (4G/5G) for long-range wireless transmission.
- LoRaWAN/NB-IoT for low-power, long-range wireless transmission. These protocols are best suited for industrial applications.

3.5.2 Feature Engineering

One of the most essential steps in predictive maintenance is feature engineering. It involves creating new, more relevant features from the original data to help the data-driven model better understand the underlying patterns, making predictions about machine health and failures more accurate. The common feature extraction techniques are as follows:

(i) Time-Domain Features: These are derived directly from raw sensor signals over time. They are easy to compute and often provide valuable insights into machine health. Table 3.2 gives the mathematical formula of several time-domain features. Here, x_i denotes the sensor value at time i, and N is the total number of observations in the time window.

(ii) Frequency-Domain Features: In industrial systems, many faults manifest as changes in the frequency content of original sensor signals. In such cases, frequency-domain features need to be extracted by transforming raw time-series data into the frequency domain using techniques such as Fourier transform. The mathematical representation of different frequency-domain features is given in Table 3.3. Here, $x(n)$ is the discrete time-domain signal, j is the imaginary term, N denotes the total number of samples, and C represents the spectral centroid.

(iii) Time-Frequency Domain Features: Time-frequency domain features combine both time and frequency information to capture more complex patterns in the signal. They are particularly useful for analyzing non-stationary signals, whose frequency content changes over time [Boashash, 2015]. Some common techniques for deriving time-frequency domain features are short-time Fourier transform (STFT), wavelet transform, and Hilbert-Huang transform (HHT).

TABLE 3.2
Various Time-Domain Features and Their Formula

Time-Domain Features	Formula
Mean (μ)	$\mu = \frac{1}{N}\sum_{i=1}^{N} x_i$
Variance (Var)	$\text{Var} = \frac{1}{N}\sum_{i=1}^{N} (x_i - \mu)^2$
Standard Deviation (σ)	$\sigma = \sqrt{\frac{1}{N}\sum_{i=1}^{N} (x_i - \mu)^2}$
Root Mean Square (RMS)	$\text{RMS} = \sqrt{\frac{1}{N}\sum_{i=1}^{N} x_i^2}$
Peak-to-Peak Amplitude (P-to-P)	$\text{P-to-P} = max(x_i) - min(x_i)$
Skewness (S)	$S = \frac{\frac{1}{N}\sum_{i=1}^{N} (x_i - \mu)^3}{\sigma^3}$
Kurtosis (K)	$K = \frac{\frac{1}{N}\sum_{i=1}^{N} (x_i - \mu)^4}{\sigma^4}$
Crest factor (CF)	$\text{CF} = \frac{max(x_i)}{\text{RMS}}$
Energy (E)	$E = \sum_{i=1}^{N} x_i^2$

TABLE 3.3
Various Frequency-Domain Features and Their Formula

Frequency-Domain Features	Formula
Discrete Fourier Transform/DFT ($X(f_k)$)	$X(f_k) = \sum_{n=0}^{N-1} x(n) e^{-j2\pi kn/N}$
Power Spectral Density (PSD)	$\text{PSD}(f_k) = \frac{\lvert X(f_k)\rvert^2}{N}$
Peak Frequency	Peak Frequency = f_k where max $\lvert X(f_k)\rvert$
Spectral Bandwidth	Spectral Bandwidth = $\sqrt{\frac{\sum_{k=0}^{N-1} (f_k - C)^2 \lvert X(f_k)\rvert}{\sum_{k=0}^{N-1} \lvert X(f_k)\rvert}}$
Spectral Entropy	Spectral Entropy = $-\sum_{k=0}^{N-1} P(f_k) \log_2 P(f_k)$

TABLE 3.3 (Continued)
Various Frequency-Domain Features and Their Formula

Frequency-Domain Features	Formula
Band Energy Ratio	$\text{Band Energy Ratio} = \dfrac{\sum_{f_{low}}^{f_{high}} \lvert X(f_k)\rvert^2}{\sum_{k=0}^{N-1} \lvert X(f_k)\rvert^2}$
Frequency Variance	$\text{Frequency Variance} = \dfrac{\sum_{k=0}^{N-1} (f_k - C)^2 \lvert X(f_k)\rvert}{\sum_{k=0}^{N-1} \lvert X(f_k)\rvert}$

After extracting a wide variety of features, it becomes essential to select the most relevant and informative features while eliminating the irrelevant or redundant ones. Proper feature selection can significantly improve model accuracy and reduce overfitting and computational complexity. The feature selection methods can be broadly categorized into three types:

(i) Filter Methods: In this method, the features are ranked on the basis of statistical criteria and the top-ranked features are selected. Examples: Pearson correlation, chi-square test, etc.
(ii) Wrapper Methods: This method uses an ML model to evaluate subsets of features. The optimal feature subset is determined by iteratively adding or removing features and evaluating model performance. It is a computationally expensive process. Examples: forward selection, backward elimination, and recursive feature elimination.
(iii) Embedded Methods: This method performs feature selection during the training process and is typically embedded in the AI model. They have less computational complexity compared to wrapper methods and consider interactions between features. Examples: LASSO (L1 Regularization), ridge (L2 Regularization), random forest, gradient boosting, etc.

3.5.3 Model Training for Fault Diagnosis

After data collection, preprocessing, and feature engineering, suitable machine learning (ML) or deep learning (DL) models are developed that can detect or predict faults in industrial machines and systems. Fault detection helps to identify and react to issues in real-time, ensuring that equipment failures are addressed as they occur. For fault detection and identification of fault types, classification models must be used. On the other hand, fault prediction/prognosis aims to predict future faults, enabling proactive maintenance and reducing downtime. Regression models are chosen when we want to predict the next occurrence of fault and the remaining useful life (RUL). Thus, fault detection and prognosis models are two key components of predictive maintenance, serving different but complementary roles in maintaining machinery health and preventing breakdowns. Table 3.4 shows the comparison of the two models based on several important criteria. The dataset must be split into training, testing, and validation data for efficient model building and evaluation.

3.5.4 Model Deployment in Predictive Maintenance

Model deployment is the final step in developing a predictive maintenance system. The trained ML or DL model is moved from the development environment to the production environment to make real-time predictions. The deployed model must be capable of handling continuously evolving data and conditions. Proper deployment of the PdM model can significantly reduce downtime, improve operational efficiency, and lower maintenance costs. The deployment architectures can be broadly classified into three types, which are discussed as follows:

(i) Edge Deployment: The model is deployed on local edge devices, such as microcontrollers and embedded systems present in the sensor nodes. The data analysis is done locally, largely reducing the latency, transmission power requirement, and bandwidth usage. However, the models must be lightweight to be successfully deployed on resource-constrained edge devices.
(ii) Cloud Deployment: The model is deployed on a cloud server/infrastructure (e.g., AWS, Azure, Google Cloud, etc.), making it easily usable for large

TABLE 3.4
Comparison between Fault Detection and Prognosis Models

Criteria	Fault Detection	Fault Prognosis
Objective	Detect faults in real-time after they occur	Estimate the time before a fault occurs or predict future degradation
Model Type	Classification	Regression
Data Type	Labeled data	Historical time-series data
Time Horizon	Short-term analysis	Long-term analysis
Model Complexity	Usually simpler	More complex
Interpretability	Easily interpretable	Harder to interpret
Decision-Making	Reactive	Proactive
Algorithms Used	Decision trees, SVM, random forest, etc.	SVR, GPR, LSTM, etc.
Evaluation Metrics	Confusion Matrix, Accuracy, F1 score, etc.	RMSE, MAE, AE, RUL accuracy, etc.

Notes: SVM: support vector machine; SVR: support vector regressor; GPR: Gaussian process regressor; LSTM: long short-term memory; RMSE: root mean squared error, MAE: mean absolute error; AE: absolute error.

datasets and complex models. However, this method faces the challenge of increased latency due to network speed and is often prone to data privacy concerns.

(iii) On-Premise/In-house Deployment: The model is deployed on local servers or within the industry's own IT infrastructure. Local data processing and analysis ensures low latency and improved data security. This deployment process is unsuitable for small and medium industries since it involves high infrastructure costs and may require significant hardware upgrades.

3.5.5 User Interface for Predictive Maintenance

A suitable user interface (UI) must be designed to provide the maintenance teams, engineers, and operators in industries with easy access to the real-time predictions and insights generated by the deployed PdM models. Some desirable features of the UI designed for predictive maintenance are discussed next:

- A central dashboard for an overview of real-time machine data and predictions. This will include live data feeds, color-coded alerts, data trends, etc., for easy visualization.
- Pop-up notifications and SMS/e-mail alerts can be integrated with the UI to notify operators when the system detects an anomaly or when predicted failure is imminent.
- Data visualization elements (e.g., time-series plots, heat maps, etc.) can be incorporated into the UI to enable interactive data exploration and pattern investigation.
- Generation of a maintenance calendar for past and upcoming maintenance activities aligned with RUL predictions.
- Implementation of different access levels for the operators, technicians, and engineers so that they can see the information relevant to their tasks only.
- Display the model performance metrics such as accuracy, precision, recall, etc., so that the users can track false predictions and ensure efficient model performance.

3.6 EXPLAINABLE AI IN PREDICTIVE MAINTENANCE

The AI-based models are used for efficient and accurate predictive maintenance in modern industries. However, their *black-box* nature prevents the maintenance personnel and operators from considering them trustworthy enough for real-life deployment [Sinha and Das, 2023a]. Explainable AI (XAI) plays an important role in demystifying complex models by providing understandable explanations and root cause analysis for decisions and predictions, thereby enhancing the trust between users and AI systems [Chowdhury et al., 2023]. In industries with strict regulatory requirements (e.g., aerospace, health care), explanations are often required for automated decisions. The use of XAI ensures regulatory compliance by providing clear reasoning for model outcomes. XAI also enables the engineers to identify areas for PdM model improvement by understanding the reasons behind incorrect predictions. Among the various available XAI methods, the two most commonly used are SHAP and LIME. However, these methods usually require additional interpretation procedures other than the actual prediction models, and they may not be compatible with all types of ML models. To mitigate this drawback, explainable boosting machine (EBM) has been introduced recently to provide the result interpretation during the prediction process [Liu and Sun, 2023]. All these three methods have been explained briefly in the following subsections.

3.6.1 Shapley Additive Explanations (SHAP)

SHAP is a powerful tool used for interpreting the outputs of ML models. It identifies which input features have the most significant impact on the model's predictions. Thus, it assists in refining the models via targeted feature engineering by identifying which features have the highest contribution. SHAP utilizes several visualization techniques such as summary plot, force plot, dependence plot, and waterfall plot to help interpret the prediction results. For example, a maintenance engineer can see which sensor readings (e.g., vibration, acoustic, temperature, etc.) are most influential in predicting machine failure by using SHAP.

3.6.2 Local Interpretable Model-Agnostic Explanations (LIME)

LIME is an approach that aims to explain individual predictions rather than the overall model behavior. By focusing on local explanations for individual predictions, LIME provides insights into how specific input features contribute to the model's output, making it easier to interpret and trust the results of the ML algorithms. LIME explanations can be visualized by bar chart, decision boundary, and feature contribution values. For example, if an ML model predicts an imminent failure, LIME can help explain why that specific prediction was made by considering the current state of various sensor readings.

3.6.3 Explainable Boosting Machine (EBM)

EBM is an interpretable ML algorithm that provides human-understandable explanations for predictions while maintaining high prediction accuracy. It combines the strengths of additive models and boosting techniques to deliver accurate predictions with relevant explanations for informed decision-making. For example, in manufacturing and energy sectors, EBM can predict equipment failures while simultaneously explaining the impact of various sensor readings.

CASE STUDIES

Use Case I: Valve Failure Prognosis in Thermal Power Plants

Problem Description: Valve failure is a major concern in thermal power plants, as valves are one of the critical components of the plant. It often leads to operational disruptions, safety hazards, and increased maintenance costs. Therefore, an intelligent predictive maintenance scheme is required for the health prediction of the valves.

Dataset Description: Various process and health data, such as temperature, pressure, vibration, and steam expansion, have been obtained from a thermal power plant. The data has been acquired at intervals of 10 minutes and contains a total of 56 input features.

Data Preprocessing and Feature Engineering: The raw data contains several missing values, which have been handled by interpolation. After that, the dataset is smoothed for noise removal and standardized for data scaling. After the data has been prepared, feature selection is done using the random forest algorithm for dimensionality reduction. The top 10 input features (shown in Figure 3.4) are selected that have the highest impact on the fault occurrence.

Fault Prognosis Model: For efficient predictive maintenance, the remaining working days (RWD) of the valve before complete failure must be determined. For this purpose, the EBM model has been utilized to predict valve health and also provide useful insights into the prediction explanations. The estimation of RWD can be visualized in Figure 3.5, where the red line denotes the actual RWD and the green scatter plot indicates the predicted RWD.

Model Interpretation: The use of EBM for valve health prognosis has the added benefit of obtaining an in-built interpretation of the prediction outcome. The local interpretation of the prediction using the EBM model is given in Figure 3.6, where the orange and blue bars, respectively, indicate the positive and negative impacts of a particular input feature on the model output.

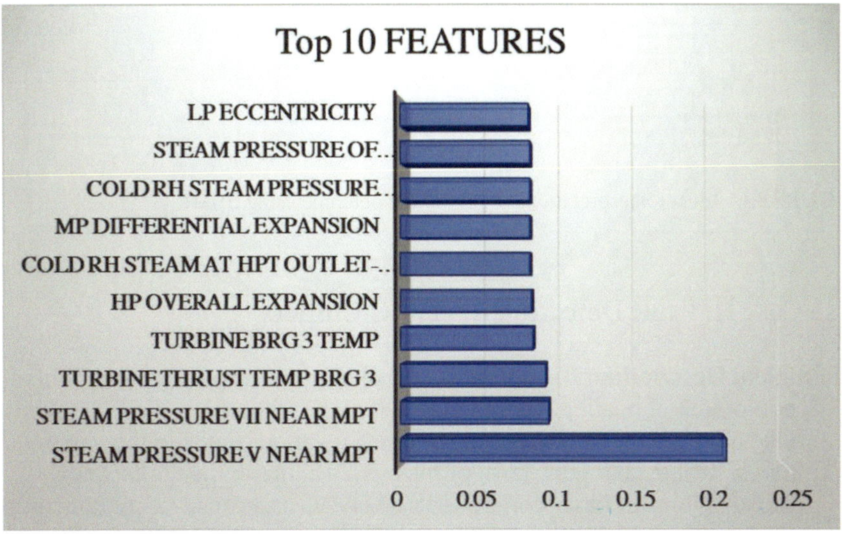

FIGURE 3.4 Top 10 high impact features obtained from random forest.

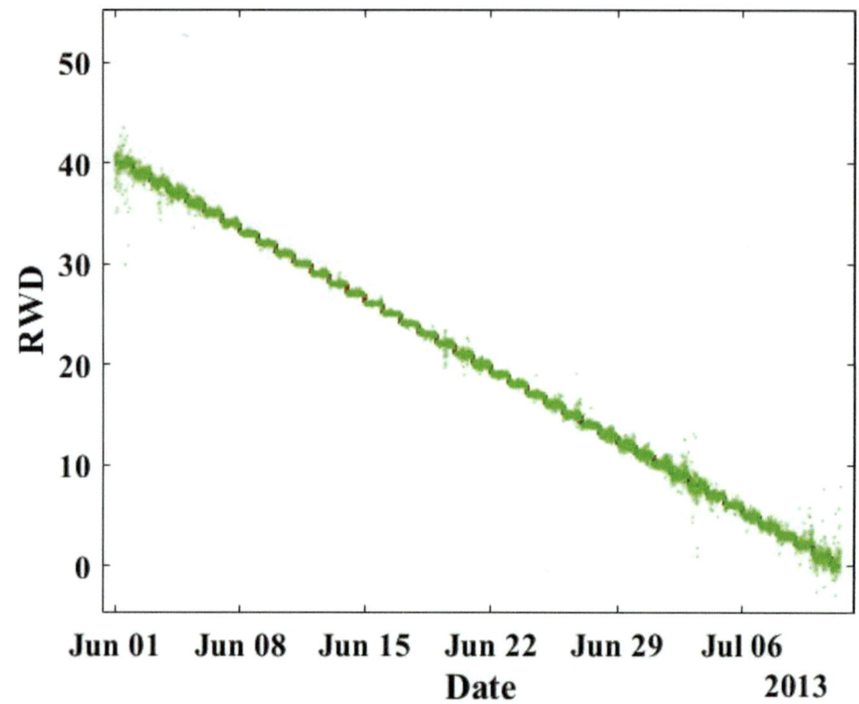

FIGURE 3.5 RWD estimation for valve health prognosis using EBM.

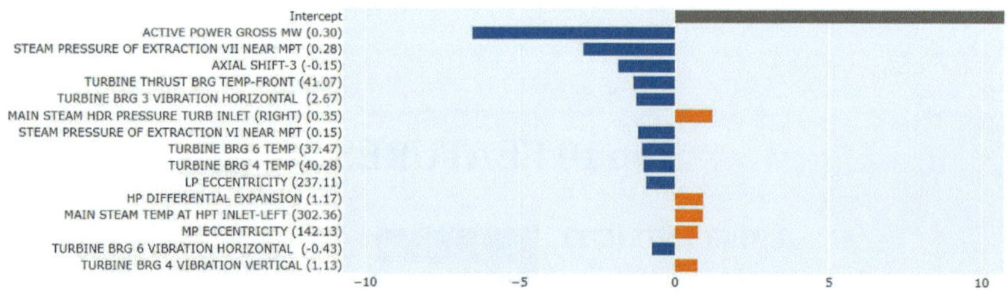

FIGURE 3.6 Local interpretations of prediction outcome using EBM.

Use Case II: Fault Detection in HVAC Chillers

Problem Description: The chiller is one of the most expensive and critical equipment of heating, ventilation, and air-conditioning (HVAC) systems. Like all other machines, it can suffer from various faults in the valves, tubes, heat exchangers, fans, pumps, etc. Failure in the chillers may cause failures in other components of HVAC and cause safety concerns.

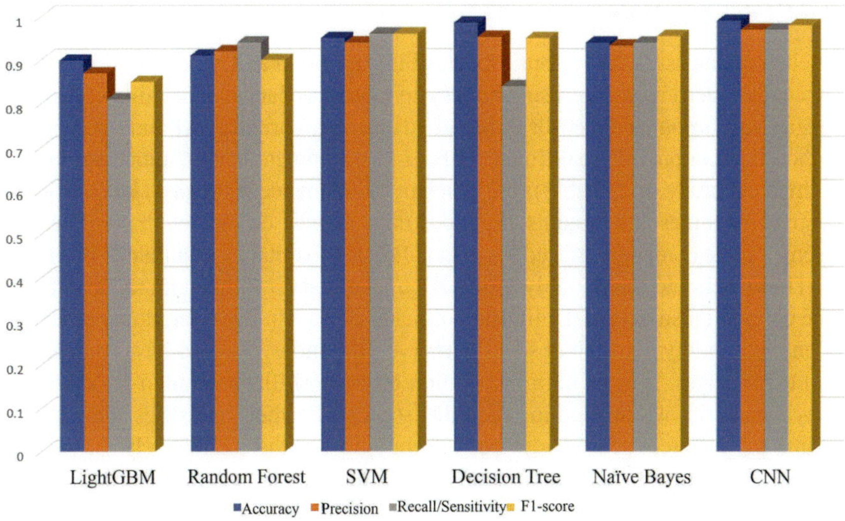

FIGURE 3.7 Evaluation metrics of various models for HVAC fault detection.

Hence, early detection and diagnosis of chiller faults are essential to reduce the maintenance costs and sudden operational disruptions in HVAC systems.

Dataset Description: Various sensor data have been obtained from the HVAC unit at the interval of 5 minutes. The data collected include exhaust air flow, water temperature, air temperature, etc., and contain 25 fault types. The number of input features in the raw dataset is 27.

Data Preprocessing and Feature Engineering: The raw data is cleaned and smoothed to remove any noise elements. The data is then normalized to make it suitable for further statistical processing and analysis. To reduce the dimension of the dataset, the random forest algorithm is applied, which selects the top 10 features with the highest impact on HVAC faults. The irrelevant and redundant features are removed to optimize the dataset and decrease the complexity of the fault detection model.

Fault Detection Model: After data preparation and feature selection, several common ML and DL classification models are trained. The dataset is split into training, testing, and validation data in the ratio of 70:15:15. The best model is chosen on the basis of the evaluation metrics (e.g., accuracy). Figure 3.7 depicts a comparison of evaluation metrics for the different ML and DL models. From this analysis, it is clear that the convolutional neural network (CNN) gives the highest accuracy (99.5%) and can be used for fault detection in this use case.

3.7 CONCLUSION

This chapter discusses the various aspects of the use of AI and ML in predictive maintenance in modern industries using both system process data and machine health data. By using vast amounts of sensor data and advanced algorithms, AI and ML with IoT handholding can provide real-time insights into equipment health, anticipate failures with high accuracy, and enable more efficient maintenance strategies. Apart from the industrial machines and systems, the focus must also be on the health monitoring of the sensor node components used for data collection to obtain a sustainable PdM solution. These technologies not only minimize unplanned downtime and reduce maintenance costs but also extend the lifespan of machinery, improve operational efficiency, and enhance safety across industries. However, the industries also have to deal with certain challenges, such as high installation costs, upskilling the industry operators, and cybersecurity while adopting the PdM strategy for their industries. This chapter explains the different sensory devices and how to use them effectively for successful PdM. The various predictive maintenance steps, such as data collection, feature engineering, fault diagnosis, and model deployment, have also been discussed with real-life case studies to give the readers a complete idea of PdM implementation. The explainability of AI models, with tools like SHAP, LIME, and EBM, strengthens their trust and transparency, making these smart solutions accessible to engineers and decision-makers. Thus, the integration of AI and ML into predictive maintenance represents a technical and cultural shift in how industries manage and maintain their critical assets. This evolution will be crucial in ensuring more reliable, cost-effective, and sustainable operations across various industries and organizations.

REFERENCES

Ahmad, Z., Rai, A., Maliuk, A. S., and Kim, J.-M. (2020). Discriminant feature extraction for centrifugal pump fault diagnosis. *IEEE Access*, 8:165512–165528.

Boashash, B. (2015). *Time-frequency signal analysis and processing: A comprehensive reference*. Academic Press.

Chowdhury, D., Sinha, A., and Das, D. (2023). XAI-3DP: Diagnosis and understanding faults of 3-D printer with explainable ensemble AI. *IEEE Sensors Letters*, 7(1):1–4.

Ciaburro, G., Padmanabhan, S., Maleh, Y., and Puyana-Romero, V. (2023). Fan fault diagnosis using acoustic emission and deep learning methods. *Informatics*, 10:24. MDPI.

Dhamande, L. S., Bhaurkar, V. P., and Patil, P. N. (2023). Vibration analysis of induced draught fan: A case study. *Materials Today: Proceedings*, 72:657–663.

Gao, Z., Cecati, C., and Ding, S. X. (2015). A survey of fault diagnosis and fault-tolerant techniques—part I: Fault diagnosis with model-based and signal-based approaches. *IEEE Transactions on Industrial Electronics*, 62(6):3757–3767.

Jafari, S., Mehdigholi, H., and Behzad, M. (2014). Valve fault diagnosis in internal combustion engines using acoustic emission and artificial neural network. *Shock and Vibration*, 2014(1):823514.

Liu, G., and Sun, B. (2023). Concrete compressive strength prediction using an explainable boosting machine model. *Case Studies in Construction Materials*, 18:e01845.

Liu, K., Peng, Q., Sun, H., Fei, M., Ma, H., and Hu, T. (2022). A transferred recurrent neural network for battery calendar health prognostics of energy-transportation systems. *IEEE Transactions on Industrial Informatics*, 18(11):8172–8181.

Liu, X., Mou, J., Xu, X., Qiu, Z., and Dong, B. (2023). A review of pump cavitation fault detection methods based on different signals. *Processes*, 11(7):2007.

Nugraha, A. D., Harianto, H., and Muflikhun, M. A. (2023). Failure in power plant system related to mitigations and economic analysis; A study case from steam power plant in Suralaya, Indonesia. *Results in Engineering*, 17:101004.

Nunes, P., Santos, J., and Rocha, E. (2023). Challenges in predictive maintenance: A review. *CIRP Journal of Manufacturing Science and Technology*, 40:53–67.

Shohet, R., Kandil, M. S., and McArthur, J. (2019). Machine learning algorithms for classification of boiler faults using a simulated dataset. *IOP Conference Series: Materials Science and Engineering*, 609:062007.

Shukla, K., Nefti-Meziani, S., and Davis, S. (2022). A heuristic approach on predictive maintenance techniques: Limitations and scope. *Advances in Mechanical Engineering*, 14(6):16878132221101009.

Sinha, A., Ahmed, S. F., and Das, D. (2023a). Explainable AI for bearing fault detection systems: Gaining human trust. In *2023 IEEE Guwahati subsection conference (GCON)*, pp. 1–6, Guwahati, India, 23–25 June 2023.

Sinha, A., and Das, D. (2023a). An explainable deep learning approach for detection and isolation of sensor and machine faults in predictive maintenance paradigm. *Measurement Science and Technology*, 35(1):015122.

Sinha, A., and Das, D. (2023b). Machine learning-based explainable stator fault diagnosis in induction motor using vibration signal. In *2023 IEEE international instrumentation and measurement technology conference (I2MTC)*, pp. 1–6.

Sinha, A., and Das, D. (2023c). SNRepair: Systematically addressing sensor faults and self-calibration in IoT networks. *IEEE Sensors Journal*, 23(13):14915–14922.

Sinha, A., and Das, D. (2023d). XAI-LCS: Explainable AI-based fault diagnosis of low-cost sensors. *IEEE Sensors Letters*, 7(12):1–4.

Sinha, A., Das, D., and Palavalasa, S. K. (2023b). dClink: A data-driven based clinkering prediction framework with automatic feature selection capability in 500 MW coal-fired boilers. *Energy*, 276:127448.

Sinha, A., Das, D., Udutalapally, V., and Mohanty, S. P. (2022). iThing: Designing next-generation things with battery health self-monitoring capabilities for sustainable IIoT. *IEEE Transactions on Instrumentation and Measurement*, 71:1–9.

Topan, P. A., Ramadan, M. N., Fathoni, G., Cahyadi, A. I., and Wahyunggoro, O. (2016). State of charge (SOC) and state of health (SOH) estimation on lithium polymer battery via Kalman filter. In *2016 2nd international conference on science and technology-computer (ICST)*, pp. 93–96.

Webert, H., Döß, T., Kaupp, L., and Simons, S. (2022). Fault handling in industry 4.0: Definition, process and applications. *Sensors*, 22(6):2205.

Xu, L., Huang, Y., Yue, J., Dong, L., Liu, L., Zha, J., Yu, M., Chen, B., Zhu, Z., and Liu, H. (2021). Improvement of slagging monitoring and soot-blowing of waterwall in a 650MWe coal-fired utility boiler. *Journal of the Energy Institute*, 96:106–120.

Xu, Y., Liu, J., Wan, Z., Zhang, D., and Jiang, D. (2022). Rotor fault diagnosis using domain-adversarial neural network with time-frequency analysis. *Machines*, 10(8):610.

Yang, D., Mahmood, A., Hassan, S. A., and Gidlund, M. (2022). Guest editorial: Industrial IoT and sensor networks in 5G-and-beyond wireless communication. *IEEE Transactions on Industrial Informatics*, 18(6):4118–4121.

4 Harnessing Machine Learning for Peptidase Inhibitor Prediction in Therapeutic Discovery

Aminu Jibril Sufyan, Muthu Kumar Thirunavukkarasu, Aliyu Zainulabidin Ashiru, and Rakesh Sengupta

4.1 INTRODUCTION

Enzymes are biological molecules, which are most commonly proteins, speeding up chemical reactions in living organisms. Since the processes include metabolism, DNA replication, and protein synthesis, they are essentially elementary to a living organism's survival. Highly selective and efficient enzymes accelerate chemical reactions without undergoing an alteration in the process themselves [1]. This is why their dysregulation plays such a significant role in preventing diseases. As biomarkers, the enzymes can act as useful diagnostic markers for disease as well as disease monitoring and treatment [2]. Diseases like cancer, diabetes, or neurological disorders may be indicated by changes in levels or activities of enzymes [3]. This is due to their specificity, drugability, and biomarker potential, which make them attractive targets for controlling diseases. This process can be modulated using small molecules, antibodies, or other therapeutic agents. Thus, enzymes form an excellent target for the treatment of any disease [4]. A bioclass of enzymes comprises functional groups of enzymes that exhibit analogous properties, such as substrate specificity, reaction mechanisms, or biological processes. Understanding this bioclass may lead to the identification of potential therapeutic targets [5]. Specific targets in disease mechanisms have become prevalent with enzyme bioclasses such as peptidases. In general, the specific enzymes offer specific targets for therapeutic intervention [6]. Targeting these enzymes can lead to effective treatments of metabolic disorders and cancer as well as inflammatory diseases, neurological disorders, and infectious diseases [7].

Peptidases is a key group of proteolytic enzymes, a target for treating cancer, cardiovascular diseases, and infectious diseases, taking part in the breakdown and processing of proteins. Enzymes break down proteins to regulate many cellular processes. Peptidase dysregulation leads to disease and can be targeted for effective treatments [8].

 DOI: 10.1201/9781003473442-4

By understanding such functions and regulations of this enzyme, individuals in research may look forward to developing the appropriate disease diagnosis, treatment, and prevention strategy. Thus, the aforementioned highlighted importance of enzymes in disease control clearly points to an area where researchers should continue their exploration of the functions, regulations, and therapeutic potential as targets for intervention [9].

It is, therefore, important to design drugs that interact with enzymes in the inhibition of enzyme activity associated with diseases. Such computational methods such as machine learning (ML) models used for predicting enzyme inhibition are found valuable by pharmaceutical companies and other industries [10]. Our study extends related models with comprehensive machine learning models, predicting ligand activity of the specific enzymes peptidase bioclass.

These models enable the predictions of ligand activity on broad scales of peptidase enzyme bioclass that will lead to quick identification of potential inhibitors and accelerates drug discovery. Contrasting with the current machine learning models that have narrow coverage and limited accuracy and are not comprehensive enough, our work intends to revolutionize the prediction of enzyme inhibition by offering a model specifically for peptidases [11].

This approach will enable researchers to quickly and reliably identify potential inhibitors for the vast variety of peptidase enzymes, thereby accelerating drug discovery and opening new avenues of treatment that could cure several diseases. This work by us will hopefully catalyze a revolution in drug discovery in general and human health in particular.

4.2 MATERIALS AND METHODS

4.2.1 Dataset Retrieval

Ligands associated with the peptidase enzyme bioclass were downloaded from the Therapeutic Target Database (https://db.idrblab.net/ttd/full-data-download). The datasets retrieved contain target information, drug information, cross-matching IDs between TTD drugs and public databases, synonyms of drugs and small molecules in TTD, and target-to-compound mappings with activity data.

4.2.2 Dataset Preparation

All ligands showing activity on the peptidase enzyme bioclass were prepared as a dataset for machine learning models creation. This bioclass contains 200 various peptidase enzymes, with a total number of 56,903 ligands showing activity on these enzymes. After duplicate removal, 31,224 unique ligands were saved. The dataset was constructed by means of SMILES of the ligands; they were divided into two categories according to their IC_{50} values: ligands, for which IC_{50} <1000 nM, were marked as active (1), and those with IC_{50} >1000 nM were marked as inactive (0). The quantities of the resulting active and inactive ligands amount to 14,384 and 16,840, respectively. PubChem IDs have been used for retrieving the corresponding SMILES in the PubChem database.

4.2.3 Molecular Representation

In machine learning, fingerprints are numerical representations of molecular structures and properties, enabling the analysis and comparison of molecules. Structural fingerprints, such as MACCS and Morgan, encode molecular information into a format that can be processed by algorithms [12]. These fingerprints are used in various applications, including virtual screening to identify potential drug candidates, QSAR modeling to predict biological activity, molecular similarity searching, and clustering/classification to group molecules by similarity or activity [13]. By leveraging fingerprints, machine learning models can efficiently process and analyze large molecular datasets, accelerating drug discovery and development [14].

MACCS (molecular access system) encodes molecular structure and properties into a 166-bit binary vector. MACCS is a widely used fingerprinting method in cheminformatics and drug discovery. In this, four different fingerprints were chosen. Utilizing a hashing algorithm, MACCS captures various molecular features, including atom types and counts, bond types and counts, ring systems and connectivity, and functional groups and fragments [15].

Morgan fingerprints, specifically Morgan 2 and Morgan 3, are circular fingerprints that capture molecular structure and atom neighborhoods, providing a more comprehensive representation of molecular topology [16].

A substructure fingerprint is a type of molecular fingerprint that identifies the presence of specific substructures or functional groups within a molecule. This fingerprinting method breaks down a molecule into its constituent parts, such as rings, chains, and functional groups, and generates a binary vector indicating the presence or absence of each substructure [17]. Machine learning models were built here with these fingerprints to choose the best with the best performing model.

4.2.4 Machine Learning Models Construction

Machine learning models were built for each of the four fingerprints, making it 32 models with each peptidase enzymes-ligands dataset. Eight ML algorithms were generated using the prepared enzymes bioclass dataset. To create ML models, Google Colab Notebook was used. First, the necessary Python packages were imported onto the workspace, including Matplotlib, RDKit, sklearn, and others. Subsequently, the following models were accessed to predict the status of breast cancer.

4.2.4.1 Random Forest Classifier

This is an ensemble technique for machine learning that makes multiple decision trees based on random subsets of data for the purpose of classifying, regressing, and more [18].

4.2.4.1.1 Logistic Regression

Logistic regression focuses on the relationship between a predictor variable and an outcome variable that would have applications in predicting binary or multi-class outcomes and thus is an important technique in health care and beyond [19].

4.2.4.1.2 Naïve Bayes (NB)

The simplest Bayesian network model is built on the application of the Bayes theorem to produce "probabilistic classifiers" or, in other words, supervised machine learning methods [20].

4.2.4.1.3 Gradient Boosting

This machine learning method, called gradient boosting of trees, uses pseudo-residuals as targets, distinguishing it from other methods of boosting. It uses functional space boosting to create a strong ensemble by combining many weak prediction models, usually simple decision trees [21].

4.2.4.1.4 Extreme Gradient Boosting (XGB)

XGB is an ensemble method that builds on gradient boosting, incrementally adding models while adjusting the learning rate [22].

4.2.4.1.5 K-Nearest Neighbors (KNN)

K-nearest neighbors, in simple terms, is a non-parametric, simple, machine learning algorithm that is applicable to both regression and classification problems [23].

4.2.4.1.6 AdaBoost Classifier

It gathers the incorrectly classified data points and gives them greater weights. In the ensuing iterations, there was close monitoring of higher-weighted data points. Until a lower error rate was achieved, this process was repeated [24].

4.2.5 Feature Selection and Model Optimization

Morgan 2 fingerprint and random forest were chosen as the best model for further analysis due to their superior performance. Feature selection was performed using random forest to reduce dimensionality and enhance model interpretability. Optuna was employed to optimize the hyperparameters of the RF model with 5000 steps. The final models were generated based on the best parameters obtained from the optimization process.

4.2.6 Model Evaluation

The optimized models were evaluated using metrics such as precision, accuracy, recall, F1 score, ROC, AUC, and MCC to assess their predictive capabilities on the blind dataset.

4.3 RESULTS AND DISCUSSION

4.3.1 Model Performance Evaluation

Eight machine learning models were developed for each of the four fingerprints, resulting in a total of 32 models using the peptidase enzyme bioclass dataset (https://github.com/MuthuBIN/PeptidaseBioclassPrediction). The overall workflow of the study is mentioned in Figure 4.1. The ML algorithms that were generated using the fingerprints have been evaluated. Each of the used model was validated using external validation metrics to evaluate the predictive capacity of the model. The evaluation accuracy metrics of the models were arranged in Tables 4.1–4.4. Further evaluations were made by the following parameters: prediction accuracy as the ability of a model to correctly differentiate actives and inactive cases. Precision and recall score are the two important parameters, which are used to evaluate the predictive performance of both positive and negative targets [25]. The weighted harmonic mean of the test's precision and recall is known as the F1 measure, which quantifies the accuracy of a test.

The best performing model of the four built, according to its performance metrics, is Morgan 2. This model performed with the best accuracy, predictive power, ability to capture complex molecular relationships, and robustness in identifying potential inhibitors, as can be seen in Table 4.1.

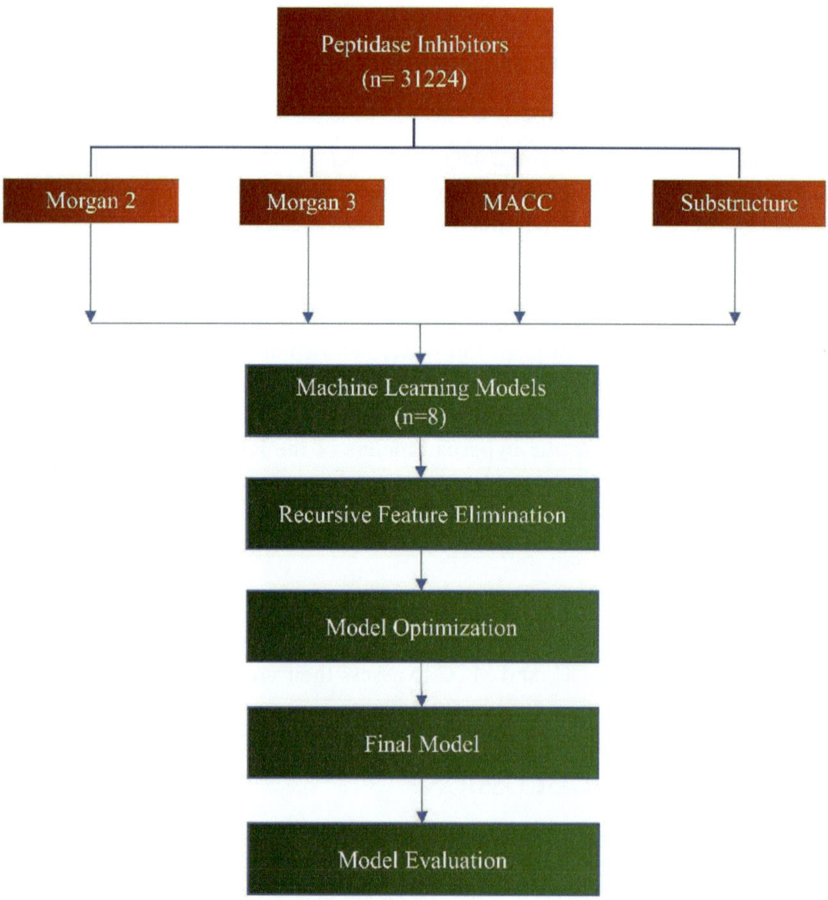

FIGURE 4.1 Overall workflow for the peptidase model generation.

TABLE 4.1
Performance Metrics of Machine Models with Morgan 2 Fingerprint on Test Peptidase Bioclass Dataset

		Precision		Recall		F1_score		
SN	Model Name	0	1	0	1	0	1	Accuracy
1	Random forest	0.84	0.84	0.87	0.81	0.86	0.83	0.84
2	Logistic regression	0.77	0.76	0.76	0.72	0.79	0.74	0.77
3	KNN	0.86	0.82	0.84	0.83	0.85	0.83	0.84
4	NB	0.74	0.68	0.72	0.70	0.73	0.69	0.71
5	XGB	0.80	0.83	0.87	0.75	0.83	0.78	0.81
6	LGB	0.79	0.82	0.86	0.73	0.82	0.77	0.80
7	AdaBoost	0.67	0.67	0.77	0.55	0.77	0.60	0.67
8	Decision tree	0.80	0.76	0.80	0.77	0.80	0.77	0.77

TABLE 4.2
Performance Metrics of Machine Models with Morgan 3 Fingerprint on Test Peptidase Bioclass Dataset

		Precision		Recall		F1_score		
SN	Model Name	0	1	0	1	0	1	Accuracy
1	Randomforest	0.84	0.85	0.88	0.81	0.86	0.83	0.84
2	Logistic regression	0.76	0.74	0.79	0.72	0.77	0.73	0.75
3	KNN	0.85	0.83	0.86	0.83	0.85	0.83	0.84
4	NB	0.72	0.70	0.76	0.65	0.74	0.67	0.71
5	XGB	0.81	0.82	0.86	0.76	0.83	0.79	0.81
6	LGB	0.79	0.82	0.86	0.74	0.82	0.77	0.80
7	AdaBoost	0.67	0.68	0.77	0.57	0.72	0.62	0.68
8	Decision tree	0.79	0.76	0.79	0.76	0.79	0.76	0.78

The performance accuracies of the assessed models were observed to be within the range of 0.71–0.84. The peptidase class of enzymes were particularly noticed to perform best using Morgan 2 fingerprint and random forest model with an accuracy of 0.84. As presented in Table 4.2, Morgan 3 despite being structurally like Morgan 2, yielded slightly lower performance metrics with accuracies ranging from 0.68–0.84. This could be because Morgan 3 captures higher-order molecular interactions more effectively than those that might have been irrelevant to peptidase activity predictions. The application of Morgan 2 facilitates confident identification of promising compounds, so that the entire drug discovery process runs faster. For instance, as opposed to the MACCS fingerprints, which have a fixed predefined length and are

TABLE 4.3
Performance Metrics of Machine Models with MACC Fingerprint on Test Peptidase Bioclass Dataset

		Precision		Recall		F1_score		
SN	Model Name	0	1	0	1	0	1	Accuracy
1	Random_forest	0.82	0.81	0.84	0.79	0.83	0.80	0.82
2	Logistic regression	0.74	0.73	0.78	0.68	0.76	0.76	0.74
3	KNN	0.83	0.79	0.81	0.80	0.82	0.79	0.81
4	NB	0.72	0.53	0.37	0.84	0.49	0.65	0.58
5	XGB	0.80	0.79	0.82	0.77	0.81	0.98	0.80
6	LGB	0.75	0.77	0.83	0.68	0.79	0.72	0.76
7	AdaBoost	0.67	0.64	0.72	0.58	0.69	0.61	0.65
8	Decision tree	0.77	0.74	0.78	0.73	0.78	0.74	0.74

TABLE 4.4
Performance Metrics of Machine Models with Substructure Fingerprint on Test Peptidase Bioclass Dataset

		Precision		Recall		F1_score		
SN	Model Name	0	1	0	1	0	1	Accuracy
1	Random_forest	0.82	0.84	0.87	0.78	0.85	0.81	0.83
2	Logistic regression	0.74	0.73	0.78	0.68	0.76	0.76	0.74
3	KNN	0.85	0.82	0.84	0.83	0.85	0.82	0.84
4	NB	0.60	0.62	0.81	0.36	0.69	0.46	0.60
5	XGB	0.82	0.82	0.86	0.78	0.84	0.86	0.82
6	LGB	0.78	0.80	0.85	0.72	0.81	0.76	0.79
7	AdaBoost	0.67	0.64	0.72	0.58	0.69	0.61	0.65
8	Decision tree	0.77	0.74	0.78	0.73	0.78	0.74	0.74

focused on predefined substructures, Morgan fingerprints are based on molecular context, including bond orders in addition to atom types, for the generation of one-of-a-kind fingerprint. As shown in Table 4.3, the accuracies achieved by MACCS fingerprints varied between 0.58–0.82. Similarly, the accuracies of the substructure fingerprints listed in Table 4.4 lie in the range of 0.65–0.83. Although they may be beneficial for certain applications, these fingerprints were not as useful in this study. The fixed-length nature of MACCS probably omitted nuanced molecular features captured by circular Morgan fingerprints. Similarly, the substructure fingerprints, which focus on the presence or absence of specific fragments, were less informative for the task at hand compared to Morgan 2, which captures more intricate relationships between molecular features.

Morgan 2 differs in their radius values, with Morgan 3 being more comprehensive, capturing longer-range interactions. These fingerprints are particularly useful for identifying complex molecular relationships, making them well-suited for applications like virtual screening, QSAR modeling, and molecular similarity searching. Their ability to capture nuanced molecular features make Morgan 2 a valuable tool for researchers, enabling the identification of possible drug candidates and the exploration of molecular structure-activity relationships. By leveraging this fingerprint, scientists can gain a deeper understanding of molecular interactions and accelerate drug discovery [26].

4.3.2 Feature Selection and Model Optimization

Important features were predicted according to the top-scoring random forest model. Recursive feature elimination (RFE) with fivefold cross-validation was applied to the Morgan 2 fingerprints, comprising a total of 2,047 features. RFE selected 1,726 features and excluded the rest (Figure 4.2 and Figure 4.3). Based on those features, a new dataset was created that was used to optimize the eight models through hyperparameter tuning using Optuna, as illustrated in Table 4.5. Efficient algorithms from the Optuna system identified the best combination of those hyperparameters, including the number of decision trees, the maximum depth, and the least amount of samples needed to split a node. It demonstrated superior performances through accuracy between 0.71 to 0.8 (Table 4.5). It is important to note that random forest and LGB displayed maximum accuracy value of 0.85 with the optimal parameters.

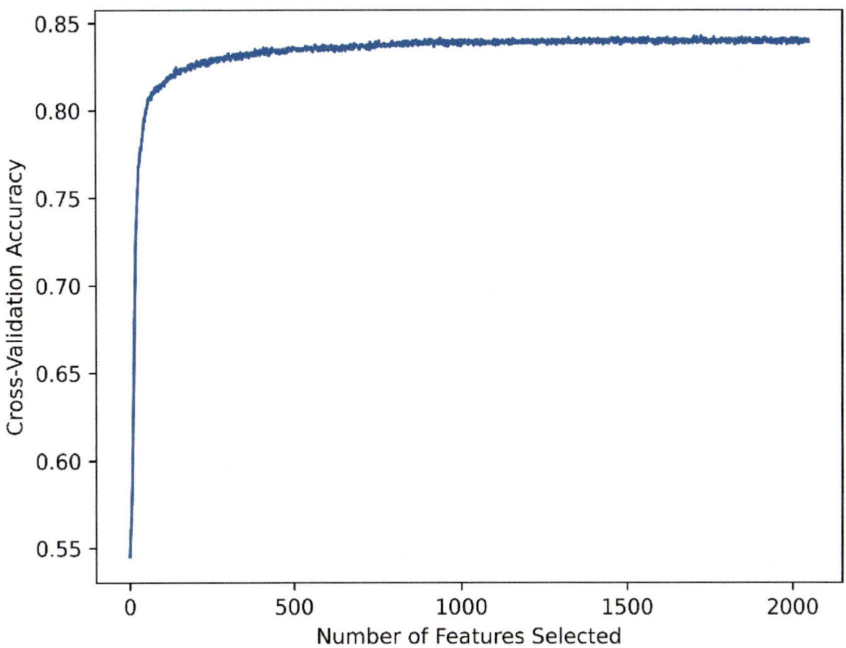

FIGURE 4.2 Recursive feature elimination (RFE) plot with 5-fold cross-validation.

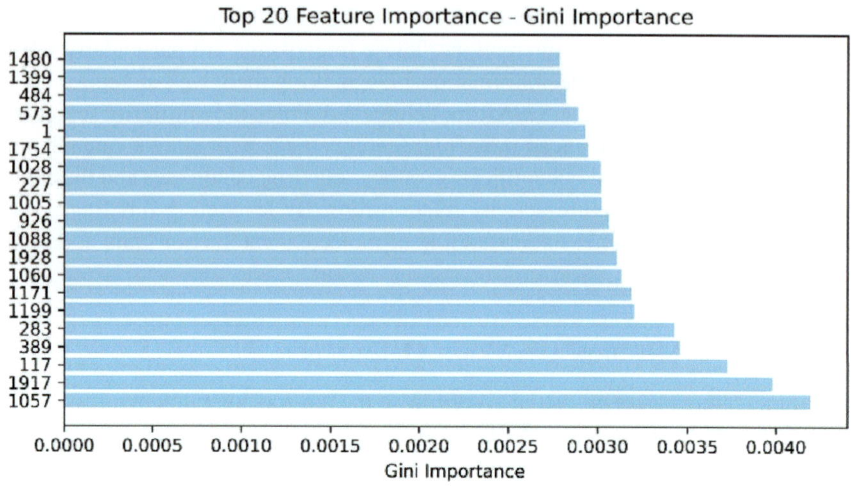

FIGURE 4.3 Top-ranked features among the 2048 Morgan fingerprints representing the importance in terms of Gini importance.

TABLE 4.5
Best Hyperparameters of the Models Obtained during Optuna Hyperparameter Tuning

SN	Model Name	Optimization Parameters	Accuracy
1	Random forest	Random_state=85, max_depth=84, n_estimators=100, min_samples_split=2	0.85
2	Logistic regression	C=0.17496662701821752, max_iter=1000, solver='liblinear')	0.77
3	KNN	KNeighborsClassifier(n_neighbors = 7, leaf_size = 39, p = 1)	0.84
4	NB	none	0.71
5	XGB	colsample_bytree=0.77, importanclearning_rate=0.09, max_depth=10, n_estimators=470,	0.85
6	LGB	max_depth=64, n_estimators=1040	0.85
7	AdaBoost	none	0.67
8	Decision tree	none	0.78

Table 4.5 displays the best combination of hyperparameters that yielded the highest performance metric during the analysis.

4.3.3 Model Evaluation

The AUC of the ROC curve was determined to evaluate the model's performance in this study by plotting the true against the false positive rate at various thresholds.

The AUC ROC has been considered an effective measure for binary classifiers [27]. Figure 4.4 displays all curves of the evaluation of the models. Notably, the mean ROC-AUC of the models was 0.91. The ROC-AUC of the produced models were observed to fall between 0.76 and 0.92. Moreover, the models proved to have a high precision both in classes, along with substantial F1-scores and recall values.

4.3.4 Matthews Correlation Coefficient (MCC)

MCC values were observed to be within the range of 0.32–0.69 as shown in Figure 4.5 indicating strong correlation between predicted and actual classes. The XGB model achieved the highest MCC score (0.69), confirming its exceptional performance. Our models appear promising on predictive grounds since a higher value of MCC means this model is both capable of labeling instances in both classes. MCC metric is useful in performance estimation of the model on imbalanced datasets since it considers both true positives and false negatives [28].

4.3.5 Model Comparison

XGB model showed the best performance with highest values of accuracy, ROC-AUC, and MCC [29]. These results indicate that the presented algorithms with optimal fingerprint are very well-correlated with ligands activity prediction on the

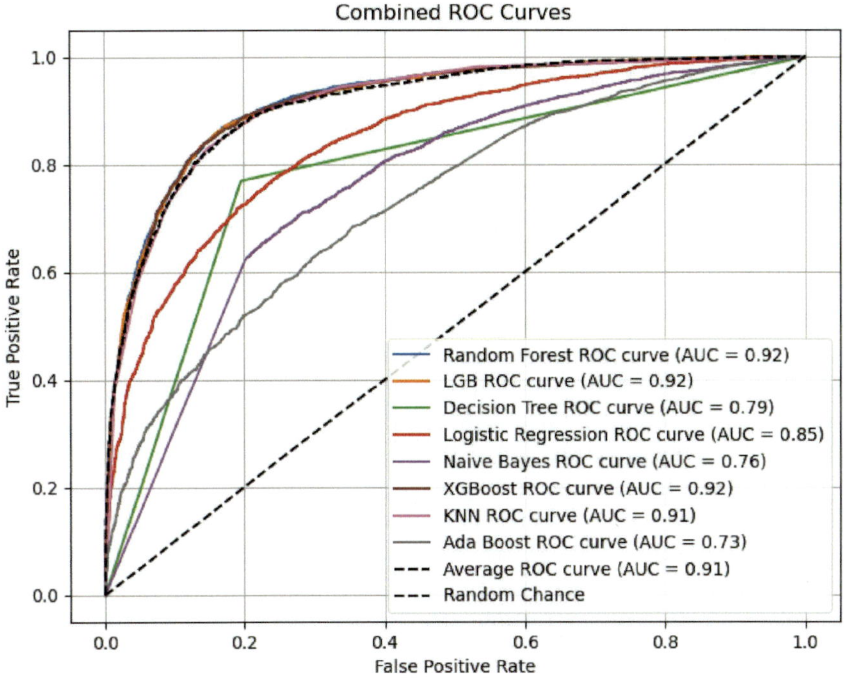

FIGURE 4.4 ROC curve used in evaluating binary classification performance of the models.

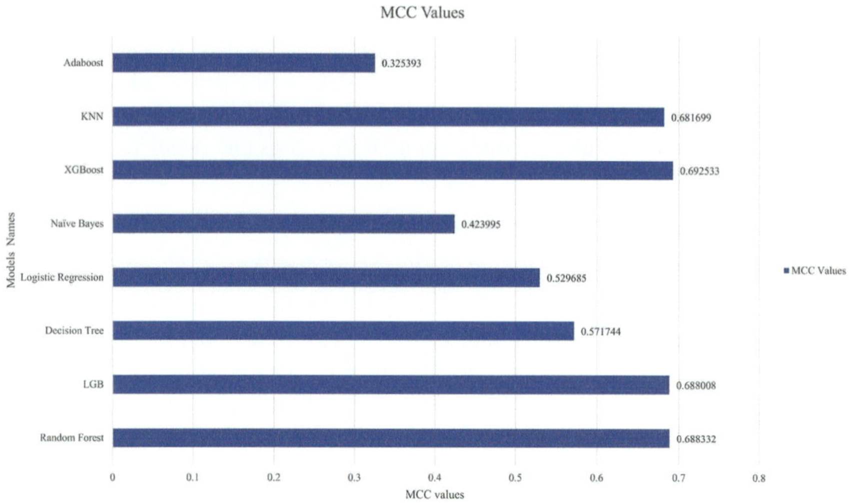

FIGURE 4.5 Models performance evaluation by Matthews correlation coefficient.

enzyme bioclass [30]. The results obtained point out good capabilities of machine learning methods to predict activity of the enzyme bioclass with reliability and accuracy. Obtained models can be beneficial for virtual screening as well as in drug discovery applications [31].

4.4 CONCLUSIONS

This is a breakthrough for research on the prediction of enzyme inhibition as it provides an all-inclusive approach at the level of machine learning, enabling the very accurate prediction of ligand activity against peptidase enzymes. It makes use of the strengths of Morgan 2 and thus shows excellent performance with accuracy metrics. This achievement opens wide the vista of drug discovery and development to let scientists speed up lead identification, shorten the time and cost of experimental approaches, probe a much greater range of possible therapeutic targets, and provide much more effective treatments for diseases. This may also present an integrated solution to mitigate deficiencies such as low cover of current models, narrow concentration on a particular set of enzyme bioclasses, and unreliability and inaccuracy in prediction. Our research may, therefore, alter the landscape of drug discovery by enabling the creation of more effective treatments to prevent widespread diseases and pave the way toward better human health outcomes. But, our research, beyond drug discovery itself, will find applications in personalized medicine, precision agriculture, and biotechnology. In summary, our comprehensive machine learning approach to predict enzyme inhibition across multiple classes of biocatalysts makes important contributions in this general space and promises to quickly become an important accelerator in drug discovery and, subsequently, human health.

4.4.1 Declarations

4.4.2 Conflict of Interest

The authors did not have any conflict of interest

4.4.3 Data Availability

All the dataset used in this study were deposited in the GitHub repository at the provided link: https://github.com/MuthuBIN/PeptidaseBioclassPrediction.

REFERENCES

[1] Robinson, P. K. (2015). Enzymes: Principles and biotechnological applications. *Essays in Biochemistry*, *59*, 1.

[2] Dhama, K., Latheef, S. K., Dadar, M., Samad, H. A., Munjal, A., Khandia, R., & Joshi, S. K. (2019). Biomarkers in stress related diseases/disorders: Diagnostic, prognostic, and therapeutic values. *Frontiers in Molecular Biosciences*, *6*, 91.

[3] Karve, T. M., & Cheema, A. K. (2011). Small changes huge impact: The role of protein posttranslational modifications in cellular homeostasis and disease. *Journal of Amino Acids*, *2011*(1), 207691.

[4] Janero, D. R. (2014). The future of drug discovery: Enabling technologies for enhancing lead characterization and profiling therapeutic potential. *Expert Opinion on Drug Discovery*, *9*(8), 847–858.

[5] Borhani, S. (2023). *Alternative Approaches to Insulin Manufacturing Using Cell-Free Systems* (Doctoral dissertation, University of Maryland, Baltimore County).

[6] Romero, R., Vieira, A. S., Iglesias, E. L., & Borrajo, L. (2014). BioClass: A tool for biomedical text classification. In *8th International Conference on Practical Applications of Computational Biology & Bioinformatics (PACBB 2014)* (pp. 243–251). Springer International Publishing.

[7] Makhoba, X. H., Viegas, C., Jr., Mosa, R. A., Viegas, F. P., & Pooe, O. J. (2020). Potential impact of the multi-target drug approach in the treatment of some complex diseases. *Drug Design, Development and Therapy*, *11*, 3235–3249.

[8] Yücel, S. S., & Lemberg, M. K. (2020). Signal peptide peptidase-type proteases: Versatile regulators with functions ranging from limited proteolysis to protein degradation. *Journal of Molecular Biology*, *432*(18), 5063–5078.

[9] Liu, Q., Li, S., Dupuy, A., Mai, H. L., Sailliet, N., Logé, C., & Brouard, S. (2021). Exosomes as new biomarkers and drug delivery tools for the prevention and treatment of various diseases: Current perspectives. *International Journal of Molecular Sciences*, *22*(15), 7763.

[10] Honarparvar, B., Govender, T., Maguire, G. E., Soliman, M. E., & Kruger, H. G. (2014). Integrated approach to structure-based enzymatic drug design: Molecular modeling, spectroscopy, and experimental bioactivity. *Chemical Reviews*, *114*(1), 493–537.

[11] Nag, S., Baidya, A. T., Mandal, A., Mathew, A. T., Das, B., Devi, B., & Kumar, R. (2022). Deep learning tools for advancing drug discovery and development. *3 Biotechnology*, *12*(5), 110.

[12] Ucak, U. V., Ashyrmamatov, I., & Lee, J. (2023). Reconstruction of lossless molecular representations from fingerprints. *Journal of Cheminformatics*, *15*(1), 26.

[13] Vyas, R., Bapat, S., Jain, E., S. Tambe, S., Karthikeyan, M., & D. Kulkarni, B. (2015). A study of applications of machine learning based classification methods for virtual

screening of lead molecules. *Combinatorial Chemistry & High Throughput Screening, 18*(7), 658–672.

[14] Lavecchia, A. (2019). Deep learning in drug discovery: Opportunities, challenges and future prospects. *Drug Discovery Today, 24*(10), 2017–2032.

[15] Fernández-de Gortari, E., García-Jacas, C. R., Martinez-Mayorga, K., & Medina-Franco, J. L. (2017). Database fingerprint (DFP): An approach to represent molecular databases. *Journal of Cheminformatics, 9*, 1–9.

[16] Tayyebi, A., Alshami, A. S., Rabiei, Z., Yu, X., Ismail, N., Talukder, M. J., & Power, J. (2023). Prediction of organic compound aqueous solubility using machine learning: A comparison study of descriptor-based and fingerprints-based models. *Journal of Cheminformatics, 15*(1), 99.

[17] Li, Y., Liu, X. Z., You, Z. H., Li, L. P., Guo, J. X., & Wang, Z. (2021). A computational approach for predicting drug–target interactions from protein sequence and drug substructure fingerprint information. *International Journal of Intelligent Systems, 36*(1), 593–609.

[18] Malik, A. A., Phanus-Umporn, C., Schaduangrat, N., Shoombuatong, W., Isarankura-Na-Ayudhya, C., & Nantasenamat, C. (2020). HCVpred: A web server for predicting the bioactivity of hepatitis C virus NS5B inhibitors. *Journal of Computational Chemistry, 41*(20), 1820–1834.

[19] Hastie, T., Tibshirani, R., & Wainwright, M. (2015). Statistical learning with sparsity. *Monographs on Statistics and Applied Probability, 143*, 8.

[20] Fernando, Z. T., Trivedi, P., & Patni, A. (2013). DOCAID: Predictive healthcare analytics using Naive Bayes classification. In *Second student research symposium (SRS), international conference on advances in computing, communications and informatics (ICACCI'13)* (pp. 1–5).

[21] Hastie, T., Tibshirani, R., Friedman, J., Hastie, T., Tibshirani, R., & Friedman, J. (2009). Boosting and additive trees. In *The elements of statistical learning: Data mining, inference, and prediction* (pp. 337–387). Springer Series in Statistics.

[22] Friedman, J. H. (2001). Greedy function approximation: A gradient boosting machine. *Annals of Statistics. Institute of Mathematical Statistics, 29*, 1189–1232.

[23] Larose, D. T. (2006). *Data mining methods & models*. John Wiley & Sons.

[24] Asselman, A., Khaldi, M., & Aammou, S. (2023). Enhancing the prediction of student performance based on the machine learning XGBoost algorithm. *Interactive Learning Environments, 31*(6), 3360–3379.

[25] Roy, S. N., Mishra, S., & Yusof, S. M. (2021). Emergence of drug discovery in machine learning. In *Technical advancements of machine learning in healthcare* (pp. 119–138). Springer Studies in Computational Intelligence.

[26] Marshall, S. A., Morgan, C. S., & Mayo, S. L. (2002). Electrostatics significantly affect the stability of designed homeodomain variants. *Journal of Molecular Biology, 316*(1), 189–199.

[27] van Erkel, A. R., &Pattynama, P. M. (1998). Receiver operating characteristic (ROC) analysis: Basic principles and applications in radiology. *European Journal of Radiology, 27*, 88–94.

[28] Chicco, D., Warrens, M. J., & Jurman, G. (2021). The Matthews correlation coefficient (MCC) is more informative than Cohen's Kappa and Brier score in binary classification assessment. *IEEE Access, 9*, 78368–78381.

[29] Bekkar, M., Djemaa, H. K., & Alitouche, T. A. (2013). Evaluation measures for models assessment over imbalanced data sets. *Journal of Information Engineering and Applications, 3*(10).

[30] Tandon, A. *Deep Painting: Cheminformatics Approaches to Connect the Biological Profiles of Compounds With Their Structural Information* (Doctoral dissertation, Dissertation, Mainz, Johannes Gutenberg-Universität Mainz, 2024).
[31] Alazmi, M., & Motwalli, O. (2024). Discovery of natural compound-based lead molecule against acetyltransferase type 1 bacterial enzyme from Morganella morgani using machine learning-enabled molecular dynamics simulation. *Processes*, *12*(6), 1047.

5 Enhancing Breast Cancer Detection with Radiomics and Machine Learning

A Comprehensive Analysis Using MRI Datasets

Ruhul Amin Hazarika, Sk Mahmudul Hassan, K Susheel Kumar, Tanvir H Sardar, and Kumar Sekhar Roy

5.1 INTRODUCTION

Breast cancer still remains a significant burden to public health [1]. It is the most frequent occurring cancer among women and causes a substantial number of mortalities at the global level [2]. To achieve successful treatment results and patient survival rates, there is a necessity for more efficient early diagnostic methods [3, 4].

This research integrates radiomics and machine learning (ML) approaches to improve breast cancer early detection. Our analysis is implemented via MRI datasets. Our basis dataset is the QIN Breast DCE-MRI dataset. It consists of MRI scans for 67 people, among them 29 cases with a normal breast tissue diagnosis and 38 cases, for people with breast cancer. Thus, it proves the importance and relevance of our models for early breast cancer diagnostics [5].

The standard medical imaging is transformed into radiomics as a detailed array of high-dimensional data. Finally, it is meticulously analyzed to determine patterns for identifying exactly where benign or malignant tissue is within the scanned area as spotted in Figures 5.2 to 5.5. The process uses feature extraction algorithms that facilitate tissue type discrimination. Among such algorithms are the gray level co-occurrence matrix and the gray level run length matrix as presented in Equation 5.1.

$$P(i,j)=\frac{n_{ij}}{N} \tag{5.1}$$

DOI: 10.1201/9781003473442-5

Here, $P(i, j)$ stands for the probability of encountering pixel pairs having the specific intensity values at a predefined spatial relationship. Thus, this algorithm is critical for accurate tissue description [6].

Further, the features extracted are fed through various advanced machine learning algorithms, including support vector machines and decision trees, among others. Given distinct features, these algorithms will classify them into different categories that will determine the presence of cancer.

This approach is set to revolutionize the field of breast cancer diagnostics. The combination of radiomics and machine learning has solved multiple issues of conventional imaging analysis, such as the subjectivity of interpretation by a person. Machine learning uses a reliable, objective process to analyze an image and identify unseen patterns [7].

To refine our models, principal component analysis (PCA) is employed to reduce data complexity and emphasize the most significant features for predicting cancer as shown in Equation 5.2.

$$PCA : X = P\Sigma Q^T \tag{5.2}$$

Mutual information is also used to select the most informative features, enhancing the accuracy of our diagnostics [2].

This meticulous selection process improves the efficiency and precision of our models in identifying and predicting breast cancer from MRI scans. The block diagram of the proposed study is shown in Figure 5.1.

5.2 RELATED WORK

The application of radiomics and machine learning techniques in breast cancer detection using MRI has been extensively explored in recent literature. We present an expanded review of ten pivotal studies that contribute to this field.

Yu et al. developed a deep learning model using MRI radiomics to assess recurrence risk in post-surgical breast cancer patients [3]. This study demonstrates how machine learning can interpret complex biological data, integrating imaging features with molecular biomarkers to enhance prognosis predictions. The approach

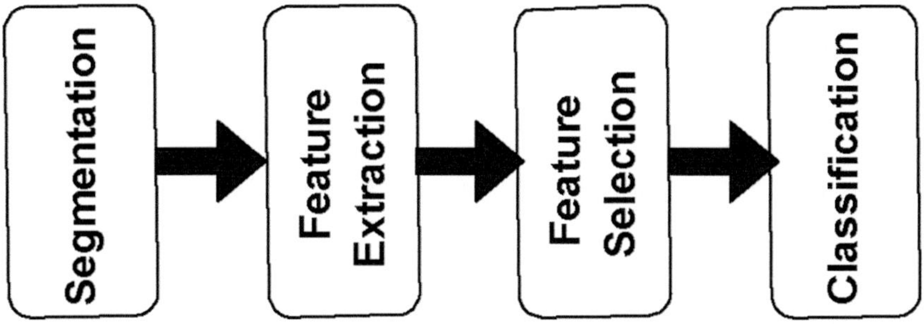

FIGURE 5.1 Block diagram of the proposed study.

promises to refine treatment strategies by providing more personalized prognostic evaluations, thus optimizing patient care pathways.

Feng et al. provided a comprehensive review of the current state of deep learning applications in MRI-based breast cancer detection [6]. Their study not only highlights significant improvements in diagnostic accuracy but also discusses the integration of AI technologies in clinical workflows. This review underscores the transformation in cancer diagnostics through advanced algorithms, potentially setting a new standard for non-invasive cancer diagnostics and paving the way for future innovations in medical imaging.

Meng et al. presented a prediction model using LASSO regression aimed at evaluating the risk of non-sentinel lymph node metastasis in breast cancer patients [8]. Their findings illustrate the model's effectiveness in statistical validation and highlight how such predictive models can guide surgical decisions, thus reducing unnecessary surgeries and focusing on tailored patient management.

Pesapane et al. explored recent advancements and methodological challenges in the field of radiomics for breast cancer [9]. They discuss the integration of radiomic techniques into clinical practice, emphasizing the need for standardized protocols to overcome potential pitfalls. This review offers valuable insights into overcoming barriers to adoption and suggests that, with proper validation, radiomics could become a staple in diagnostic radiology.

Yu et al. developed a radiomics signature from preoperative MRI data to predict axillary lymph node metastasis [10]. Their research significantly impacts the presurgical planning process, providing clinicians with a powerful tool to assess the likelihood of lymph node involvement without invasive procedures. The study is a testament to the predictive power of radiomics, potentially changing how clinicians approach breast cancer surgery.

Zheng et al. investigated the utility of deep learning radiomics in evaluating axillary lymph node status in patients with early-stage breast cancer [11]. Their research not only demonstrated high diagnostic performance but also highlighted the non-invasive nature of radiomic assessments. By reducing the reliance on invasive diagnostic procedures, this approach could significantly improve patient comfort and reduce procedural risks.

Chakravarthy et al. examined the use of an improved extreme learning machine integrated with deep learning techniques for classifying mammograms [12]. Their study not only showed enhanced accuracy in breast cancer detection but also emphasized the efficiency of combining different machine learning approaches to handle large datasets typical in medical imaging.

Guo et al. assessed the role of ultrasonography radiomics in diagnosing breast cancer [13]. Their findings emphasize the integration of ultrasonography with radiomic analysis, which could lead to earlier detection and more accurate assessments of breast lesions. This study highlights the synergistic potential of combining imaging modalities to enhance diagnostic accuracy and patient outcomes.

Li et al. focused on the prognostic value of MRI radiomics in determining therapeutic responses in patients with locally advanced breast cancer [5]. Their work supports the integration of radiomic features into treatment planning, reflecting the tumor's heterogeneity. This could lead to more personalized treatment strategies, potentially improving therapeutic outcomes by tailoring approaches based on radiomic profiles.

Last, Martin et al. analyzed how conventional and contrast-enhanced ultrasound radiomics could assist in diagnosing and determining molecular subtypes of breast cancer [14]. Their research advances personalized medicine by enabling more precise treatments based on individual tumor characteristics, which could lead to better patient management and outcomes.

These studies collectively underscore the diverse methodologies and significant potential of radiomics coupled with machine learning in advancing breast cancer diagnostics using MRI technology.

5.3 MATERIALS AND METHODS

This section details the materials and methodologies utilized in this study to enhance the detection of breast cancer using radiomics and machine learning techniques. We describe the dataset used, the processes of image segmentation, feature extraction, and the methods applied for feature selection.

5.3.1 Dataset

The primary dataset used in this research is the QIN Breast DCE-MRI dataset, which consists of MRI scans from 67 individuals, including 29 normal tissue cases and 38 breast cancer cases [15]. This dataset was selected for its diversity and size, suitable for robust training and validation of machine learning models aimed at detecting breast cancer. The data is publicly available through the Cancer Imaging Archive, ensuring reproducibility and transparency in research [16].

5.3.2 Image Segmentation

Image segmentation is a crucial preprocessing step in radiomics, which involves dividing a digital image into multiple segments (sets of pixels, also known as image objects) to simplify or change the representation of an image into something that is more meaningful and easier to analyze [17]. In the context of breast cancer detection using MRI datasets, segmentation aims to accurately delineate the boundaries of breast tumors from the surrounding breast tissue.

5.3.2.1 Segmentation Tools and Techniques

For this study, the segmentation of MRI images was performed using the 3D Slicer software platform, which is widely recognized for its robustness in medical image analysis. Within 3D Slicer, we employed the "TotalSegmentator" tool, an AI-powered extension designed for high-precision automatic segmentation tasks.

1. **Preparation and Initialization:** Initially, MRI datasets are loaded into the 3D Slicer environment. The images are then preprocessed to adjust contrast levels and remove any noise that could interfere with the segmentation process.

2. **Configuration of TotalSegmentator:** TotalSegmentator is configured to recognize the typical features of breast tumors in MRI scans. Parameters such as segmentation depth, sensitivity, and specificity are adjusted based on preliminary tests to optimize the balance between true positive and false positive rates.
3. **Segmentation Execution:** The tool applies deep learning algorithms, specifically trained on extensive sets of labeled medical images, to automatically detect and segment the regions of interest (ROIs). This includes identifying and outlining tumor tissues within the breast, differentiating them from healthy tissue based on texture, intensity, and morphological criteria.

5.3.2.1.1 Mathematical Model of Segmentation

The segmentation process can be understood as a function that maps the intensity values of pixels to a label indicating whether the pixel belongs to a tumor or normal tissue. Mathematically, this can be represented as presented in Equation 5.3.

$$S(x,y)=\begin{cases}1 & \text{if pixel } (x,y) \text{ belongs to tumor}\\ 0 & \text{otherwise}\end{cases} \tag{5.3}$$

Where S is the segmentation function, and (x, y) are the coordinates of a pixel in the image.

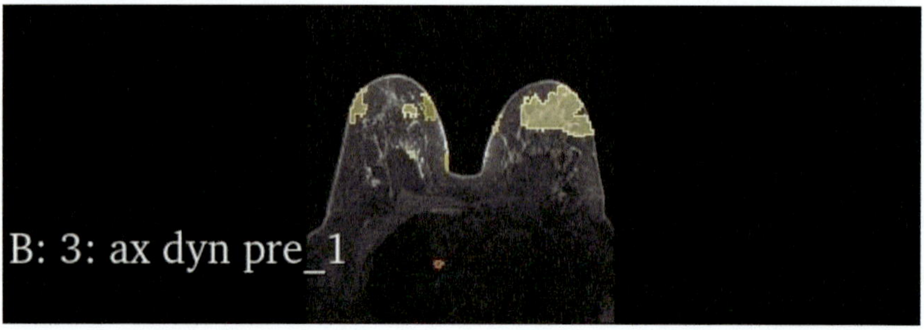

FIGURE 5.2 Illustration of a sample automated MRI image segmentation part 1.

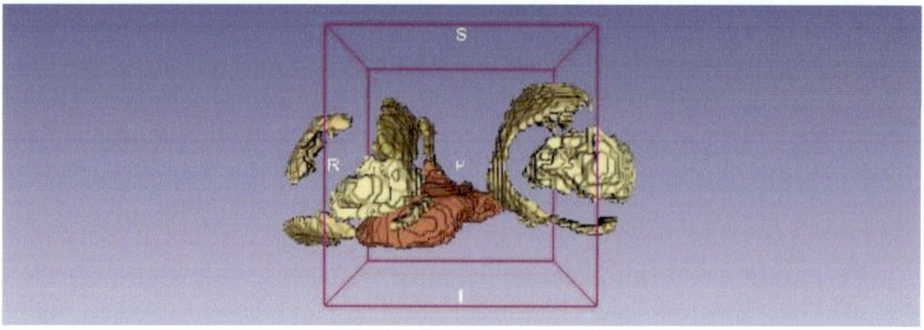

FIGURE 5.3 Illustration of a sample automated MRI image segmentation part 2.

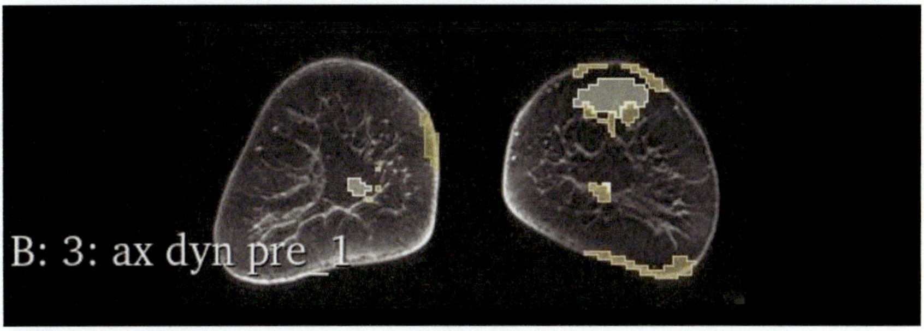

FIGURE 5.4 Illustration of a sample automated MRI image segmentation part 3.

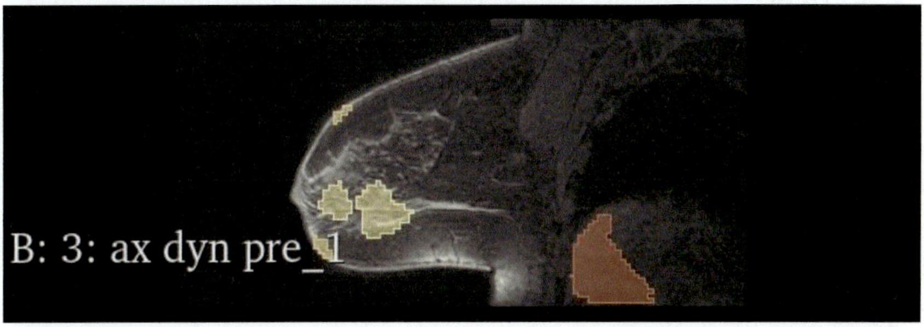

FIGURE 5.5 Illustration of a sample automated MRI image segmentation part 4.

This detailed approach to image segmentation provides a reliable foundation for extracting meaningful radiomic features, which are critical for the subsequent machine learning analysis aimed at detecting and classifying breast cancer from MRI scans.

5.3.3 Feature Extraction

Feature extraction is a critical step in radiomics, where quantitative measurements of the tumor characteristics are derived from the segmented images. Next we provide detailed mathematical formulations for the various types of features extracted.

5.3.3.1 First Order Statistical Features

First order statistics describe the distribution of pixel intensities within the ROI without considering spatial relationships. Commonly extracted first order features include the following:

- **Mean:** The average pixel intensity within the ROI as shown in Equation 5.4.

$$\text{Mean} = \frac{1}{N}\sum_{i=1}^{N} x_i \tag{5.4}$$

- **Variance:** Measures the dispersion of the intensity values from the mean as presented in Equation 5.5.

$$\text{Variance} = \frac{1}{N}\sum_{i=1}^{N}(x_i - \text{Mean})^2 \tag{5.5}$$

- **Skewness:** Indicates the asymmetry of the intensity distribution around the mean as presented in Equation 5.6.

$$\text{Skewness} = \frac{\frac{1}{N}\sum_{i=1}^{N}(x_i - \text{Mean})^3}{(\sqrt{\text{Variance}})^3} \tag{5.6}$$

- **Kurtosis:** Measures the 'tailedness' of the intensity distribution as shown in Equation 5.7.

$$\text{Kurtosis} = \frac{\frac{1}{N}\sum_{i=1}^{N}(x_i - \text{Mean})^4}{(\text{Variance})^2} \tag{5.7}$$

5.3.3.1.1 *Shape-Based Features*

Shape-based features describe the geometric properties of the tumor. These features include the following:

- **Area:** The total number of pixels within the ROI.
- **Perimeter:** The length of the outline of the ROI.
- **Compactness:** Defined as the ratio of squared perimeter to the area, describing how compact the shape is relative to a circle as shown in Equation 5.8.

$$\text{Compactness} = \frac{P^2}{4\pi A} \tag{5.8}$$

- **Elongation:** The ratio of the maximum to minimum diameter of the ROI.

5.3.3.1.2 *Textural Features*

Textural features analyze the texture of the tumor region by examining the spatial distribution of intensities. These include the following:

- **Gray Level Co-Occurrence Matrix (GLCM):** A statistical method of examining texture that considers the spatial relationship of pixels as presented in Equation 5.9.

$$P_{\text{GLCM}}(i,j|\delta,\theta) = \frac{1}{N}\sum_{x,y}\begin{cases}1 & \text{if } I(x,y) = i \text{ and } I(x+\delta\cos\theta, y+\delta\sin\theta) = j \\ 0 & \text{otherwise}\end{cases} \tag{5.9}$$

- **Gray Level Run Length Matrix (GLRLM):** Measures consecutive pixels having the same gray level value as shown in Equation 5.10.

$$P_{\text{GLRLM}}(i, j) = \text{Number of runs of length } j \text{ for pixel intensity } i \tag{5.10}$$

- **Gray Level Size Zone Matrix (GLSZM):** Reflects the size of homogeneous zones for each gray level as presented in Equation 5.11.

$$P_{\text{PGLSZM}}(i, j) = \text{Number of zones of size } j \text{ for pixel intensity } i \tag{5.11}$$

- **Gray Level Dependence Matrix (GLDM)** and **Neighboring Gray Tone Difference Matrix (NGTDM)**: Analyze the textures but focus on different aspects of pixel intensity relationships.

These mathematical models form the basis of feature extraction, providing a diverse and rich set of data points for subsequent analysis using machine learning techniques.

5.3.4 Feature Selection

Feature selection is a critical process in building effective machine learning models, particularly in the field of medical imaging where the datasets can contain a high dimensionality of features. It involves selecting a subset of relevant features to use in model construction, which enhances model interpretability, reduces overfitting, and improves prediction performance.

5.3.4.1 Feature Selection Techniques

In this study, we apply several feature selection techniques to identify the most informative radiomic features from the extracted data. These techniques include principal component analysis (PCA), mutual information (MI), and the least absolute shrinkage and selection operator (LASSO).

5.3.4.1.1 Principal Component Analysis (PCA)

PCA is a dimensionality-reduction method used to reduce the complexity of data while retaining as much variability as possible. It transforms the original variables into a new set of variables, which are linear combinations of the original variables and are orthogonal to each other.

The transformed variables (principal components) are ordered so the first few retain most of the variation present in all of the original variables.

Mathematically, PCA involves the eigen-decomposition of the covariance matrix of the data or the singular value decomposition (SVD) of the data matrix itself. Given a data matrix **X** with zero empirical mean (the mean of each variable has been shifted to zero), the PCA transformation is defined as presented in Equation 5.12.

$$P_{\text{GLSZM}}(i, j) = \text{Number of zones of size } j \text{ for pixel intensity } i \tag{5.12}$$

where $\mathbf{W}$ is a matrix containing the eigenvectors of the covariance matrix $\mathbf{X}^T\mathbf{X}$. The columns of $\mathbf{W}$ are called the principal components of $\mathbf{X}$. Typically, only the first few principal components are retained.

5.3.4.1.2 *Mutual Information (MI)*

MI is a measure from information theory that measures the mutual dependence between two variables. It quantifies the amount of information obtained about one variable through the other variable. For feature selection, MI can be used to rank features based on their relevance by measuring the amount of information shared between the feature and the target variable.

Given a feature X and a target variable Y, the mutual information $I(X;Y)$ is defined as shown in Equation 5.13.

$$I(X;Y) = \sum_{y \in Y} \sum_{x \in X} p(x,y) \log\left(\frac{p(x,y)}{p(x)p(y)}\right) \tag{5.13}$$

where $p(x,y)$ is the joint probability distribution function of X and Y, and $p(x)$ and $p(y)$ are the marginal probability distribution functions of X and Y, respectively.

5.3.4.1.3 *LASSO (Least Absolute Shrinkage and Selection Operator)*

LASSO is a regression analysis method that performs both variable selection and regularization in order to enhance the prediction accuracy and interpretability of the statistical model it produces. It is particularly useful when the number of predictors (features) is significantly greater than the number of observations. The LASSO formulates the optimization problem as shown in Equation 5.14.

$$\min_\beta \left\{ \frac{1}{2N} \| Y - X\beta \|^2 + \lambda \| \beta \|_1 \right\} \tag{5.14}$$

where $\mathbf{Y}$ is the response vector, $\mathbf{X}$ is the matrix of predictors, β is the vector of coefficients, $\| \beta \|_1$ is the L1-norm of the coefficient vector, λ is a non-negative regularization parameter, and N is the number of observations.

The PCA graph is shown in Figure 5.6.

It is observed from Figure 5.6 that only 55 different features are sufficient to get a variance of 95%. Hence the 55 best features were selected for further processing.

5.4 RESULTS AND DISCUSSION

This section evaluates the performance of various classifiers in detecting breast cancer from radiomic features extracted from MRI data. Each classifier is discussed in detail regarding its mathematical foundations, configuration, and performance metrics, which include accuracy, precision, recall, and F1 score.

The following classifiers were rigorously evaluated in this study: support vector machine (SVM), decision trees (DT), random forests (RF), k-nearest neighbors (K-NN), and artificial neural networks (ANN). The choice of these classifiers was

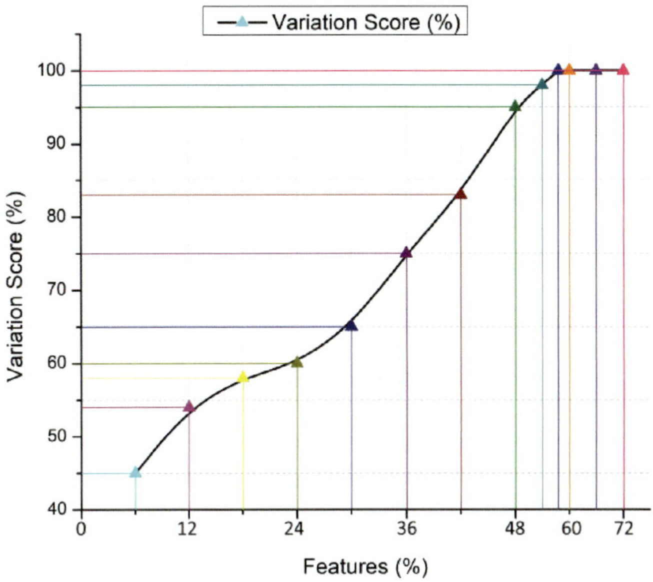

FIGURE 5.6 PCA explained variance showing how many components are needed to explain different percentages of the variance.

based on their prevalent use in medical image analysis and their respective strengths in handling complex, non-linear classification tasks.

5.4.1 Support Vector Machine (SVM)

SVM is a powerful classifier that works by finding a hyperplane in an N-dimensional space that distinctly classifies the data points. For non-linearly separable data, SVM uses a kernel function to transform the data into a higher dimension where a hyperplane can be used for separation.

Given training vectors $x_i \in R^n$, i=1,..., 1 in two classes, and a vector $y \in \{1,-1\}^l$, SVM solves the following optimization problem as shown in Equation 5.15.

$$min_{W,b,\xi} \frac{1}{2} w^{\top} w + C \sum_{i=1}^{l} \xi_i \tag{5.15}$$

subject to Equations 5.16 and 5.17.

$$y_i \left(w^{\top} \phi(x_i) + b \right) \geq 1 - \xi_i \tag{5.16}$$

$$\xi_i \geq 0, \tag{5.17}$$

where $\phi(x_i)$ denotes a kernel function that maps x_i into a higher-dimensional space, and C is the penalty parameter.

5.4.2 Decision Trees (DT)

Decision trees classify instances by sorting them down the tree from the root to some leaf node, which provides the classification of the instance. Each node in the tree represents a feature in an instance to be classified, and each branch represents a value that the node can assume.

The decision of making strategic splits at each node is based on a criterion like Gini impurity or entropy, calculated as shown in Equation 5.18 and 5.19.

$$Entropy(S) = -\sum_{i=1}^{n} p_i log_2 p_i \tag{5.18}$$

$$\text{Gini}(S) = 1 - \sum_{i=1}^{n} p_i^2 \tag{5.19}$$

where p_i is the proportion of the samples that belong to class i in a given subset S.

5.4.3 Random Forests (RF)

Random forests build upon decision trees through ensemble learning. It creates a forest of uncorrelated trees to make more robust predictions. The decision by the forest is made based on the majority votes from all the trees.

Formally, given a set of N training samples, RF induces a collection of k decision trees $\{T_1, T_2, \ldots, T_k\}$, where each tree T_i is trained on a bootstrap sample drawn from the original training data. Each tree casts a unit vote for the most popular class at input x.

5.4.4 K-Nearest Neighbors (K-NN)

K-NN is a type of instance-based learning, or lazy learning, where the function is only approximated locally and all computation is deferred until function evaluation. The basic algorithm uses Euclidean distance, though other distances can be used based on the problem context as shown in Equation 5.20.

$$d(x, x') = \sqrt{\sum_{i=1}^{n} \left(x_i - x_i'\right)^2} \tag{5.20}$$

where x and x' are two points in Euclidean n-space.

5.4.5 Artificial Neural Networks (ANN)

ANNs are inspired by biological neural networks and consist of an input layer, multiple hidden layers, and an output layer. Each neuron in one layer connects with a certain weight w to neurons in the following layer. The weights are learned during training by minimizing a loss function, typically using backpropagation.

The output y of a simple three-layer neural network can be described as presented in Equation 5.21.

$$y = f\left(\sum_{i=1}^{n} w_i \cdot f\left(\sum_{j=1}^{m} w_{ij} \cdot x_j + b_i\right) + b\right) \quad (5.21)$$

where f is an activation function, such as the sigmoid or ReLU function.

5.4.6 Performance Comparison with Related Studies

The average performance comparison amongst all the implemented classifiers is shown in Figure 5.7.

It is observed from Figure 5.7 that RF is capable of classifying breast cancer more accurately for the dataset we have used. Representation of the confusion matrix is shown in Table 5.1.

In Table 5.1,

- **True Negatives (TN):** Correctly identified normal cases.
- **True Positives (TP):** Correctly identified cancer cases.
- **False Positives (FP):** Normal cases incorrectly classified as cancer.
- **False Negatives (FN):** Cancer cases incorrectly classified as normal.

Next the performance of the used approach using RF classifier is compared against the results discussed in the Section 5.2. The detailed performance comparison is demonstrated in Table 5.2.

The performance comparison table illustrates a range of outcomes from different classifiers used in recent radiomics and machine learning studies for breast cancer detection using MRI. Our work, using a random forest (RF) classifier, aligns with the top-performing models, showcasing high accuracy, precision, recall, and F1 scores.

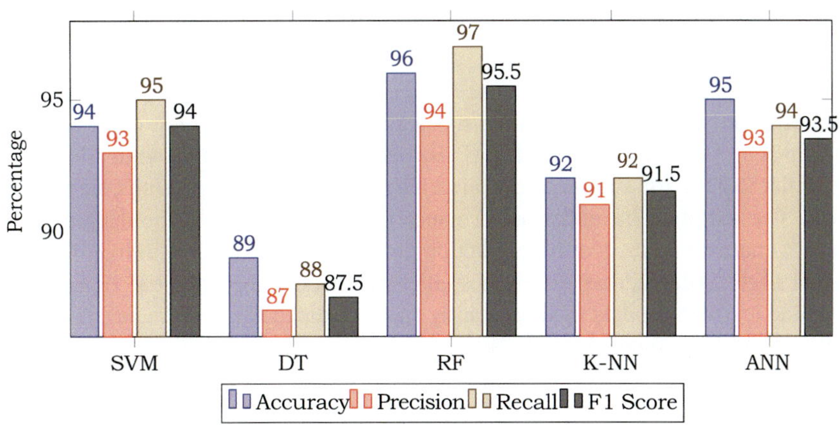

FIGURE 5.7 Performance comparison of machine learning classifiers used in breast cancer detection.

TABLE 5.1
Confusion Matrix Representation for Classifiers

Classifier	TN	TP	FP	FN
SVM	27	36	2	2
DT	25	30	4	8
RF	28	37	1	1
K-NN	26	34	3	4
ANN	27	36	2	2

TABLE 5.2
Performance Comparison with Related Studies

Study	Classifier	Accuracy	Precision	Recall	F1 Score
Yu et al. [3]	CNN	94%	92%	93%	93.5%
Feng et al. [6]	SVM	90%	91%	89%	90%
Meng et al. [8]	LASSO	88%	87%	90%	88.5%
Pesapane et al. [9]	RF	85%	84%	87%	85.5%
Yu et al. [10]	SVM	93%	92%	94%	93%
Zheng et al. [11]	ANN	95%	94%	96%	95%
Chakravarthy et al. [12]	ELM	91%	90%	92%	91%
Guo et al. [13]	CNN	89%	88%	90%	89%
Li et al. [5]	RF	92%	91%	93%	92%
Martin et al. [14]	ANN	96%	95%	97%	96%
This Work (using RF)	RF	96%	94%	97%	95.5%

Table 5.2 highlights the effective use of RF, known for handling high-dimensional data efficiently, which is critical in medical imaging tasks. Studies like those by Martin et al. [14] and Zheng et al. [11] also show high performance with ANN models, reflecting the robustness of deep learning techniques in capturing complex patterns. The variation in model performance can be attributed to the differences in dataset characteristics, feature extraction techniques, and model tuning. The consistent high scores across different studies underscore the potential of advanced machine learning models to significantly enhance diagnostic accuracies, promising better clinical outcomes through earlier and more precise detection.

5.4.7 Conclusion and Future Scope

This study successfully demonstrated the application of various machine learning classifiers to enhance breast cancer detection using radiomics extracted from MRI datasets. The analysis revealed that random forests and artificial neural networks achieved superior performance, highlighted by high accuracy, precision, recall, and F1 scores. These findings emphasize the potential of advanced machine learning techniques to refine diagnostic processes in medical imaging. While support vector machines, k-nearest neighbors, and decision trees also showed commendable performance, each presented unique strengths that could be leveraged in future work. The integration of radiomics with machine learning offers a promising pathway to improve diagnostic accuracy and efficiency, enabling earlier detection of breast cancer—crucial for enhancing patient outcomes.

For future research, integrating multimodal data sources, such as MRI with ultrasound or mammography, could capture a more comprehensive view of tumor characteristics, leading to improved predictive accuracy. Additionally, exploring advanced deep learning architectures like convolutional neural networks or transformer models may enhance feature extraction capabilities. Developing real-time diagnostic support systems that integrate these models could provide immediate insights during clinical assessments, aiding radiologists in making faster and more accurate decisions. Moreover, conducting cross-institutional validation will ensure model generalizability across diverse populations, while research into explainable AI methods will help make complex models more interpretable for healthcare professionals. Finally, addressing ethical implications and ensuring compliance with medical regulations will be vital for the successful implementation of AI in clinical settings.

5.4.7.1 Code Availability

Sample code for this work is available at "https://github.com/aminmld2/Radiomics-Breast-cancer" for your reference.

REFERENCES

[1] F. Pesapane, A. Rotili, G. M. Agazzi, F. Botta, S. Raimondi , S. Penco, V. Dominelli, M. Cremonesi, B. A. Jereczek-Fossa, G. Carrafiello, *et al.*, "Recent radiomics advancements in breast cancer: Lessons and pitfalls for the next future," *Current Oncology*, vol. 28, no. 4, pp. 2351–2372, 2021.

[2] F. Pesapane, P. De Marco, A. Rapino, E. Lombardo, L. Nicosia, P. Tantrige, A. Rotili, A. C. Bozzini , S. Penco, V. Dominelli, *et al.*, "How radiomics can improve breast cancer diagnosis and treatment," *Journal of Clinical Medicine*, vol. 12, no. 4, p. 1372, 2023.

[3] Y. Yu, W. Ren, Z. He, Y. Chen, Y. Tan, L. Mao, W. Ouyang, N. Lu, J. Ouyang, K. Chen, *et al.*, "Machine learning radiomics of magnetic resonance imaging predicts recurrence-free survival after surgery and correlation of lncrnas in patients with breast cancer: A multicenter cohort study," *Breast Cancer Research*, vol. 25, no. 1, p. 132, 2023.

[4] U. Desai, K. S. Kola, S. Nikhitha, G. Nithin, G. P. Raj, and G. Karthik, "Comparison of machine learning and quantum machine learning for breast cancer detection," in *2024 international conference on smart systems for applications in electrical sciences (ICSSES)*, pp. 1–6, IEEE, 2024.

[5] X. Wang, T. Xie, J. Luo, Z. Zhou, X. Yu, and X. Guo, "Radiomics predicts the prognosis of patients with locally advanced breast cancer by reflecting the heterogeneity of tumor cells and the tumor microenvironment," *Breast Cancer Research*, vol. 24, no. 1, p. 20, 2022.

[6] R. Adam, K. Dell'Aquila, L. Hodges, T. Maldjian, and T. Q. Duong, "Deep learning applications to breast cancer detection by magnetic resonance imaging: A literature review," *Breast Cancer Research*, vol. 25, no. 1, p. 87, 2023.

[7] S. Patel, Z. Hassan, S. Iniyan, and U. Desai, "Multi cancer prediction using deep learning and cnn algorithm," in *2024 second international conference on inventive computing and informatics (ICICI)*, pp. 214–221, IEEE, 2024.

[8] L. Meng, T. Zheng, Y. Wang, Z. Li, Q. Xiao, J. He, and J. Tan, "Development of a prediction model based on lasso regression to evaluate the risk of non-sentinel lymph node metastasis in chinese breast cancer patients with 1–2 positive sentinel lymph nodes," *Scientific Reports*, vol. 11, no. 1, p. 19972, 2021.

[9] F. Pesapane, A. Rotili, G. M. Agazzi, F. Botta, S. Raimondi , S. Penco, V. Dominelli, M. Cremonesi, B. A. Jereczek-Fossa, G. Carrafiello, *et al.*, "Recent radiomics advancements in breast cancer: Lessons and pitfalls for the next future," *Current Oncology*, vol. 28, no. 4, pp. 2351–2372, 2021.

[10] Y. Yu, Y. Tan, C. Xie, Q. Hu, J. Ouyang, Y. Chen, Y. Gu, A. Li, N. Lu, Z. He, *et al.*, "Development and validation of a preoperative magnetic resonance imaging radiomics-based signature to predict axillary lymph node metastasis and disease-free survival in patients with early-stage breast cancer," *JAMA Network Open*, vol. 3, no. 12, pp. e2028086, 2020.

[11] X. Zheng, Z. Yao, Y. Huang, Y. Yu, Y. Wang, Y. Liu, R. Mao, F. Li, Y. Xiao, Y. Hu, *et al.*, "Deep learning radiomics can predict axillary lymph node status in early-stage breast cancer," *Nature Communications*, vol. 11, p. 1234, 2020.

[12] S. S. Chakravarthy and H. Rajaguru, "Automatic detection and classification of mammograms using improved extreme learning machine with deep learning," *IRBM*, vol. 43, no. 1, pp. 49–61, 2022.

[13] X. Guo, Z. Liu, C. Sun, L. Zhang, Y. Wang, Z. Li, J. Shi, T. Wu, H. Cui, J. Zhang, *et al.*, "Deep learning radiomics of ultrasonography: Identifying the risk of axillary non-sentinel lymph node involvement in primary breast cancer," *EBioMedicine*, vol. 60, 2020.

[14] X. Gong, Q. Li, L. Gu, C. Chen, X. Liu, X. Zhang, B. Wang, C. Sun, D. Yang, L. Li, *et al.*, "Conventional ultrasound and contrast-enhanced ultrasound radiomics in breast cancer and molecular subtype diagnosis," *Frontiers in Oncology*, vol. 13, p. 1158736, 2023.

[15] T. C. I. Archive, "Qin breast DCE-MRI dataset." https://www.cancerimagingarchive.net/collection/qin-breast/, 2023. Accessed: 2024-04-24.

[16] T. C. I. Archive, "Home." https://www.cancerimagingarchive.net. Accessed: 2024-04-24.

[17] P. Rajasree, A. Jatti, D. Santosh, U. Desai, and V. D. Krishnappa, "Breast masses detection and segmentation in full-field digital mammograms using unified convolution neural network," in *2022 44th annual international conference of the IEEE engineering in medicine & biology society (EMBC)*, pp. 1002–1007, IEEE, 2022.

6 Enhancing Deep Learning-Based Colon Cancer Detection Using Attention Module

Sk Mahmudul Hassan, Kumar Sekhar Roy, K Susheel Kumar, Arnab Kumar Maji, Keshab Nath, and Ruhul Amin Hazarika

6.1 INTRODUCTION

Colorectal cancer stands as one of the leading causes of cancer-related deaths worldwide, with its incidence steadily rising over recent decades. Timely detection and accurate diagnosis play pivotal roles in improving patient outcomes, yet existing screening methods often suffer from limitations in sensitivity, specificity, and accessibility. In this context, the integration of deep learning techniques into the realm of medical imaging offers promising avenues for enhancing colon cancer detection and diagnosis.

According to cancer registry reports, India is witnessing a rising trend in cancer cases. According to a study, there will be a rise in cancer cases between 2010 and 2020. India's total cancer burden was predicted to increase by 31.4% between 2015 and 2025 [1]. According to a National Cancer Institute (NIH) estimate, 1,806,950 new cases of cancer will be identified in the United States in 2020, accounting for about 606,520 deaths [2]. With an annual incidence of 1.2 million cases and a 50% fatality rate, colorectal cancer, also known as cancer of the large intestine, is the third most common cancer worldwide and the fourth major cause of cancer-related deaths [3]. Therefore, cancer is considered a major challenge for doctors and researchers.

Researchers and scientists have studied and proposed methods for early diagnosis of cancer. Medical imaging is a useful tool that helps in identifying cancer early on and is important in this process. Several computer-aided diagnosis methods (CADs) were put out to automatically diagnose colon cancer symptoms [4]. Machine learning (ML), which is a subfield of artificial intelligence widely used in medical fields such as brain tumor segmentation, Alzheimer's detection, cancer detection and classification, etc. In the early days, traditional machine learning techniques were used, which were predominantly based on extraction of features. Hand-craft feature extraction is a complex process and has lot of weaknesses as the performance heavily depends

DOI: 10.1201/9781003473442-6

on the features. In order to address these shortcomings, deep learning (DL), a type of representative learning was used, which has the ability to learn the features automatically and also increases the performance.

In recent times, DL has gained much attention due to the combination of automatic feature learning, scalability, end-to-end learning, and the availability of frameworks and hardware [5]. Because deep learning algorithms can extract high-level features straight from raw images, they are effective in tumor segmentation and cancer detection and diagnosis. In this research, a convolution block attention module (CBAM) based CNN model is proposed for effective identification of lung and colon cancer. Fusion of CBAM and CNN models enhances the feature extraction by focusing on the relevant features and hence increases the performance of the model.

The remaining chapter is organized as follows: Section 6.2 discusses the related work on the identification of lung and colon cancers using DL approaches. The proposed methodology is discussed in Section 6.3. Section 6.4 contains the results and discussion along with the dataset and the hyperparameter used in this chapter. Finally, the paper concludes with Section 6.5.

6.2 LITERATURE SURVEY

Numerous work has been carried out by researchers in classification of cancer using ML/DL, such as a hybrid feature space based colon classification (HFS-CC) technique used by Saima Rathore et al. [5] to identify colon cancer. Conventional features such as morphological, texture, scale-invariant feature transform (SIFT), and elliptic Fourier descriptors (EFDs) are used to extract the features, and a kernel SVM classifier was used for classification and achieved an accuracy rate of 98.07%. Mehedi Masud et al. [6] used 2D Fourier and 2D discrete wavelet features to identify colon and lung cancers. After extraction of features, the author used CNN model for classification and achieved an accuracy rate of 96.33%. Jianpeng Zhang et al. [7] classify medical images along with colorectal cancer images. In this paper, the author proposed a CDHVF algorithm that combines three pre-trained DL model and two hand-crafted based feature extraction techniques. A. Karthikeyan et al. [3] designed one CNN architecture consisting of eighteen CNN layers to identify the stages in colon cancer. The author fused CNN and LSTM in this work and achieved an accuracy rate of 91%.

Ben Hamida et al. [8] reviewed several DL architectures such as AlexNet, VGG16, InceptionV3, ResNet, and DenseNet architectures to identify colon cancer and proposed UNet and SegNet architecture. They also used patch level image classification, and using SegNet they achieved an accuracy rate of 98.66%.

Md. Alamin Talukder et al. [9] proposed a hybrid ensemble feature extraction based model to identify lung and colon cancers. In this paper, the authors extracted the features using transfer learning on five different DL architectures namely VGG16, VGG19, MobileNet, DenseNet169, and DenseNet201. After extraction of features some well-known ML classifiers such as SVM, RF, XGB, etc. are used for classification. Indu Chhillar et al. [10] proposed one feature engineering based ML approach to identify lung and colon cancers. In this paper, they extracted 52 Haralick-based texture features and color-based features. With a combine feature set and light gradient boosting machine (LightGBM) classifier they achieved maximum performance accuracy.

Ahmed S. Sakr et al. [11] designed several end-to-end lightweight DL architectures to identify colon cancer. Out of those architectures 12 layer CNN with dropout rate 0.5 and batch size of 8, the authors recorded the highest accuracy rate of 99.50%.

Maha Sharkas [12] proposed one color-CADx approach to classify colon cancer. In this approach the author has used three DL architecture (AlexNet, ResNet, and DenseNet) to extract the features from the input images. The features are then reduced using DCT. The acquired DCT features from the DL models are then concatenated, and analysis of variance (ANOVA) is applied to select the important features, and SVM is applied to classify the images. They have recorded an accuracy rate of 96.80% on Kather texture 2016 image tiles dataset.

Amit Seth et al. [13] detected lung and colon cancer using cascade CNN. In this paper, the authors segmented the ROI using the Swin Transformer and applied two phase CNN to extract both high-level and low-level features. The ATDO algorithm is used to optimize the network parameter and achieved an accuracy rate of 97.40%.

6.3 MATERIALS AND METHODOLOGY

6.3.1 Convolution Block Attention Model

Convolutional neural networks and attention mechanisms in vision, with encouraging outcomes in terms of enhancing the network's performance in the field of computer vision. The CNN network is aided by attention mechanisms in a variety of ways. CNN networks, such as VGGNet, GoogLeNet, and residual-style networks, work by widening and deepening the network to improve its capacity for detection, while the attention mechanism works to improve the network's performance by focusing on important details and information about the features. Woo et al. [14] proposed CBAM, which uses both spatial and channel attention module. Spatial attention module designed to selectively focus on certain spatial regions of an image, enhancing the model's capability to capture relevant features. The goal of channel-wise attention is to highlight more significant channels by assigning weights to each channel according to its relevance. The channel attention module and the spatial attention module are two sequential submodules of CBAM that are applicable to feed-forward CNN models. The block diagram of CBAM is shown in Figure 6.1.

6.3.2 Proposed Model

In this chapter, we have proposed a CNN architecture, and for better feature extraction we have incorporated CBAM in the CNN. The block diagram of the proposed model is shown in Figure 6.2. The proposed model is a 13-layer CNN architecture that consists of input layer, 5 convolution layers, 3 max-pooling layers, 1 global average pooling layer, 1 CBAM layer, a dense layer, and a SoftMax (output) layer. At first, the images in the dataset are resized to 224×224 and fed into the input of the CNN model. The convolution and max-pooling layers are used to extract the basic features from the images. The convolution layer uses filter size of 3×3. Convolutions

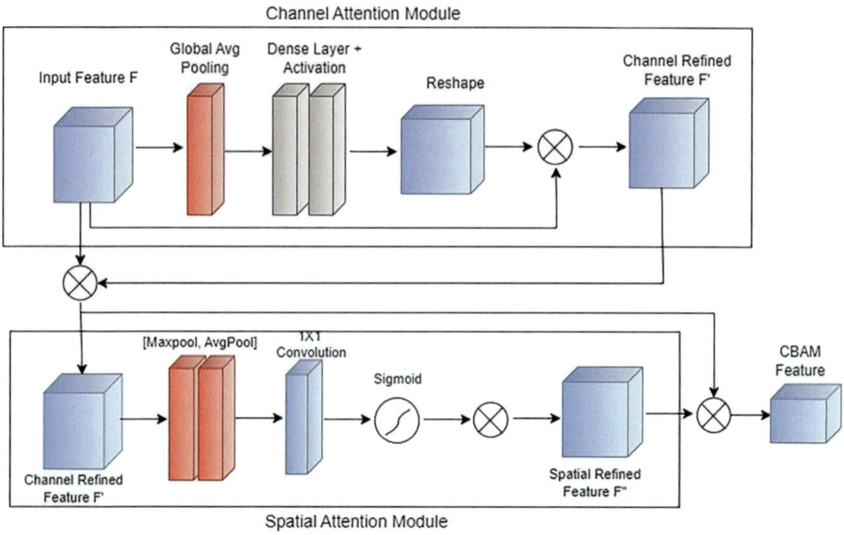

FIGURE 6.1 Block diagram of CBAM.

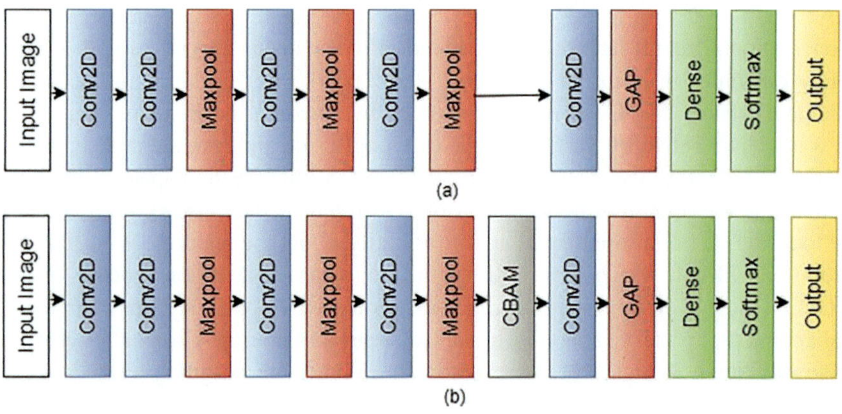

FIGURE 6.2 Proposed CNN architecture.

with various filters are used to create a set of representation maps, which are then subjected to a non-linearity function and batch normalization. We have incorporated rectified linear unit (ReLu) as non-linearity function to normalize the input image pixels. For subsampling and dimension reduction purposes the max-pooling layer is used with a filter size of 2×2. More condensed features, which have considerably fewer dimensions than the previous ones, can be extracted by the pooling operator. This leads to a reduction in computing complexity as well. It is crucial to further enhance the roughly extracted features because the ultimate performance is significantly influenced by the quality of the learned features. For this purpose, one CBAM layer is used to highlight the important information and simultaneously suppress the unimportant ones. After that one global average pooling (GAP) layer is used, which reduces the number of parameters over the flattened layer. Finally, one SoftMax layer is used for the classification of lung and colon cancer.

6.4 RESULTS

6.4.1 DATASET

In this work, we have considered an open-access lung and colon cancer dataset called the LC25000 dataset [15]. This dataset consists of 25,000 images of lung and colon cancer. All the images are colored images and of size 768×768. The dataset consists of three categories of lung cancer cell images, namely lung benign tissue, lung adenocarcinoma, and lung squamous cell carcinoma, and two colon cancer cells, namely colon adenocarcinoma and colon benign tissue. In this work we have considered 1000 images per class. The dataset are split into 80% training and 20% test set. Table 6.1 shows the dataset details used in this chapter. Figure 6.3 shows some sample images from the dataset.

6.4.2 EXPERIMENTAL SETUP

The experiment was carried out using Google Colab pro with GPU. The experiment implemented in Jupyter notebook with common Python libraries as NumPy, Keras, Tensorflow, Matplotlib, etc. are used. The model is trained with learning rate 0.001, the batch size is set to 32, and the training epoch is set to 50.

Performance metrics determine the efficiency of the model. The performance metrics evaluated are accuracy, precision, recall, and F1 score. The Equations 6.1 to 6.4 define the expression of these matrices.

$$Accuracy = \frac{TP + TN}{TP + FP + TN + FN} \tag{6.1}$$

$$Precision = \frac{TP}{TP + FP} \tag{6.2}$$

$$Recall = \frac{TP}{TP + FN} \tag{6.3}$$

TABLE 6.1
Dataset Description

Disease Class	No of Train Image	No of Test Image	Total Image
Lung benign tissue	800	200	1000
Lung adenocarcinoma	800	200	1000
Lung squamous cell carcinoma	800	200	1000
Colon adenocarcinoma	800	200	1000
Colon benign tissue	800	200	1000

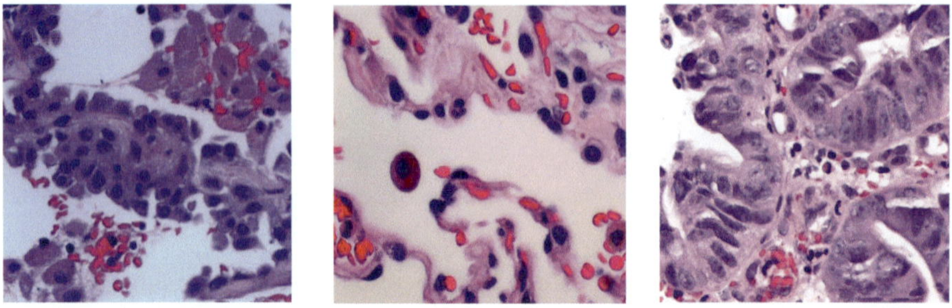

(a) Lung denocarcinoma (b) Lung cell carcinoma (c) Colon adenocarcinoma

FIGURE 6.3 Sample images from the dataset.

TABLE 6.2
Hyperparameter Used

Parameter	Value
Epoch	50
Batch size	32
Learning rate	0.001
Optimizer	Adam
Loss	Categorical cross entropy

$$f1-score = \frac{2 \times Precision \times Recall}{Precision + Recall} \quad (6.4)$$

6.4.3 Result Analysis and Discussion

This section briefly discusses the performances of the proposed model and compares the performances with some state-of-art DL approaches. The hyperparameter used in the proposed CNN model is shown in Table 6.2. Performances of the proposed CNN model with CBAM are compared with the performances of CNN without CBAM. Table 6.3 shows the performance of the proposed model in terms of accuracy and loss. From Table 6.3 it is seen that the proposed CNN with CBAM model achieves an accuracy rate of 98.34%, whereas CNN without attention achieves an accuracy rate of 95.34% on both lung and colon images. Figure 6.4 shows the accuracy and loss curve of the proposed model on the datasets (only lung, only colon, both lung and colon images). From Figure 6.4, it is seen that the proposed CNN with CBAM model achieves high performances in all the cases.

The performances of the proposed models are evaluated in terms of the confusion matrix also. The confusion matrix obtained from the model is shown in Figure 6.5. From Figure 6.5, it is seen that the proposed CNN with CBAM has a better ability to classify the images. Moreover, we have evaluated the performances of the proposed

TABLE 6.3
Performances of the Proposed Model

Model	Dataset	Train Accuracy	Train Loss	Val Accuracy	Val Loss	Epoch
CNN without CBAM	Lung	0.9804	0.0509	0.9567	0.1523	50
	Colon	0.9912	0.0082	0.9621	0.1283	50
	Both Lung and Colon	0.9805	0.0491	0.9534	0.1473	50
CNN with CBAM	Lung	1.0000	0.0012	0.9859	0.1244	50
	Colon	1.0000	0.0027	0.9923	0.1026	50
	Both Lung and Colon	1.0000	0.0056	0.9834	0.1362	50

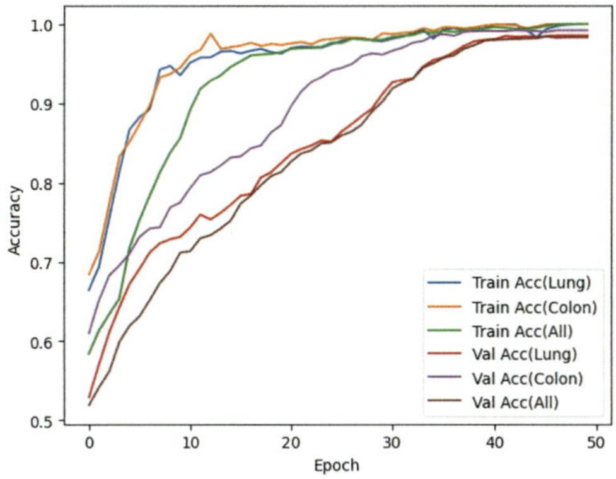

(a) Accuracy

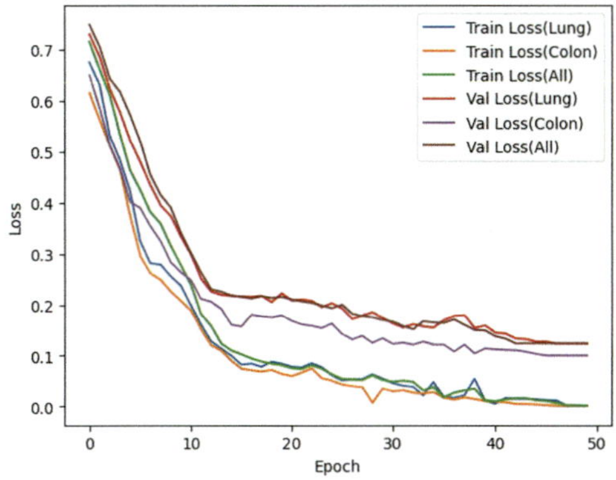

(b) Loss

FIGURE 6.4 Performance measure in terms of accuracy and loss.

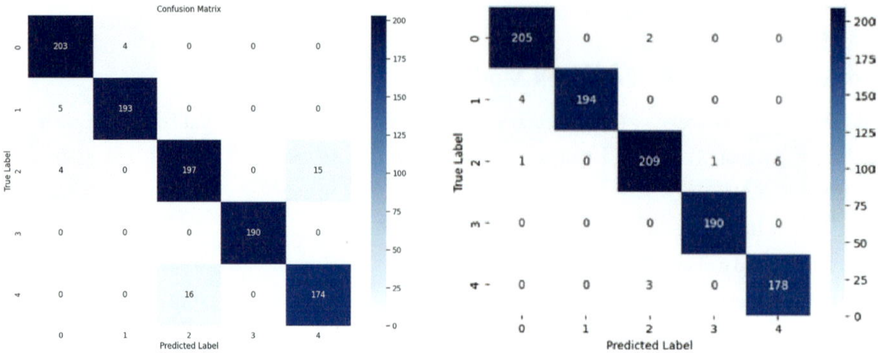

(a) CNN without CBAM (b) CNN with CBAM

FIGURE 6.5 Confusion matrix of the proposed CNN model.

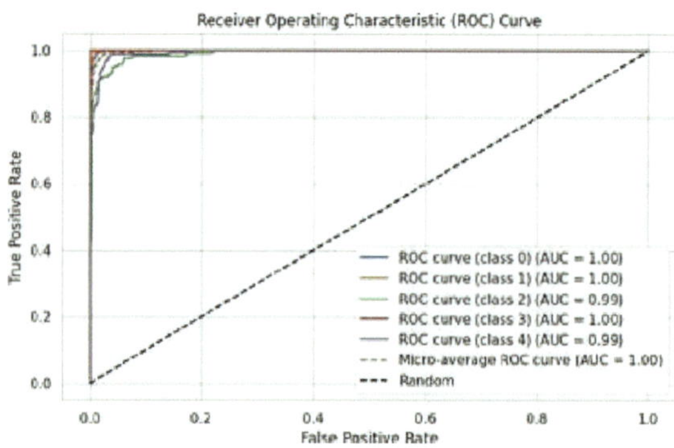

(a) CNN without CBAM

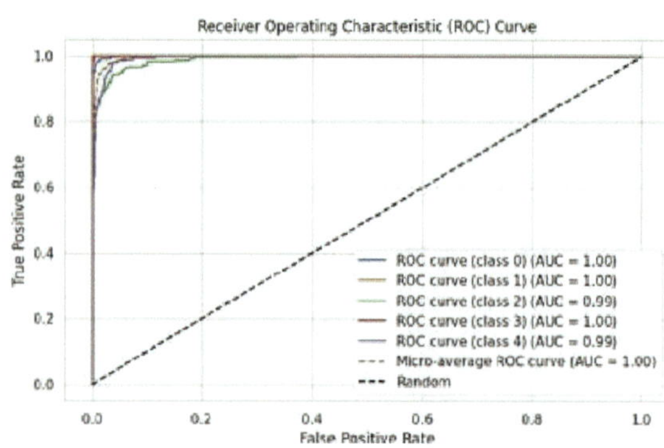

(b) CNN with CBAM

FIGURE 6.6 Performance measure in terms ROC-AUC curve.

TABLE 6.4
Performance Comparison

Model Name	Parameter	Depth	Accuracy (%)
VGG16 [16]	138.4M	16	96.23
VGG19 [16]	143.7M	19	96.51
InceptionV3 [17]	23.9M	189	97.20
ResNet50 [18]	25.6M	107	97.43
DenseNet121 [19]	8.1M	242	96.07
MobileNetV2 [20]	3.5M	105	94.50
Proposed	0.0565M	13	98.34

model in terms of the ROC-AUC curve. Figure 6.6 shows the ROC-AUC curve of the proposed model, and the figure shows that the proposed model classifies the images with high-performance accuracy.

To better demonstrate the feature extraction capability in the proposed model, some state-of-the-art DL models are implemented for comparison. Different variants of DL such as VGG16, VGG19, InceptionV3, ResNet50, DenseNet, EfficientNetB0, and MobileNetV2 are considered for comparison. The performance comparison is shown in Table 6.4. From Table 6.4, it is seen the proposed model gives higher performance accuracy as compared to the state-of-the-art DL architectures with fewer parameters.

6.5 CONCLUSION

This study demonstrates the effectiveness of incorporating attention modules into deep learning-based models for enhancing colon cancer detection from medical imaging data. The integration of attention modules allows the model to dynamically adapt its focus based on the saliency of features within the image, enabling it to prioritize areas with potentially malignant lesions while suppressing irrelevant background noise. In this chapter, we have proposed one lightweight DL model with CBAM in the identification of lung and colon cancers. The performance of the proposed CNN with CBAM model is compared with CNN architecture without self-attention model and several state-of-the-art DL architectures. The result shows that CNN with attention has the better ability to identify the images and achieves an accuracy rate of 98.34%. Further, the proposed model is compared with several DL models in terms of parameters, and it is seen that the proposed model used a few parameter and less model depth.

REFERENCES

[1] Shafi, L., Iqbal, P., Khaliq, R.: Cancer burden in india: A statistical analysis on incidence rates. Indian Journal of Public Health **67**(4), 582–587 (2023)

[2] Pacal, I., Karaboga, D., Basturk, A., Akay, B., Nalbantoglu, U.: A comprehensive review of deep learning in colon cancer. Computers in Biology and Medicine **126**, 104003 (2020)

[3] Karthikeyan, A., Jothilakshmi, S., Suthir, S.: Colorectal cancer detection based on convolutional neural networks (CNN) and ranking algorithm. Measurement: Sensors **31**, 100976 (2024)
[4] Giger, M.L., Doi, K., MacMahon, H.: Image feature analysis and computer-aided diagnosis in digital radiography. 3. Automated detection of nodules in peripheral lung fields. Medical Physics **15**(2), 158–166 (1988)
[5] Rathore, S., Hussain, M., Khan, A.: Automated colon cancer detection using hybrid of novel geometric features and some traditional features. Computers in Biology and Medicine **65**, 279–296 (2015)
[6] Masud, M., Sikder, N., Nahid, A.-A., Bairagi, A.K., AlZain, M.A.: A machine learning approach to diagnosing lung and colon cancer using a deep learning-based classification framework. Sensors **21**(3), 748 (2021)
[7] Zhang, J., Xia, Y., Xie, Y., Fulham, M., Feng, D.D.: Classification of medical images in the biomedical literature by jointly using deep and handcrafted visual features. IEEE Journal of Biomedical and Health Informatics **22**(5), 1521–1530 (2017)
[8] Hamida, A.B., Devanne, M., Weber, J., Truntzer, C., Derang'ere, V., Ghiringhelli, F., Forestier, G., Wemmert, C.: Deep learning for colon cancer histopathological images analysis. Computers in Biology and Medicine **136**, 104730 (2021)
[9] Talukder, M.A., Islam, M.M., Uddin, M.A., Akhter, A., Hasan, K.F., Moni, M.A.: Machine learning-based lung and colon cancer detection using deep feature extraction and ensemble learning. Expert Systems with Applications **205**, 117695 (2022)
[10] Chhillar, I., Singh, A.: A feature engineering-based machine learning technique to detect and classify lung and colon cancer from histopathological images. Medical & Biological Engineering & Computing **62**(3), 913–924 (2024)
[11] Sakr, A.S., Soliman, N.F., Al-Gaashani, M.S., Pławiak, P., Ateya, A.A., Hammad, M.: An efficient deep learning approach for colon cancer detection. Applied Sciences **12**(17), 8450 (2022)
[12] Sharkas, M., Attallah, O.: Color-CADX: A deep learning approach for colorectal cancer classification through triple convolutional neural networks and discrete cosine transform. Scientific Reports **14**(1), 6914 (2024)
[13] Seth, A., Kaushik, V.D.: Automatic lung and colon cancer detection using enhanced cascade convolution neural network. Multimedia Tools and Applications **83**, 1–22 (2024)
[14] Woo, S., Park, J., Lee, J.-Y., Kweon, I.S.: CBAM: Convolutional block attention module. In: Proceedings of the European Conference on Computer Vision (ECCV), pp. 3–19 (2018)
[15] Borkowski, A.A., Bui, M.M., Thomas, L.B., Wilson, C.P., DeLand, L.A., Mastorides, S.M.: Lung and colon cancer histopathological image dataset (LC25000). arXiv preprint arXiv:1912.12142 (2019)
[16] Karen, S.: Very deep convolutional networks for large-scale image recognition. arXiv preprint arXiv: 1409.1556 (2014)
[17] Szegedy, C., Vanhoucke, V., Ioffe, S., Shlens, J., Wojna, Z.: Rethinking the inception architecture for computer vision. In: Proceedings of the IEEE Conference on Computer Vision and Pattern Recognition, pp. 2818–2826 (2016)
[18] He, K., Zhang, X., Ren, S., Sun, J.: Deep residual learning for image recognition. In: Proceedings of the IEEE Conference on Computer Vision and Pattern Recognition, pp. 770–778 (2016)
[19] Huang, G., Liu, Z., Van Der Maaten, L., Weinberger, K.Q.: Densely connected convolutional networks. In: Proceedings of the IEEE Conference on Computer Vision and Pattern Recognition, pp. 4700–4708 (2017)
[20] Sandler, M., Howard, A., Zhu, M., Zhmoginov, A., Chen, L.-C.: Mobilenetv2: Inverted residuals and linear bottlenecks. In: Proceedings of the IEEE Conference on Computer Vision and Pattern Recognition, pp. 4510–4520 (2018)

7 Acoustic-Based Parkinson's Disease Diagnosis Using Transfer Learning

Combining VGG16 with Light Gradient Boosting Machine (LGBM) Classifier

Shibina V and Thasleema T M

7.1 INTRODUCTION

Parkinson's disease (PD) is a chronic neurological impairment that progresses over time, mainly influencing motor control. The condition arises from the gradual destruction of dopamine-producing neurons in the substantia nigra, which is a region of the brain critical for mobility coordination. Patients commonly experience indications like tremors, slowness of movement, muscle rigidity, speech disorder, and balance problems. In addition to these motor symptoms, non-motor issues like sleep problems, cognitive decline, and mood disturbances are prevalent [1, 2]. Speaking difficulties are frequently among the first indications of Parkinson's disease. Research has indicated that 90% of PD patients have some degree of vocal dysfunction. PD impairs muscular function and voluntary movement; it significantly impacts the vocal system [3]. Speech disorders can include decreased vocal tract volume and tongue flexibility, decreased pitch range and intensity of speaking, poor speech quality, and untimely pauses. As a result, it makes sense and is a crucial topic to predict Parkinson's disease via speech cues, particularly during its initial phases [4]. Automated speech analysis has been explored in recent studies to diagnose Parkinson's disease. Deep learning (DL) and machine learning (ML) methods have been applied to verbal analytics to identify and monitor PD [5].

PD symptoms can differ from one individual to another. Researchers have developed several imaging and signaling tests to detect PD. The examinations for PD are diffusion tensor imaging (DATscan) and magnetic resonance imaging (MRI) [6]. Though biomarkers, genes, and neuroimaging have advanced, the medical detection

DOI: 10.1201/9781003473442-7

of Parkinson's disease remains difficult, especially in its initial phases or with unusual Parkinsonism [7]. Nevertheless, speech recording-based diagnostic methods have attracted considerable interest among these other approaches because alterations in speech or challenges with speech are one of the earliest motor indicators of PD, appearing up to 10 years before the disease is officially diagnosed, long before rigidity, gait abnormalities, and limb bradykinesia manifest [6–8]. The voice signals piqued additional curiosity because they were non-invasive and inexpensive and could be used remotely from patients' homes. Research shows that vocal cord injury is one of the first biomarkers of Parkinson's disease in 90% of individuals. These difficulties with vocal production first manifest in Parkinson's illness. Patients with Parkinson's disease often talk with a raspier sound, less vibrato, and more breathiness. Dysarthria is the manifestation of voice problems in people with Parkinsonism. When the brain regions responsible for speech become inactive, a disorder known as dysarthria develops, mostly manifesting as a lack of control over one's muscles. Damage to the basal ganglia causes hypokinetic dysarthria. Disabilities in phonation, prosody, and articulation are indications among the PD community. Disfluency in speech is indicated by articulatory impairment, and phonatory impairment is a decrease in vocal volume. Prosodic impairment is pausing anomalies, syllabic stress, and mono-pitch [6].

Data science has been used in multiple types of studies to make progress in medical research for disease identification and categorization by considering different factors. Software platforms can deliver precise and quick diagnoses of illnesses in the medical field by utilizing newly developed artificial intelligence techniques. Thus, methods such as data mining (DM), deep learning, and machine learning are employed to select relevant features and cluster them for proper disease detection and prediction [6, 7]. The precise causes of Parkinson's disease are not completely identified but are thought to entail both biological and ecological exposures such as chemicals or pollutants. Diagnosis is often challenging and based on clinical evaluations and medical history, with imaging tests sometimes used to rule out other conditions. Although Parkinson's disease has no approved remedy at the moment, there are therapies that can help lessen symptoms. These treatments include deep brain stimulation, dopamine agonists, and levodopa. Research currently being conducted attempts to understand the disease mechanisms better, identify early diagnostic markers, and develop innovative treatments, including advanced computational methods for monitoring disease progression. After Alzheimer's disease, Parkinson's disease is the second most prevalent neurological ailment and the second most common cause of cognitive loss [9]; it has a significant impact on patients and imposes considerable demands on healthcare systems globally [1, 2]. The literature outlines a broad range of approaches [10] applied for study of physiological signal characteristics. This study used the phoneme /a/ from the PC-GITA dataset to assess the transfer learning approach for PD diagnosis. Figure 7.1 illustrates the classification of diseases by applying the transfer learning mechanism where speech signals are turned into mel spectrograms, analyzed by VGG16 for key features, and classified by different models to detect disease. The further research is organized in the following manner. Section 7.2 summarizes the research approach utilized for this literature evaluation. Section 7.3 addressed the dataset and technique used in the current investigation. The findings of the research are discussed in Section 7.4. In addition, Section 7.5 illustrated the study's conclusions.

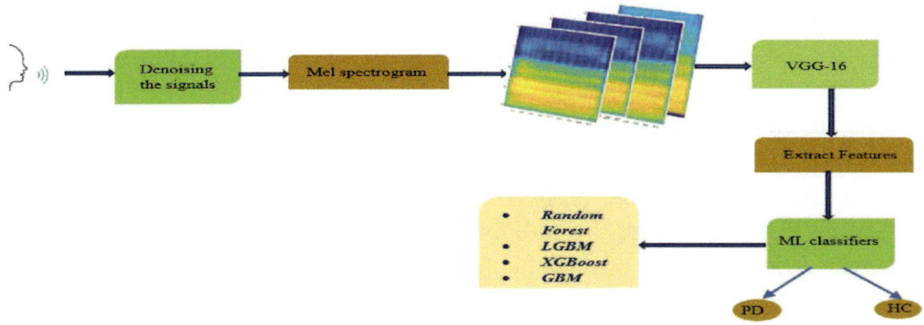

FIGURE 7.1 Overall diagram of disease classification using transfer learning mechanism.

7.2 RELATED WORK

Recent advancements in Parkinson's disease detection have increasingly utilized speech signal analysis due to the observable speech impairments associated with the condition. Acoustic features such as pitch, jitter, and shimmer are commonly extracted from voice signals to distinguish between people with Parkinsonism and healthy controls. Reddy et al. [4] introduced a sparse representation (SR) on exemplar-based classification method for PD detection from voice signals. Vectors of speech features taken from the training set are called exemplars. Regarding training speech exemplars, the detection challenge is the problem of obtaining sparse representations of test speech feature vectors. The primary benefit of employing the SR technique over traditional ML-based methods is that the training phase is not time-consuming [4]. A deep neural network (DNN) based strategy for identifying Parkinson's disease was proposed by the authors of [6]. This approach makes use of spectrograms of speech signals that are created utilizing Superlet Transform (SLT). The SLT converts 1-D voice inputs to 2-D spectrograms. The spectrograms of the speech signal are subsequently applied to various DNN classifiers, including InceptionResNetV2, VGG16, and ResNet50v2, to detect PD. The ItalianPVS dataset's vowels and the PC-GITA dataset's isolated words, modulated vowels, DDK analysis, and sustainable vowels are all evaluated using the proposed method. Warule et al. [8] presented that Chirplet Transform (CT) was implemented to obtain the time-frequency matrix (TFM) of each speech sample. Subsequently, time-frequency-based entropy (TFE) features were extracted from the TFM. The TFE features accurately reflect the alterations in speech exhibited in people with Parkinson's disease. This means it can be applied to distinguish people with Parkinson's disease from healthy individuals (HC). The suggested model is tested against vowels and words from the PC-GITA database. Bilal et al. [9] utilized mel spectrograms generated from denoised speech signals with variational mode decomposition (VMD) are employed to detect PD from voice signals. This novel method relies on pre-trained deep networks and long short-term memory (LSTM). ResNet18, ResNet50, and ResNet101 models serve as pre-trained deep networks, and this approach is explored in the PC-GITA dataset. Karan et al. [11] research delves into the joint use of Hilbert spectrum analysis

(HSA) and variational mode decomposition (VMD) to investigate voice vibrations in Parkinson's disease patients. Researchers in this study developed a novel set of traits called Hilbert cepstral coefficients (HCCs). Words and vowels from the PC-GITA database are employed to evaluate the proposed features. Zhang et al. [12] explored fractional attribute topology (FrAT) based voice feature, which is connected with energy points and directional properties. This approach results in sound accuracy in detecting PD. In addition, the authors of [13] conducted a study on gender-based feature extraction, which is enabled by the statistical-based feature score (SBFS) and classification-based feature score (CBFS) and is employed as the feature ranking. The accuracy rates for the classification of Parkinson's disease were 86% and 84% for men and women groups, utilizing 14 and 12 features, respectively. These classifications were achieved through several classifiers, including linear and nonlinear support vector machine (LSVM and NSVM, respectively), k-nearest neighborhood (KNN), naïve Bayesian (NB), and random forest (RF) methods. In another study, the authors of [14] described multilevel feature extraction and selection on isolated words in the PC-GITA dataset for the purpose of classification. Karan et al. [15] discussed that the speaker's information about the vocal folds and tract is retrieved using the Hilbert spectrum. The instantaneous energy deviation cepstral coefficient (IEDCC) is presented to bring important information to models. Vowels in the PC-GITA database have an average accuracy of 82% to 90%, whereas words have an average accuracy of 80% to 91%. The classification accuracy is improved by 20% when compared to the traditional MFCC and auditory characteristics. According to Narendra et al. [16], the baseline auditory features, which include articulation, phonation, and prosody features, were calculated while the features were being extracted. Quasi-closed phase (QCP) was utilized to compute glottal features, and speech source information was retrieved utilizing iterative adaptive inverse filtering (IAIF) glottal inverse filtering processes. This approach makes use of deep learning models built on raw speech and voice source waveforms. The latter included zero frequency filtering and two glottal inverse filtering techniques (IAIF and QCP). A multilayer perceptron comes before a convolutional layer combination in a deep learning architecture. To conduct experiments, the PC-GITA speech database was used. A combination of baseline and QCP-based glottal features in typical pipeline systems produced the highest classification accuracy (67.93%). Of all the end-to-end systems, the system trained with glottal flow signals based on QCP had the best accuracy (68.56%). The study found that voice source information extraction was the most successful strategy overall, even if classification accuracy declined across the board. An architecture for diagnosing Parkinson's disease from speech signals was presented by the authors of [17]. The architecture consists of an RF algorithm generated by machine learning and a CNN model formed by deep learning. CNN architectures generate multidimensional feature extraction layers with minimal parameters. Multidimensional features are produced by the convolution process using different filter sizes. Table 7.1 presents a summary of the literature review.

This investigation showcased the diagnostic efficacy of these acoustic features in Parkinson's disease, emphasizing their potential for ongoing monitoring and early detection. Speech analysis is a non-invasive diagnostic method, and this research highlights its significance. In the field of disease diagnosis, deep learning approaches

TABLE 7.1
Illustrates the Summary of Previous Works on PD Diagnosis

References	Dataset	Technique Used	Approach	Result
Reddy et al. [4]	PC-GITA database	Non-negative least squares (NNLS)	SVM	Accuracy 82.84% MCC 0.64 F1-score 83.17%,
Kavita et al. [6]	PC-GITA ItalianPVS dataset	Superlet Transform	InceptionResNetV2 VGG16 ResNet50v2	VGG16 Accuracy 92% sensitivity 92% specificity 91% precision 95% F1 93%
Warule et al. [8]	PC-GITA	Chirplet Transform	SVM	Accuracy vowel /a/ 98% word /atleta/ 99%
Bilal et al. [9]	PC-GITA	VMD	ResNet101 and LSTM	Accuracy 98.61%
Zhang et al. [12]	Three native datasets	Fractional attribute topology (FrAT)	—	Accuracies 99.57%, 95.33% and 94.13%
Mahboobeh et al. [13]	UCI repository	Statistical-based feature score (SBFS), Classification-based feature score (CBFS)	LSVM and NSVM (KNN), NB, RF	Accuracy of 86% and 84% for men and women groups
Amato et al. [14]	PC-GITA	Multilevel features	KNN	Accuracy 94.3%
Gaffari et al. [17]	PD_Dataset	ML, DL combination	CNN + RF	98.30%
Proposed model	PC-GITA	VMD Mel spectrogram Transfer Learning	VGG16 + (RF, XGB, LGBM, GBM)	LGBM vowel /a/ Accuracy 90.33 Pre 89.54 Recall 91.33 F1 90.42

play a significant role. Most of the works examined in the literature review were based on either machine learning or deep learning techniques rather than transfer learning and the mel spectrogram approach. This research focused on signal preprocessing with mel spectrogram and VMD.

7.3 MATERIAL AND METHODOLOGY

The speech database maintained by PC-GITA [18] includes recordings of Spanish speech made by 50 people with Parkinson's disease (25 males and 25 females) as

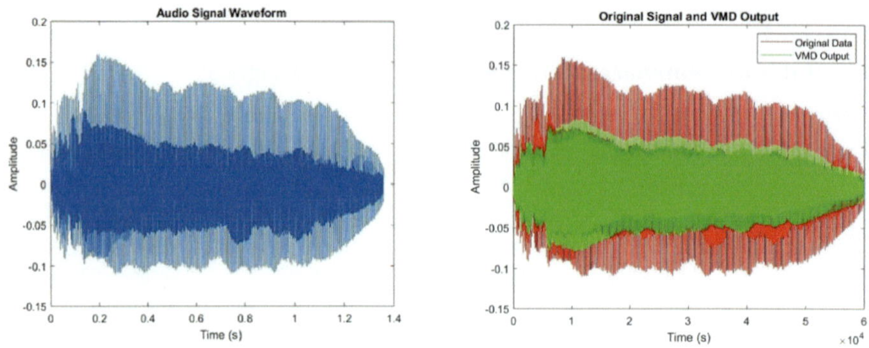

FIGURE 7.2 (a) Plots the original signal with amplitude fluctuations; (b) plots the denoised audio signal using the VMD technique.

well as 50 healthy control speakers (25 males and 25 females). A sampling rate of 44.1 kHz and a bit depth of 16 were used for the data collection. Neurologists figured out that the people had PD. No cases of Parkinson's disease or other neurodegenerative diseases have been reported in the healthy controls. The speaker's age ranges considerably between the ages of 31 and 86. The recording sessions were carried out in a sound-proof booth located at the Clínica Noel of Medellín, which is located in Colombia. This work focused on the sustained phonation of the vowel /a/ pronounced three times. Figure 7.2a shows the clean audio signal with natural sound patterns, i.e., the original signal and small variations in loudness. Figure 7.2b shows that the green waveform is the denoised version, while the red waveform is the original noisy signal. Denoising using VMD smooths the green waveform by eliminating noise but keeping the original sound patterns, making it clearer for analysis.

7.3.1 Preprocessing

Two steps are covered in this preprocessing step, which is being discussed. In the initial step, the noise is eliminated, and then a mel scale spectrogram is generated. Algorithm1 detailed the methodology behind preprocessing.

7.3.1.1 Noise Removal Using VMD

In variational mode decomposition, IMF6 refers to the sixth intrinsic mode function derived from the decomposition of a noisy signal. Each IMF represents a specific frequency component of the original signal. Analyzing IMF6 involves examining its frequency content and energy to determine if it contains significant noise or useful information [19]. VMD parameters, such as alpha, influence the characteristics of IMF6 (α), which controls the smoothness of the modes and is set around 2000, and the number of modes k=6, which defines how many components the signal is decomposed into six. Based on this analysis, IMF6 may be retained or discarded in reconstructing the denoised signal, depending on whether it primarily represents noise or contributes valuable information.

Algorithm1: VMD and mel spectrogram implementation
Steps: **Input:** ***raw signal, IMF=6,*** **output:** ***denoised signal***

1. ***Input the speech signal raw_signal and its sampling frequency fs.***
2. ***Decompose the raw_signal into NumIMF as 6 Intrinsic Mode Functions (IMFs) using the VMD algorithm.***
3. ***Store the output IMFs in a matrix vmd_output and the residual (if any) in residual.***
4. ***Denoise the Signal:***
   - ***Select specific IMFs (IMFs 2, 3, and 4) to reconstruct the denoised signal.***
   - ***Sum these selected IMFs along the rows to form the denoised_signal.***
5. ***Plot Raw Signal vs. Denoised Signal:***
6. ***Calculate the mel spectrogram of the denoised_signal using parameters like Hamming window, overlap length 50%, and filter bank normalization.***
7. ***End.***

An integral part of the variational mode decomposition procedure for decomposing complicated signals like speech waveforms into more straightforward oscillatory modes is the intrinsic mode functions (IMFs). Each of the six IMFs in the provided code represents a distinct frequency band in the original audio source. The value for tolerance for convergence of the decomposition process is 1e–7. It sets a threshold for terminating the iterative optimization when variations fall below this number. Reduced tolerance values result in more accurate decompositions but require increased computing time. IMF 1 is good at picking up noise and high-frequency oscillations, which can be present in speech or background noise. IMF 2 has a slightly lower frequency range, making speech transitions more quickly. Mid-range frequencies are included in IMF 3, which frequently captures the basic phonetic elements; lower-frequency components, such as sustained vowel sounds, are reflected in IMF 4. With IMF 6 capturing the overall baseline trends, IMF 5 and IMF 6 represent even slower oscillations. Denoising works by re-creating the signal by adding IMFs 2, 3, and 4, believed to have the most important speech qualities with the least noise and unimportant frequency components. The denoised signal improves clarity by removing interference from intermodulation frequencies (IMFs) 1 and 5, which may convey high-frequency noise and slower, less informative trends. It is compared to the source signal to find where the denoised signal excels. To better comprehend the acoustic characteristics of the speech signal following noise reduction, a mel spectrogram is created from the denoised signal to display its frequency content over time [9, 11, 19]. Figure 7.3 plots the IMF from 1 to 6 plotted against the time axis, which enables a thorough examination of the signal's underlying patterns and frequencies; each IMF represents a unique oscillatory mode extracted from the original signal.

7.3.1.2 Mel Spectrogram from Denoised Signal

The mel spectrogram of a signal is a frequency vs time representation that translates the input signal into the mel frequency scale, which aligns more closely with human

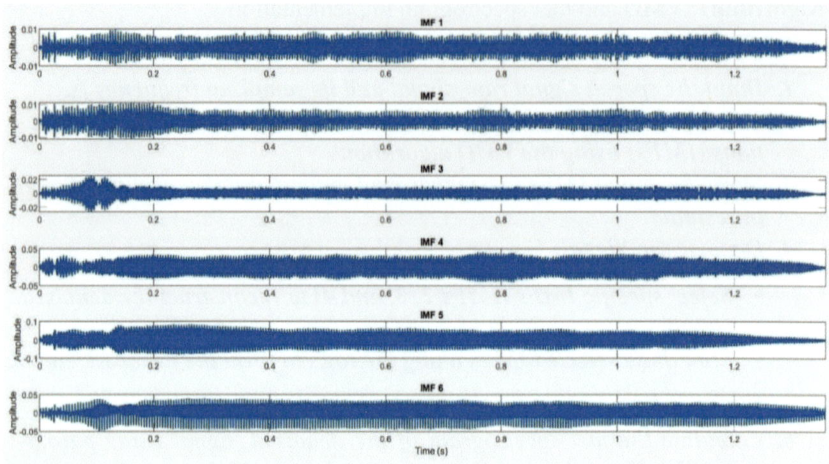

FIGURE 7.3 Depicts the time plot of IMF from 1 to 6 plotted extracted from the audio signal.

auditory perception. The process begins with preprocessing the signal, which may involve normalization and framing using a window function. Next, the short-time Fourier transform (STFT) is applied to each frame to capture the signal's frequency content over time. The resulting frequency spectrum is then transformed into the mel scale, a logarithmic scale that reflects how humans perceive pitch. This is achieved using a mel filter bank, which applies overlapping triangular filters spaced according to the mel scale. Logarithmic compression may be applied to the mel spectrogram to enhance contrast and highlight significant features. The final mel spectrogram is a 2D representation where the time is represented in the x-axis, the y-axis holds the intensity of color shows the magnitude of the frequencies and mel frequency bands. This representation is beneficial for audio and speech analysis as it captures the essential features of the signal in a manner that mimics human hearing [3, 9, 11].

After decomposition, the signal undergoes denoising. This is done by reconstructing the signal using only the second, third, and fourth IMFs, which carry the most useful speech information. Summing these IMFs results in a denoised version of the signal, which is compared to the original via visual plots. Finally, a mel spectrogram is created for the denoised signal using a 256-length Hamming window, 128-sample overlap, and bandwidth normalization. The mel spectrogram visually represents the signal's frequency content over time, mapped to the mel scale, which aligns with human auditory perception. This approach is useful for visualizing speech patterns and can be applied to speech analysis and diagnosing speech-related disorders. Optionally, apply logarithmic compression to the mel spectrogram to enhance the dynamic range and highlight significant features. This involves taking the logarithm of the power spectrum, often with a small constant added to prevent taking the logarithm of zero. Finally, the mel spectrogram may be resized to meet specific dimensions required for input into machine learning models, such as 224x224 pixels for compatibility with VGG16, ensuring it is properly formatted for further analysis or classification tasks. Figure 7.4 plots the preprocessed signals from PD and HC (healthy control) individuals.

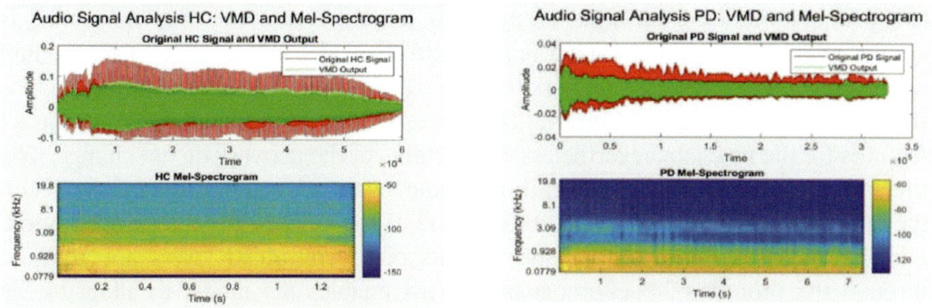

FIGURE 7.4 (a) Plots the preprocessed healthy control signal; (b) plots the preprocessed PD patient signal.

7.3.2 Transfer Learning Approach

A method used in machine learning is termed transfer learning, in which a pattern generated and optimized for one function is recreated as the base point for a subsequent task. In contrast to traditional machine learning, transfer learning starts with an additional task by employing a pre-trained model as a launching pad. The evident limitations of conventional machine learning methods and the increasing volume of multimodal signal data in biomedical treatments prompted researchers to adopt deep learning for signal processing [20]. The pre-trained deep transfer learning (DTL) frameworks and traditional machine learning models serve as an automated method for diagnosing Parkinson's disease from voice data. This study aggregated the retrieved features from the deep pre-trained architectures, VGG16, to produce the discriminative feature vectors. Transfer learning is a widely used approach that uses a pre-trained model to address new tasks. A pre-trained model has been trained using a comprehensive benchmark dataset, such as ImageNet. Transfer learning primarily entails leveraging knowledge gained from solving one problem with a large dataset to address a related problem with a smaller or different dataset. The domain and task components delineate transfer learning. Two components make up a domain ‘d’: the first is the feature space, which is represented by the ‘x’, and the second is the probability distribution, which is represented by the fraction p(x) [21].

$$d = (x, p(x)) \tag{7.1}$$

An element of the set x is denoted by the expression $x = \{x1,\ x2,\ x3,\ ......xn\}$. The predictive function ‘f(x)’ and the label space “z” are the two components of task ‘t’. The first component is the predictive function [21].

$$t = \big(z, f\left(x\right)\big) \tag{7.2}$$

Deep learning can be difficult to handle when dealing with datasets that are either limited or unlabeled. This issue is mitigated by using transfer learning, which utilizes knowledge from a big dataset for models with a limited amount of data. The implementation of transfer learning can be accomplished through the use of two primary methods: the first is known as feature extraction, and the second is known as fine tuning. As a fixed feature extractor, the feature extraction method uses a convolutional neural network (ConvNet) pre-trained on a big dataset, such as ImageNet. The weights of ConvNet that have been pre-trained are used to extract features for the new job; nevertheless, the weights of the network do not change. The fine tuning technique involves re-training some layers of the pre-trained ConvNet on the new dataset while preserving some layers of the ConvNet in a static condition. For the purpose of fine tuning, the weights of the retrained layers are adjusted through the process of backpropagation. This enables the model to adapt to the new data. Using these strategies, transfer learning makes it possible to effectively apply already trained models to increase performance on new tasks that need to be completed with limited datasets [21, 22]. VGG16, built by the Visual Geometry Group at Oxford, is a convolutional neural network (CNN) architecture that prevailed in the ILSVRC (ImageNet) competition in 2014. It is additionally referred to as OxfordNet. This design has 13 convolutional layers and 3 fully linked layers. The input dimensions are set to 224x224 RGB images by default. Convolutional layers utilize a fixed 3x3 filter size. VGG16 was trained on a large dataset (ImageNet); therefore, it has learned to recognize numerous low- and high-level features that are generalizable across other datasets, even though the target dataset (spectrogram images) differs significantly from the ImageNet data (natural images) [21]. In the preprocessing phase for preparing spectrogram images for machine learning models, several crucial steps are undertaken to ensure the data is suitable for model training and evaluation. First, images are loaded from the input set and are resized to 224×224, a standard dimension for many deep learning models such as VGG16, ensuring consistency in the input size. Normalization follows, where pixel values, initially ranging from 0 to 255, are scaled to a [0, 1] range by dividing by 255.0. This step helps the model converge faster and perform better by providing input data on a consistent scale. Label encoding is then applied to convert categorical labels, such as 'healthy' and 'patient', into numerical values using the LabelEncoder. This encoding translates categorical data into integers, making it compatible with machine learning algorithms that require numerical input. By following these preprocessing steps—loading and resizing images, normalizing pixel values, encoding labels, and splitting the data—the dataset is effectively prepared for subsequent model training and evaluation. A sequential model is built on top of VGG16, and it flattens the features and adds a dense layer with 256 units, followed by batch normalization and 0.5 dropout for regularization. The final layer is a single unit with a sigmoid activation function, making it suitable for binary classification. The model is compiled using the Adam optimizer with a learning rate of 0.0001 and binary cross-entropy loss. Finally, the VGG16 model undergoes training for 5 epochs, utilizing 80% of the data for training and 20% for validation. Early halting is employed to mitigate overfitting. This split is performed with a fixed random state to ensure reproducibility. For the classification PD and HC here, four types of classifiers have been used.

7.3.2.1 LGBM

Parkinson's disease is a complicated neurological condition that affects millions of individuals annually throughout the world. A gradient boosting framework known for its strong prediction capabilities, the LightGBM classifier effectively distinguishes between Parkinson's disease patients and healthy controls. LightGBM predominantly uses decision trees as basis models to accelerate training and improve efficiency. In LightGBM, "decision tree" refers to the base model utilized in the boosting ensemble. LightGBM enhances the speed and efficiency of training by employing a unique form of decision tree known as "histogram-based decision trees". The classifier's accuracy heavily depends on tweaking the appropriate hyperparameters to find patterns hidden in the data. Grid Search is a methodical way to investigate combinations of parameters like the number of estimators (*n_est*), learning rate (*lr*), number of leaves (*n_leaf*), lambda (*l*), and alpha (*a*) to maximize these hyperparameters [22, 23].

7.3.2.2 XGBoost

An ensemble machine learning method called XGBoost is built on top of the gradient boosting framework. In terms of regression, classification, ranking, and predictive analysis, this algorithm seems to be one of the best. The algorithm uses gradient descent to enhance inadequate dataset features, making it suitable for numerous purposes. Scalability is a key characteristic of XGBoost, enabling efficient memory management and training via parallel and distributed computation [22]. Data can be classified and predicted with the use of XGBoost, which is a gradient boosting classifier. The idea is to boost and transform average learners into exceptional ones by combining their results. Error-fixing methods from earlier stages are used to create new models until no more changes need to be made [22, 24].

7.3.2.3 Random Forest

This approach is frequently applied as a component of an ensemble and is very beneficial for problems involving regression and classification. Data samples are randomly selected for each decision tree. Each decision tree is trained on an alternate portion of the dataset, resulting in varied outputs for each tree. Voting on each decision tree's outcomes yields the best outcomes [24].

7.3.2.4 Gradient Boost

Gradient boosting (GB) reduces the loss function with each new model iteratively created from subpar models.

The loss function is computed using the gradient descent approach. Consequently, it is utilized to fit new models more correctly. Therefore, the findings lead to an improvement in total accuracy. Conversely, boosting can't go on indefinitely; doing so would lead to overfitting of the model [22].

7.4 RESULTS AND DISCUSSION

7.4.1 Evaluation Parameters

The four factors considered during evaluation are accuracy, recall, precision, and F1 score. The accuracy of the proposed research model serves as an indicator of its effectiveness. Recall describes how the suggested study project can predict persons with PD, HD, and healthy individuals. The precision of the proposed model's positive predictions for PD and healthy patients is measured. The model's accuracy, precision, and recall are calculated using a confusion matrix, shown using Equations 7.3

to 7.6. True positive (TP) denotes an accurate decision classification. False positives (FP) denote wrong decision classification; TN indicates proper negative classification, while incorrect positive classification is indicated by FN [19].

$$Accuracy = \frac{TP + TN}{TP + TN + FP + FN} \tag{7.3}$$

$$Precision = \frac{TP}{TP + FP} \tag{7.4}$$

$$Recall = \frac{TP}{TP + FN} \tag{7.5}$$

$$F1 - Score = 2\frac{Precision * Recall}{Precision + Recall} \tag{7.6}$$

7.4.2 Experimental Findings

Four machine learning models were assessed in this study—random forest, LightGBM, XGBoost, and gradient boosting machine (GBM)—using features extracted from the VGG16 deep learning model to distinguish Parkinson's disease patients from healthy individuals. Four primary measures were used to evaluate the models: mean F1 score, mean test accuracy, mean precision, and mean recall. LightGBM was the model that performed the best out of all of them, with an accuracy of 90.33% and recall and precision of 89.54% and 91.33%, respectively. With an F1 score of 90.42%, LightGBM is the most successful classifier for this job, reflecting this balance. With an accuracy of 88.66% and an F1 score of 88.82%, XGBoost trailed slightly behind LightGBM but still demonstrated strong performance. With an accuracy of 87.00%, random forest was deemed reliable; however, its precision (85.35%) and recall (89.33%) were marginally lower than those of LightGBM and XGBoost, suggesting a greater false positive rate. Due to a rather uneven precision and recall performance, GBM received the lowest F1 score (86.79%) despite having the best precision (92.00%). LightGBM fared better than all other models overall, exhibiting a well-rounded performance across all criteria when handling the classification assignment. The features extracted from VGG16 provided a robust foundation for these machine learning models, highlighting the potential of combining deep learning-based feature extraction with traditional classifiers for complex tasks such as Parkinson's disease diagnosis. While GBM achieved the highest precision, LightGBM's superior balance between precision, recall, and F1 score makes it the most suitable model for this classification task. Further research and development may entail optimizing hyperparameters or improving the feature extraction procedure to improve the performance of the other models. Images are fed into this modified VGG16 model using a series of convolutional and pooling layers, producing feature maps that capture different elements of the input images. With a few layers, an image that is 224 × 224 × 3 can be changed into a feature map that is

7 × 7 × 512 [25]. The resulting 1D vectors are then flattened from these feature maps. Subsequently, these flattened features are appropriate for inclusion in machine learning classifiers, including random forest, GBM, XGB, and LGBM. Stratified fivefold cross-validation is evaluated on these models to ensure a more robust performance estimate. This method uses the pre-trained weights of VGG16 was selected as the foundation for feature extraction in this study which efficiently extract fine-grained features from image data that diverge greatly from ImageNet, like spectrograms. As a result, this technique saves time and resources while offering strong and broadly applicable feature representations for various applications, such as the classification of diseases, without requiring a lot of retraining or large datasets. The result is tabulated in Table 7.2, which displays the experimental overview across important performance indicators for every model that was tested. Figure 7.5 plotted the graph of evaluation parameters such as accuracy, recall, precision, and F1 score.

TABLE 7.2
Results Obtained from the Experiment over Performance Metrics

Model	Mean Test Accuracy	Mean Precision	Mean Recall	Mean F1 Score
Random Forest	87.00	85.35	89.33	87.29
LightGBM	90.33	89.54	91.33	90.42
XGBoost	88.66	87.66	90.00	88.82
GBM	88.99	92.00	89.32	86.79

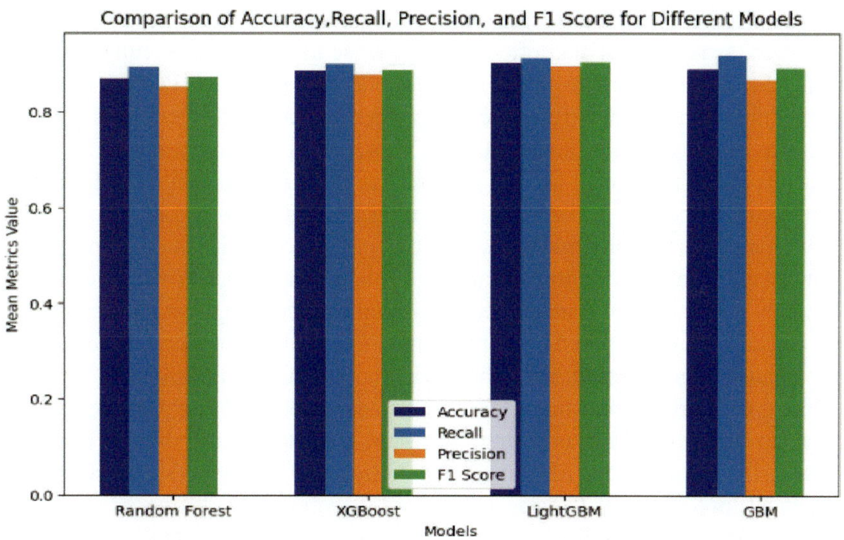

FIGURE 7.5 Plot of the comparison graph for evaluation parameters across four models.

The LightGBM model's cross-validation results demonstrate strong performance, with most accuracy scores tightly clustered around 0.92, indicating consistent reliability. Random forest cross-validation accuracy scores ranging from 0.80 to 0.88, with a median around 0.84, indicating moderate variability across folds. The model achieved 87.00% accuracy, 85.35% precision, 89.33% recall, and an F1 score of 87.29%, performing well. The cross-validation accuracy scores for XGBoost across five-folds, ranging from 0.85 to 0.91, with a median of around 0.88. This stability reflects the model's reliability. With an accuracy of 88.66%, precision of 87.66%, recall of 90.00%, and F1 score of 88.82%, XGBoost performs well, especially in correctly identifying positive cases. Among these, the LightGBM classifier achieved the most impressive results. Overall, LightGBM achieves high accuracy, though its performance may for the task fluctuate slightly depending on the data subset. This stability with occasional variation underscores its potential effectiveness. LightGBM, a boosting algorithm designed for high-speed and efficient gradient boosting, demonstrated its capability to handle large volumes of complex data, delivering an F1 score of 90.42%, a precision of 89.54%, a recall of 91.33%, and an accuracy of 90.33%. These metrics reflect LightGBM's capacity to achieve equilibrium between precision (minimizing false positives) and recall (reducing false negatives), which is crucial for diagnostic accuracy in a medical context. The high accuracy achieved by LightGBM suggests that this classifier is well-suited for this task, indicating its potential for broader clinical application.

The proposed strategy for detecting early Parkinson's disease utilizes speech features and transfer learning mechanisms, which have potential, but there are certain constraints to consider. The comparatively short dataset size is one drawback that could restrict the model's functionality to fully capture the variety of verbal traits linked to Parkinson's disease. A larger dataset might enhance the model's capability to learn and increase its precision in identifying subtle speech features associated with the disease. Additionally, the reliance on high-quality audio recordings poses challenges, as real-world data often includes noise that may not be fully addressed by the denoising technique used. Furthermore, the ability of VGG16 to extract PD-specific characteristics from mel spectrograms may be limited due to the fact that it was initially trained on picture data. This approach's computing demands may restrict its use in areas with limited resources or in therapeutic settings. To confirm the robustness and appropriateness of the model as a diagnostic tool, evaluation on larger, more diverse real-world datasets is crucial. More sophisticated preprocessing methods might be used in future iterations to enhance model performance. Currently, the model uses variational mode decomposition for denoising, but adding adaptive filtering, deep learning-based noise reduction, or data augmentation tailored specifically to audio signals could make the model more robust to variations in recording quality and environmental noise. These enhancements would help the model generalize to real-world data, ensuring consistent accuracy across diverse and noisy datasets. Ultimately, these refinements could increase the model's effectiveness as a practical tool for early Parkinson's disease detection, broadening its applicability in varied clinical and field settings. This research marks a significant advancement in the prompt identification of Parkinson's disease by harnessing the potential of artificial intelligence (AI) to analyze voice signals—a non-invasive biomarker of PD symptoms. By leveraging sophisticated deep learning and machine learning approaches, this study developed a robust methodology that may aid in timely and accurate PD diagnosis, ultimately facilitating individualized patient management. Furthermore, integrating multimodal data, such as combining voice features with other biomarkers like gait patterns or handwriting analysis, could enhance the robustness and applicability of the diagnostic tool, creating a more comprehensive profile of PD symptoms.

7.5 CONCLUSION

This study represents a substantial leap in the prompt identification of Parkinson's disease by applying powerful AI techniques. The VGG16 model was utilized for robust feature extraction. This was accomplished by transforming voice signals into mel spectrogram pictures and utilizing variational mode decomposition to decrease noise. The features were subsequently classified using a variety of machine learning algorithms, and the LightGBM classifier demonstrated exceptional performance, attaining an F1 score of 90.42%, a precision of 89.54%, a recall of 91.33%, and an accuracy of 90.33%. In the future, the dataset could be expanded to include a broader variety of data, improved preprocessing and deep learning architectures could be incorporated, and multimodal data could be incorporated to provide a more comprehensive diagnostic tool. Additionally, advancements in preprocessing techniques could further enhance the clarity and relevance of the input data, allowing the models to focus more effectively on the subtle features associated with PD. Similarly, adopting advanced or novel deep learning frameworks, like transformer-based models or ensembles combining multiple neural networks, could potentially enhance the framework's ability to observe and generalize PD-related features. Furthermore, hyperparameter tuning has the potential to increase model performance further, and real-time monitoring and clinical integration have the potential to revolutionize early Parkinson's disease identification, hence enabling timely and individualized patient management. In conclusion, this research indicates the viability of employing mel spectrograms and powerful AI algorithms to detect PD with high accuracy, offering a promising pathway for non-invasive diagnosis. As future research builds upon these findings with improved data, refined models, and clinical integration, this approach could become an invaluable tool in the fight against Parkinson's disease.

7.5.1 Data Availability

The datasets used and/or analyzed during the current study are available from the corresponding author on reasonable request.

REFERENCES

[1] Laganas, Christos, Dimitrios Iakovakis, Stelios Hadjidimitriou, Vasileios Charisis, Sofia B. Dias, Sevasti Bostantzopoulou, Zoe Katsarou, L. Klingelhoefer, H. Reichmann, D. Trivedi, and K. R. Chaudhuri. "Parkinson's Disease Detection Based on Running Speech Data From Phone Calls." *IEEE Transactions on Biomedical Engineering* 69, no. 5 (2021): 1573–84. https://doi.org/10.1109/TBME.2021.3116935.

[2] Keserwani, Pankaj Kumar, Suman Das, and Nairita Sarkar. "A Comparative Study: Prediction of Parkinson's Disease Using Machine Learning, Deep Learning and Nature Inspired Algorithm." *Multimedia Tools and Applications* 83, no. 27 (2024): 69393–441. https://doi.org/10.1007/s11042-024-18186-z.

[3] Veetil, Iswarya Kannoth, V. Sowmya, Juan Rafael Orozco-Arroyave, and E. A. Gopalakrishnan. "Robust Language Independent Voice Data Driven Parkinson's Disease Detection." *Engineering Applications of Artificial Intelligence* 129 (2024): 107494. https://doi.org/10.1016/j.engappai.2023.107494.

[4] Reddy, Mittapalle Kiran, and Paavo Alku. "Exemplar-Based Sparse Representations for Detection of Parkinson's Disease From Speech." *IEEE/ACM Transactions on Audio, Speech, and Language Processing* 31 (2023): 1386–96. https://doi.org/10.1109/TASLP.2023.3260709Jj.

[5] Hireš, Máté, Peter Drotár, Nemuel Daniel Pah, Quoc Cuong Ngo, and Dinesh Kant Kumar. "On the Inter-Dataset Generalization of Machine Learning Approaches to Parkinson's Disease Detection From a Voice." *International Journal of Medical Informatics* 179 (2023): 105237. https://doi.org/10.1016/j.ijmedinf.2023.105237.

[6] Bhatt, Kavita, N. Jayanthi, and Manjeet Kumar. "High-Resolution Superlet Transform Based Techniques for Parkinson's Disease Detection Using Speech Signal." *Applied Acoustics* 214 (2023): 109657. https://doi.org/10.1016/j.apacoust.2023.10965.

[7] Abumalloh, Rabab Ali, Mehrbakhsh Nilashi, Sarminah Samad, Hossein Ahmadi, Abdullah Alghamdi, Mesfer Alrizq, and Sultan Alyami. "Parkinson's Disease Diagnosis Using Deep Learning: A Bibliometric Analysis and Literature Review." *Ageing Research Reviews* 96 (2024): 102285. https://doi.org/10.1016/j.arr.2024.102285.

[8] Warule, P., S. P. Mishra, and S. Deb. "Time-Frequency Analysis of Speech Signal Using Chirplet Transform for Automatic Diagnosis of Parkinson's Disease." *Biomedicine Engineering Letters* 13 (2023): 613–23. https://doi.org/10.1007/s13534–023–00283-x.

[9] Er, Mehmet Bilal, Esme Isik, and Ibrahim Isik. "Parkinson's Detection Based on Combined CNN and LSTM Using Enhanced Speech Signals With Variational Mode Decomposition." *Biomedical Signal Processing and Control* 70 (2021): 103006. https://doi.org/10.1016/j.bspc.2021.103006.

[10] Desai, U., C. G. Nayak, and G. Seshikala. "An Application of EMD Technique in Detection of Tachycardia Beats." *2016 International Conference on Communication and Signal Processing (ICCSP)*, Melmaruvathur, India (2016): 1420–24.

[11] Karan, Biswajit, and Sitanshu Sekhar Sahu. "An Improved Framework for Parkinson's Disease Prediction Using Variational Mode Decomposition-Hilbert Spectrum of the Speech Signal." *Biocybernetics, and Biomedical Engineering* 41, no. 2 (2021): 717–32. https://doi.org/10.1016/j.bbe.2021.04.014.

[12] Zhang, Tao, Liqin Lin, and Zaifa Xue. "A Voice Feature Extraction Method Based on Fractional Attribute Topology for Parkinson's Disease Detection." *Expert Systems with Applications* 219 (2023): 119650. https://doi.org/10.1016/j.eswa.2023.119650.

[13] Hasanzadeh, Mahboobeh, and Hamid Mahmoodian. "A Novel Hybrid Method for Feature Selection Based on Gender Analysis for Early Parkinson's Disease Diagnosis Using Speech Analysis." *Applied Acoustics* 211 (2023): 109561. https://doi.org/10.1016/j.apacoust.2023.109561.

[14] Amato, Federica, Luigi Borzì, Gabriella Olmo, and Juan Rafael Orozco-Arroyave. "An Algorithm for Parkinson's Disease Speech Classification Based on Isolated Words Analysis." *Health Information Science and Systems* 9 (2021): 32. https://doi.org/10.1007/s13755-021-00162-8.

[15] Karan, Biswajit, Sitanshu Sekhar Sahu, Juan Rafael Orozco-Arroyave, and Kartik Mahto. "Hilbert Spectrum Analysis for Automatic Detection and Evaluation of

Parkinson's Speech." *Biomedical Signal Processing and Control* 61 (2020): 102050. https://doi.org/10.1016/j.bspc.2020.102050.

[16] Narendra, N. P., B. Schuller, and P. Alku. "The Detection of Parkinson's Disease From Speech Using Voice Source Information." *IEEE/ACM Transactions on Audio, Speech, and Language Processing* 29 (2021): 1925–36. https://doi.org/10.1109/TASLP.2021.3078364.

[17] Celik, Gaffari, and Erdal Başaran. "Proposing a New Approach Based on Convolutional Neural Networks and Random Forest for the Diagnosis of Parkinson's Disease From Speech Signals." *Applied Acoustics* 211 (2023): 109476. https://doi.org/10.1016/j.apacoust.2023.109476.

[18] Orozco-Arroyave, J. R., J. D. Arias-Londono, J. F. Vargas-Bonilla, M. C. Gonzalez-Rátiva, and E. Noth. "New Spanish Speech Corpus Database for the Analysis of People Suffering From Parkinson's Disease." *Proceedings of the 13th Language Resources and Evaluation Conference* (2014): 342–47.

[19] Visvanathan, P., and P. M. D. R. Vincent. "Prediction of Gait Neurodegenerative Diseases by Variational Mode Decomposition Using Machine Learning Algorithms." *Applied Artificial Intelligence* 38, no. 1 (2024). https://doi.org/10.1080/08839514.2024.2389375.

[20] Rezaee, Khosro, Somayeh Savarkar, Xiaofeng Yu, and Jingyu Zhang. "A Hybrid Deep Transfer Learning-Based Approach for Parkinson's Disease Classification in Surface Electromyography Signals." *Biomedical Signal Processing and Control, Part A* 71 (2022): 103161. https://doi.org/10.1016/j.bspc.2021.103161.

[21] Jahan, Nusrat, Arifatun Nesa, and Md. Abu Layek. "Parkinson's Disease Detection Using ResNet50 with Transfer Learning." *International Journal of Computer Vision and Signal* 11 (2021): 17–23.

[22] Nishat, M. M., T. Hasan, S. M. Nasrullah, F. Faisal, M. A.-A.-R. Asif, and M. A. Hoque. "Detection of Parkinson's Disease by Employing Boosting Algorithms." *2021 Joint 10th International Conference on Informatics, Electronics & Vision (ICIEV) and 2021 5th International Conference on Imaging, Vision & Pattern Recognition (icIVPR)*, Kitakyushu, Japan (2021): 1–7. https://doi.org/10.1109/ICIEVicIVPR52578.2021.9564108.

[23] Swain, B. K., S. Mohapatra, M. Mishra, and Renu Sharma. "A Unified Approach for Parkinson's Disease Recognition: Imbalance Mitigation and Grid Search Optimized Boosting With LightGBM." *Medical & Biological Engineering & Computing* 62, no. 11 (2024): 3471–91. https://doi.org/10.1007/s11517-024-03139-3.

[24] Lamba, Rohit, Tarun Gulati, Anurag Jain, and Pooja Rani. "A Speech-Based Hybrid Decision Support System for Early Detection of Parkinson's Disease." *Arabian Journal for Science and Engineering* 48 (2023): 2247–60. https://doi.org/10.1007/s13369-022-07249-8.

[25] Kumar, S., P. Kaur, and G. Singh. "An Improved Deep Learning Approach for Detecting Malignant and Benign in Lung CT-Scan Images." *Cluster Computing* 22, no. 5 (2019): 11369–80. https://doi.org/10.1007/s10586-017-1590-4.

8 Advances in Machine Learning for QSAR Modeling

Enhancing Drug Discovery through Predictive Precision and Data Integration

Hadagali Ashoka, Pradeep S, Manjunath K, Nijaguna G S, and D Ramesh Babu

8.1 INTRODUCTION

One of the leading challenges facing in health care today is the growing prevalence of many diseases, many of which have complex and multifactorial causes (Vaishya et al., 2024). A complex interaction of environmental, genetic, and lifestyle factors contributes to the advancement of conditions like cancer, neurodegenerative diseases, and metabolic disorders (Hotamisligil, 2006; Bray et al., 2012; Wyss-Coray, 2016). Due to their limited effectiveness, unfavorable adverse effects, or higher levels of toxicity, existing therapeutic alternatives often fall short, highlighting the urgent need to develop new, more effective and safer medications (Vos et al., 2020).

The difficulty of identifying suitable candidate molecules and the higher costs involved in pre-clinical and clinical trials make conventional drug discovery and development procedures still slow and expensive. Implementing these procedures in the initial stage of drug discovery can make it favorable to identify the chemical compounds with high standard quality pharmacological patterns, ensuring the most promising and optimized lead molecules for target specific interactions and exceptional pharmacokinetic (PK) properties. These advancements may aid in identifying compounds that are more effective with the least adverse effects.

This chapter explores an essential drug discovery tool, quantitative structure-activity relationship (QSAR) modelling with the sophisticated applications through machine learning (ML) approach. The prediction of biological activity of compounds based on their chemical structure using QSAR models have been beneficial in fostering the identification of promising pharmacological compounds while reducing the cost associated with drug development process. Nevertheless, conventional QSAR

 DOI: 10.1201/9781003473442-8

methods may face issues in accuracy, interpretation, and generalization, particularly when handling with large and complex datasets.

The machine learning method is a revolutionary approach that overcomes these constraints by combining a number of methods, such as ensemble models, deep learning, and hybrid approaches. QSAR models based on machine learning can enhance the ability to interpret, assist in more robust feature selection, and increase the prediction performance by implementing these strategies. While deep learning and neural networks contribute to improved pattern recognition, ensemble methods, which combine many models, provide assurance in minimizing overfitting and improving generalization (Cherkasov et al., 2014). This chapter explores a wide range of machine learning methods in QSAR, focusing on developments that enhance accuracy in prediction and selecting the drug candidates.

Modeling QSAR has been further advanced by integrating data fusion techniques and cheminformatics tools, which aids the researchers to combine various chemical and biological data sources. This approach produces more extensive models that accurately predict the behavior and effectiveness of compounds. Such improvements not only accelerate drug discovery and development but also influence the advent of personalized medicine by customizing drug development to specific disease patterns.

A similar data-driven approach utilizing QSAR modeling is also gaining importance due to its ability to enhance translational medicine by relating practical findings with clinical applications. Large-scale, in silico research are made feasible by the accessibility of open-access databases such as ChEMBL, ZINC, and other databases. This enhances the reliability of predictive models while reducing the resources needed for drug development.

Researchers can identify helpful molecular descriptors that are vital for predicting biological properties of a compound through QSAR modeling. As demonstrated in some studies, feature selection and feature learning can improve model precision by removing unnecessary data and concentrating on pertinent molecular descriptors focused in predicting properties like intestinal absorption and blood-brain barrier penetration, both of which are vital for evaluating drug bioavailability (Dara et al., 2022).

The chapter provides the path to personalized medicine and efficient drug development pipelines, making it an invaluable resource for researchers and experts in the area of computational drug discovery. These efforts contribute to the development of effective, economical, and customized therapeutic solutions by intensifying our understanding of machine learning techniques toward QSAR and their applications. These attempts enhance the capacity of pharmaceutical industry for streamlined drug discovery and help unveil viable therapeutic agents for complex diseases.

8.2 METHODOLOGY FOR QSAR WITH HYBRIDIZED MULTI-FEATURE SELECTION AND FEATURE LEARNING APPROACHES

An extensive machine learning pipeline customized to develop and optimize models efficiently, especially in the QSAR modeling space for drug discovery is represented by a flow diagram as shown in Figure 8.1. It demonstrates the sequential steps, from preliminary data collection and preprocessing to the concluding documentation and

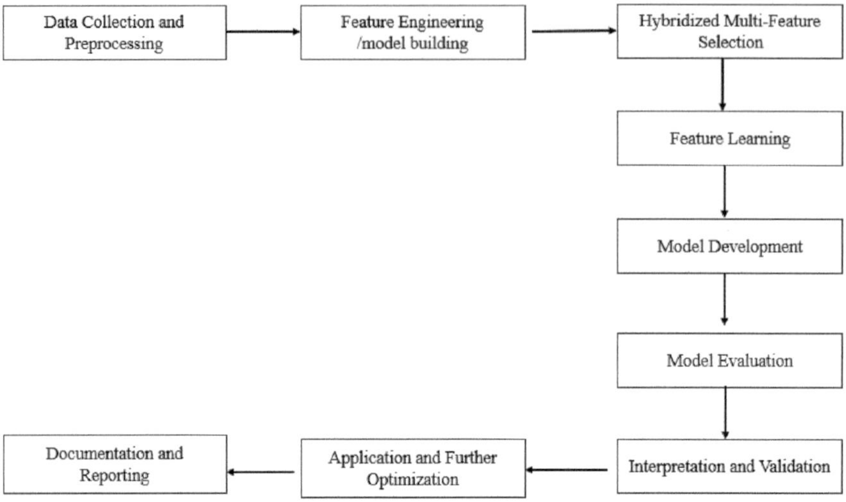

FIGURE 8.1 Machine learning pipeline for model development and optimization.

reporting phase. Every step in the pipeline assembled upon the previous one, assuring a comprehensive approach for model development, evaluation, and usage. This organized workflow aid in consistently addressing key tasks like feature engineering, selection, learning, and validation of model, finally facilitating the refinement and deployment of model in real-life applications. The process initiates with data collection and preprocessing, which involves collection of raw data from diverse sources and preparing it through cleaning, normalization, and transformation to make sure about its consistency and preparedness for analysis. The next step is model building or feature engineering that recognizes and designs key molecular descriptors and structures an initial model that covers related data characteristics. Further it is hybridized multi-feature selection, which applies innovative selection techniques to enhance feature sets and dimensionality reduction and improve efficiency of the model by focusing mainly on the most applicable variables. In feature learning, the model revels complex patterns within the chosen feature, which is a vital step in understanding non-linear relationships in data. The next step is model development, where refined algorithms are applied to create and train the predictive model. Once formulated, model evaluation precisely assesses performance metrics, like accuracy, to ensure reliability and robustness. Interpretation and validation let researchers realize the predictions of model, verify its validity with external standards, and make essential adjustments. The model is then applied in real-life applications. In the applications and further optimization step, it is refined for practical usage and improved with additional data. Finally, documentation and reporting guarantee comprehensive documentation of the performance of model and gain insights and future suggestions, making the work convenient and consistent for other professionals in this field. This organized flow aids the creation of a precise, robust, and interpretable model for effective and significant applications of QSAR in drug discovery.

8.2.1 Data Collection and Preprocessing

8.2.1.1 Data Acquisition

To carry out research or studies using models including chemical compounds and their biological activities, obtaining a well-structured dataset is crucial. Such datasets usually comprise information on chemical compounds along with their related data pertaining to their biological activity, such as half-maximal dissociation constant (Ki), inhibitory concentration (IC50), or other activity metrics that show the effectiveness of a compound in interacting with precise biological targets.

Common Data Sources:

- **ChEMBL:** One of the most extensively used open-access databases, this database provides a widespread library of bioactive compounds and their activities. ChEMBL is maintained by the European Bioinformatics Institute (EBI), which comprises a massive amount of quantitative bioactivity statistics on drug-like compounds, coping numerous targets, pathways, and organisms. EC50, Ki, IC50, and other values essential for compound assessment are accessible for researchers (Mendez et al., 2019).
- **PubChem:** PubChem, achieved by the National Center for Biotechnology Information (NCBI), is an alternative open-access resource that offers comprehensive information on chemical compounds. It comprises biological activity data for many small molecules, which are derived from high-throughput screening (HTS) and other experimental tests. It is predominantly valuable for retrieving both compound data and bioactivity, allowing researchers to investigate the trends and associations between chemical structures and biological activity (Kim et al., 2021).
- **Proprietary Databases:** Some researchers or organizations may also depend on proprietary databases, like the databases generated through in-house experimental findings or the CAS (chemical abstracts service) databases. These regularly provide exclusive or curated datasets that may include dedicated bioactivity data not found in public resources. Such proprietary datasets can be appreciated for finding high-quality, tailored data but often involve licensing agreements.
- **Importance of Data Quality and Standardization:** High-quality datasets permit more precise and reliable analysis, specifically when combining data from diverse sources. Researchers commonly use standard formats and apply strict quality checks to confirm that data points, like IC50 and Ki values, which are comparable over diverse compounds and test conditions. Data cleaning and standardization can include removing duplicates, standardizing formats of compound, and confirming activity values to minimize any potential discrepancies from different experimental circumstances.

8.2.1.2 Data Cleaning

Data cleaning is a vital step in expressing a high-quality dataset for analysis. This process involves multiple steps intended to ensure data accuracy, consistency, and completeness, which are important for producing significant results in studies involving chemical compounds and biological activities. Researchers can improve the reliability of their discoveries by addressing common issues, such as missing values, duplicate entries, and irrelevant features.

8.2.1.2.1 Removing Duplicates

Duplicates can arise from combining numerous datasets or due to repeated records of the same compound. Duplicate entries can misrepresent results by over-representing certain data points, particularly in statistical analysis or machine learning models. Removal of duplicates typically involves finding and deleting records with similar chemical identifiers, such as SMILES strings or InChI keys, which illustrate the molecular structure exclusively. Careful inspection confirms that only redundant records are removed without losing important information (Spelmen & Porkodi, 2018).

8.2.1.2.2 Handling Missing Values

Missing values in datasets comprising bioactivity data are quite common, normally due to insufficient experimental outcomes or limitations in evaluating certain properties for all compounds. Numerous approaches are there to handle missing data:

- **Deletion:** Rows with missing values may be omitted if the missing data is minimal.
- **Imputation:** If the data is large and random missingness is assumed then methods like mean, median, or model-based imputation can be used to approximate missing values.
- **Advanced Techniques:** For datasets with widespread missing values, approaches like model-based imputations (e.g., regression or expectation-maximization algorithms) or k-nearest neighbors (KNN) imputation can help preserve integrity of dataset without presenting bias (Little & Rubin, 2019).

8.2.1.2.3 Filtering Irrelevant Compounds or Features

Not all compounds or features are pertinent to the objectives of study. Unrelated compounds, such as those with non-target biological activity or molecules outside the intended molecular weight range, can limit the quality of downstream analysis. Moreover, irrelevant features (e.g., variables not related to the compound's activity in a particular analysis) should be filtered out to rationalize analysis and prevent computational inefficiencies. Feature selection algorithms, such as recursive feature elimination (RFE) or variance thresholding, can help recognize and retain only the most relevant variables (Hastie et al., 2009).

8.2.1.2.4 Ensuring Data Consistency and Integrity

Consistency across the dataset is essential, particularly in multicenter studies where data may have been collected or labeled differently. This step involves the following:

- **Standardizing Units and Formats:** Standardizing chemical identifiers (InChI or SMILES) and converting values to a uniform scale (e.g., uM for IC50 values).
- **Verifying Compound Identity:** To confirm that each compound is labeled properly and can be recognized, repeatedly by cross-referencing with databases like ChEMBL or PubChem.

- **Validation of Bioactivity Values:** Confirming that activity measurements fall within the tolerable ranges to notice any probable data entry errors or outliers.

Efficient data cleaning enhances the data integrity significantly, which makes it suitable for meaningful analysis and predictive modeling.

8.2.1.3 Normalization

In data analysis normalization is an important preprocessing step and machine learning that modifies the scale of features so they contribute similarly to model training and evaluation. This process confirms that features with higher ranges do not control the model's learning process, which is particularly significant for algorithms sensitive to feature scales, such as distance-based models (e.g., k-nearest neighbors and clustering algorithms) and gradient-based models (e.g., neural networks and linear regression). Commonly used normalization techniques are discussed next.

8.2.1.3.1 Min-Max Scaling

This technique scales the data to a fixed range, usually [0,1] or [–1,1] by implementing the following formula:

$$\mathrm{Xscaled} = \frac{(\mathrm{X} - \mathrm{Xmin})}{(\mathrm{Xmax} - \mathrm{Xmin})}$$

where X represents the feature values, and Xmin and Xmax are the minimum and maximum values of X, respectively. This method conserves the relationships and proportions within the data while ensuring all values are within a consistent range, improving model performance and convergence time.

8.2.1.3.2 Normalization (Standardization)

This technique scales the data around a mean of zero and a standard deviation of one, calculated as

$$\mathrm{X}_{\mathrm{standardized}} = \frac{(\mathrm{X} - \mu)}{\sigma}$$

where σ is the standard deviation and u is the mean of the feature values, and Z-score normalization is mainly helpful when features follow a normal distribution and is normally used in algorithms that presume the data is normally distributed.

Selecting a normalization technique depends on the explicit dataset and model requirements. Min-max scaling is frequently used for bounded data, while Z-score normalization is preferred when feature distributions are approximately normal (Goodfellow et al., 2016; Kuhn & Johnson, 2013).

8.2.2 Feature Engineering/Model Building

In computational drug discovery and cheminformatics, feature engineering includes creating useful variables (descriptors) from raw molecular structures, which are further used in model building for predictive analysis. The method of calculating the descriptors relates to the process of calculating these molecular descriptors, which are quantitative illustrations capturing various physical, chemical, and structural properties of molecules. These descriptors are used as inputs for machine learning models, facilitating predictions about toxicity, biological activity, or other chemical properties.

8.2.2.1 Types of Molecular Descriptors

8.2.2.1.1 2D Descriptors

The 2-dimensional descriptors which represent molecular properties not considering 3D spatial arrangements. Atom counts, molecular weight, and topological indices are the typical examples that review features of molecular structure, such as shape, size, and degree of branching.

8.2.2.1.2 3D Descriptors

Consider the 3D arrangement of atoms in a molecule, covering spatial features like surface area, molecular volume, and shape indices. These descriptors are crucial when the 3D conformation influences biological activity.

8.2.2.1.3 Fingerprint-Based Descriptors

Molecular fingerprints signify molecules as binary vectors, where each bit specifies the presence or absence of specific chemical fragments (e.g., substructures or pathways) or structural subunits. Prevalent fingerprint types comprise the Morgan (circular) and MACCS keys fingerprints, which are mainly suitable in similarity-based searches and clustering.

8.2.2.2 Tools for Descriptor Calculation

Several tools and libraries assist in the calculation of these descriptors, including the following:

8.2.2.2.1 PaDEL

PaDEL-Descriptor is a software tool intended for calculating a wide collection of fingerprints and molecular descriptors, advocating 797 descriptors (663 1D and 2D descriptors, and 134 3D descriptors) along with 10 types of fingerprints. The fingerprints and descriptors are mainly computed using the Chemistry Development Kit, with added features like atom-type electro topological state descriptors, molecular linear free energy relation descriptors, McGowan volume, ring counts, and substructure identifiers from Laggner, Klekota, and Roth. PaDEL-Descriptor has developed a flexible design that includes a library component that can easily be integrated into quantitative structure-activity relationship (QSAR) software, along with a standalone interface. It applies a master/worker pattern to influence multiple CPU cores, optimizing the rapidity of descriptor calculations. PaDEL-Descriptor is an open source and freely available software, which makes it stand out from other descriptor calculation tools, offering both command-line and graphical user interfaces compatible with Linux, Windows, and macOS, and it supports over 90 molecular file formats. With its extensive descriptor library and multithreading capabilities, PaDEL serves as a valuable resource for cheminformatics research. The software is available to download at http://padel.nus.edu.sg/software/padeldescriptor (Yap, 2011). It is an open-source software that computes a wide range of molecular descriptors and fingerprints (e.g., PubChem and MACCS fingerprints). It is mainly preferred for its widespread set of 2D and 3D descriptors and user-friendly Java-based interface kit. RD Kit is a common open-source cheminformatics library for Python and C++ that offers a broad range of fingerprinting algorithms (like Morgan and RDK fingerprints) and molecular descriptors. It is extensively used in machine learning pipelines owing to its integration with Python, allowing absolute usage with libraries and TensorFlow and scikit-learn for model training (Bento et al., 2020).

8.2.2.2.2 Molecular Operating Environment (MOE)

MOE is a commercial software suite with widespread cheminformatics features, which includes the calculation of 2D, 3D, and descriptors based on quantum mechanics. MOE is normally applicable for drug discovery and development in pharmaceutical research because of its robust graphical user interface and its ability to integrate with the workflows of molecular modeling (Vilar et al., 2008).

8.2.2.3 Role of Deep Learning Model Building

The role of descriptors are crucial for model building since they convert raw chemical structures into machine-readable features that cover essential molecular characteristics. This illustration allows models to learn and predict numerous molecular properties or biological activities efficiently. The quality and significance of descriptors directly influence the accuracy of prediction and the ability of the model to interpret, making descriptor selection a crucial step in machine learning and cheminformatics.

A critical step in machine learning is feature selection, which helps advance the performance of model, minimize overfitting, and make models more interpretable by selecting the most appropriate features. There are various methods to realize this, which are broadly categorized into univariate and multivariate approaches.

8.2.2.3.1 Univariate Feature Selection

The association between each feature and the target variable is evaluated separately in this method. ANOVA, t-tests, and chi-square tests are often applied as statistical tools. Univariate feature selection is easy and efficient in recognizing features that have a correlation that is statistically significant with the result variable but does not reflect interactions between the features. This approach is extensively utilized in preprocessing steps, particularly when working with high-dimensional datasets, as it offers a preliminary filter to remove unrelated features (Chandrashekar & Sahin, 2014).

8.2.2.3.2 Multivariate Feature Selection

These techniques consider interactions among features and their collective effect on the model, unlike univariate methods. These techniques include the following:

8.2.2.3.2.1 Recursive Feature Elimination (RFE)

An iterative approach that trains a model on the complete set of features, ranking them by importance, and eliminates the least significant feature(s) iteratively. It works well with algorithms that automatically rank the features like SVM and linear regression.

8.2.2.3.2.2 LASSO Regression

A form of standardized regression that complements a penalty to the model for large coefficients, efficiently driving fewer significant feature coefficients to zero. This technique is beneficial in linear models and is frequently favored when handling highly correlated features.

8.2.2.3.2.3 Tree-Based Methods (e.g., Random Forests)

Random forests and other collective tree-based methods rank features on their influence in minimizing impurity in the model. These methods are reliable and capable to handle both linear and non-linear relationships between target and features (Guyon & Elisseeff, 2003; Tibshirani, 1996).

Using a blend of univariate and multivariate methods can improve model performance by primarily filtering unrelated features and then refining the selection by investigating interactions, producing a more robust feature set for training machine learning models.

8.2.3 Hybridized Multi-Feature Selection

Hybridized multi-feature selection is a progressive feature selection technique in machine learning that influences the strengths of multiple techniques to improve the feature subset and advance model performance. This approach combines methods such as wrapper, filter, and embedded techniques to provide a more thorough and effective feature selection process. Hybridized selection is particularly valuable in multifaceted datasets where a single method might not cover all relevant patterns.

8.2.3.1 Key Components of Hybridized Multi-Feature Selection

8.2.3.1.1 Combining Techniques

A hybrid approach integrates numerous feature selection approaches to improve the feature set. For example, combining a filter method like a wrapper technique like recursive feature elimination (RFE) with correlation-based feature selection can assist in removing unrelated features based on correlation, then further reduce the set based on model performance. This layered selection approach takes benefit of the speed and efficiency of filter methods for initial filtering and the accuracy of wrapper methods for more sophisticated selection (Liu & Yu, 2005).

8.2.3.1.2 Consensus Approach

Features are selected by combining outcomes from multiple feature selection techniques, creating a consensus set in this method. Different consensus approaches include the following:

8.2.3.1.2.1 Voting

This strategy includes choosing features that are often identified as significant across diverse methods. Features that appear recurrently across wrapper, filter, and embedded techniques are considered reliable and robust, as they consistently display significance irrespective of the selection approach. Voting is a simple method to build a reliable feature subset, particularly when combining varied techniques (Saeys et al., 2007).

8.2.3.1.2.2 Ensemble Selection

This approach creates an ensemble feature set that can improve generalization and robustness aggregates features from top-performing models built using diverse feature subsets. Ensemble selection is frequently employed by training multiple models with varying feature subsets and choosing the features used in the most accurate models. This method exploits the variety of feature selection outcomes, combining the strengths of each to advance predictive power of the final model.

8.2.3.2 Advantages of Hybridized Multi-Feature Selection

- **Improved Accuracy:** Hybrid feature selection minimizes the risk of supervising important features that a single method might not by combining various methods.
- **Increased Robustness:** Consensus approaches, particularly ensemble selection, enhance robustness by averaging out the biases from discrete selection methods.
- **Efficiency in Large Datasets:** The preliminary application of filter methods can minimize dimensionality, allowing computationally intensive wrapper or embedded methods to emphasize only on a subset of features.

8.2.3.3 Practical Application

Hybridized multi-feature selection is appreciated in fields with high-dimensional data, like cheminformatics, genomics, and text processing, where a single feature selection method may find it hard to balance interpretability, accuracy, and computational viability.

8.2.4 Feature Learning

Feature learning in QSAR modeling is an important process that comprises transforming raw chemical descriptors into meaningful illustrations that capture relevant patterns in the data. This method typically utilizes three main tactics: deep learning models, transfer learning, and dimensionality reduction.

8.2.4.1 Deep Learning Models

Deep learning architectures, such as convolutional neural networks (CNNs) and autoencoders, are extremely effective for learning complex, non-linear feature illustrations from raw molecular data. CNNs, normally applied in image recognition, can be adapted to handle grid-like data structures, providing spatial understanding of molecular features. Autoencoders, on the other hand, are useful for unsupervised feature extraction, compressing high-dimensional data into lower-dimensional latent spaces, which can then be fed into QSAR models to improve predictive accuracy (LeCun et al., 2015).

8.2.4.2 Transfer Learning

Given that QSAR datasets are often small, transfer learning offers an effective solution by leveraging pre-trained models on similar, huge datasets. For example, models trained on huge chemical databases can extract and transfer meaningful features to smaller QSAR datasets. This technique not only decreases computational expenses but also improves model performance by letting the QSAR model to "inherit" learned knowledge from alike chemical domains, thereby refining generalization to new compounds (Pan & Yang, 2010).

8.2.4.3 Dimensionality Reduction

Techniques such as t-distributed stochastic neighbor embedding (t-SNE) and principal component analysis (PCA) are valuable for visualizing and simplifying high-dimensional molecular data. t-SNE is particularly effective for clustering and visualizing complex datasets in two or three dimensions, making it easier to interpret chemical space distributions. PCA, a linear dimensionality-reduction technique, retains the most informative components of the data, helping to reduce noise and computational demands while preserving the variance needed for QSAR modeling (van der Maaten & Hinton, 2008).

Each of these methods enhances the quality of features, leading to QSAR models with better predictive accuracy, interpretability, and robustness.

8.2.5 Model Development

The model development process is a critical phase in QSAR modeling that focuses on dividing data, selecting appropriate machine learning algorithms, and training the model. This structured approach ensures that the model can accurately predict the biological activity of compounds based on their chemical descriptors.

8.2.5.1 Splitting the Dataset

Proper dataset splitting is vital to ensure that the model can generalize to new data. Commonly, the dataset is divided into training, validation, and test sets in an 80/10/10 or 70/15/15 split. The training set is used to fit the model, the validation set helps tune hyperparameters, and the test set provides an unbiased evaluation of model performance. This approach minimizes overfitting and allows for robust performance assessment (Hastie et al., 2009).

8.2.5.2 Algorithm Selection

Selecting the appropriate machine learning algorithm is essential for accurate and efficient QSAR modeling. Some widely used algorithms include the following:

- **Random Forest (RF):** A popular ensemble method that builds multiple decision trees to improve prediction accuracy. It is known for its robustness to overfitting and its ability to handle large, high-dimensional datasets (Breiman, 2001).
- **Support Vector Machines (SVM):** A powerful classifier that works well with both linear and non-linear data by using kernel functions. SVMs are particularly effective in high-dimensional spaces, making them suitable for QSAR applications (Cortes & Vapnik, 1995).
- **Gradient Boosting Machines (GBM):** This algorithm sequentially builds models to correct errors of previous models, achieving high accuracy.

GBMs are commonly used for their versatility and strong predictive power in QSAR modeling (Friedman, 2001).

- **Neural Networks (NN):** Neural networks, especially deep neural networks, can capture complex, non-linear relationships in QSAR data, though they may require larger datasets and careful tuning to avoid overfitting (LeCun et al., 2015).

8.2.5.3 Training the Model

Once the algorithm is selected, the model is trained using the refined feature set. Hyperparameter optimization is conducted to improve model performance. Grid search and random search are two commonly used techniques for hyperparameter tuning. Grid search exhaustively assesses all combinations of hyperparameters within a specified range, whereas random search randomly samples hyperparameters from a distribution, often finding optimal values faster in high-dimensional spaces (Bergstra & Bengio, 2012). This iterative training procedure helps produce models with high predictive accuracy and generalizability.

Overall, a structured model development approach including dataset splitting, algorithm selection, and training ensures the creation of robust, predictive models that effectively capture the underlying relationships within QSAR data.

8.2.6 Model Evaluation

Model evaluation is a critical step in QSAR modeling that helps verify the model's predictive accuracy and reliability. Evaluation involves selecting appropriate performance metrics and validating model robustness through cross-validation techniques.

8.2.6.1 Performance Metrics

Selecting the right metrics for model evaluation is essential to understanding how well the model predicts outcomes. Common metrics include the following:

- **R^2 (Coefficient of Determination):** This metric explains the proportion of variance in the dependent variable that is predictable from the independent variables. It is often used in regression models to indicate how closely the model's predictions match the actual data, with values closer to 1 indicating a better fit (Draper & Smith, 1998).
- **RMSE (Root Mean Squared Error):** RMSE provides an estimate of the average magnitude of prediction error, penalizing large errors more than small ones. It is particularly useful for QSAR models where precise predictions are crucial, as it reveals how well the model performs in real-world conditions (Willmott & Matsuura, 2005).
- **MAE (Mean Absolute Error):** Unlike RMSE, MAE provides the average of the absolute differences between predictions and actual values, giving an intuitive measure of the model's accuracy without heavily penalizing large errors. MAE is particularly valuable in applications where individual prediction errors are less critical (Hyndman & Koehler, 2006).

- **Accuracy (for Classification Tasks):** In classification models, accuracy measures the percentage of correctly classified instances. This metric is essential for QSAR tasks that require categorizing compounds based on biological activity, though it should be balanced with other metrics like precision, recall, and F1 score to ensure a comprehensive evaluation (Powers, 2020).

8.2.6.2 Cross-Validation

Cross-validation is an influential technique for assessing the stability and generalizability of QSAR models. The most commonly used method is k-fold cross-validation, where the dataset is divided into k subsets (folds), and the model is trained k times, each time using a different fold as the validation set and the remaining folds as the training set. This technique reduces the likelihood of overfitting by providing a robust estimate of model performance across different subsets of data. When the data is limited, leave-one-out cross-validation (LOOCV) can be useful, as it iteratively uses each data point as a validation sample, though it may be computationally expensive (Ron Kohavi, 1995).

Using these performance metrics and cross-validation techniques ensures that QSAR models are both accurate and reliable, improving their predictive power in real-world applications.

8.2.7 Interpretation and Validation

In QSAR modeling, model interpretation and validation are crucial, as they help ensure that the model's predictions are not only accurate but also understandable and applicable to real-world data.

8.2.7.1 Model Interpretation

Interpreting a QSAR model involves understanding how individual features contribute to predictions. This can be especially challenging in complex models, like neural networks and ensemble methods, which often function as "black boxes." Two popular model-agnostic interpretation techniques for feature analysis include the following:

- **SHAP (SHapley Additive exPlanations):** SHAP is based on game theory and calculates the contribution of each feature to the model's predictions. By assigning "Shapley values" to features, SHAP provides insights into their importance and direction of impact on individual predictions. This method is widely used in QSAR modeling, as it helps identify the most influential chemical descriptors, facilitating insights into molecular properties that drive biological activity (Lundberg & Lee, 2017).
- **LIME (Local Interpretable Model-Agnostic Explanations):** LIME provides explanations for individual predictions by generating local, interpretable approximations of the model. LIME perturbs data samples and examines how these perturbations affect predictions, offering an interpretable linear model for each instance. This method allows for a better understanding of feature importance at a local level, helping researchers pinpoint specific structural elements in compounds that influence activity predictions (Ribeiro et al., 2016).

Using SHAP and LIME for model interpretation in QSAR ensures that predictions are transparent, enabling researchers to validate the biological plausibility of relationships between molecular features and bioactivity.

8.2.7.2 External Validation

External validation includes testing the model on an independent dataset that was not used through training. This is an important step in QSAR modeling, as it measures the model's ability to simplify to new data, thus verifying its predictive robustness. A well-validated model with strong external performance indicates that the model's learned relationships are not merely artifacts of the training data but are generalizable to other datasets. External validation is crucial for confirming that a QSAR model can reliably predict biological activity across diverse chemical compounds (Tropsha, 2010).

Incorporating model interpretation methods and performing rigorous external validation enhances the reliability, interpretability, and applicability of QSAR models in drug discovery and chemical safety assessment.

8.2.8 Application and Further Optimization

In QSAR modeling, the stages of application and further optimization are indispensable for leveraging the model in real-world situations and continually refining its accuracy and reliability.

8.2.8.1 Prediction

Once the QSAR model is developed and validated, it is used to predict the biological activity of novel compounds. This predictive competence is the central purpose of QSAR modeling in drug discovery, environmental toxicity assessment, and chemical safety. By entering the chemical descriptors of unverified compounds, researchers can estimate biological responses or toxicological properties, reducing the need for time-consuming and expensive experimental procedures (Cherkasov et al., 2014). Predictions from QSAR models help in screening huge libraries of chemical structures, allowing researchers to put emphasis on the greatest promising candidates for further study and development.

8.2.8.2 Iterative Refinement

QSAR models benefit from iterative enhancement, a process that comprises updating the model as new data becomes obtainable. By continuously integrating new data, re-evaluating feature sets, and experimenting with several machine learning techniques, the model's accuracy and generalizability can be enhanced over time. For example, integrating innovative molecular descriptors or using ensemble learning techniques can improve the model's predictive performance. Frequently refining the model permits it to adapt to evolving chemical data and raises its robustness, making it a more prevailing tool for real-world applications (Fourches et al., 2010). Iterative modification is predominantly valuable in fields with quickly evolving data, like pharmacology, where new compounds are continuously synthesized and verified.

By merging predictive application with iterative refinement, QSAR models can be used successfully in screening and optimizing chemical compounds, contributing significantly to fields like drug development, toxicology, and materials science.

8.2.9 Documentation and Reporting

Effective documentation and reporting in QSAR modeling are essential for transparency, reproducibility, and sharing of findings with the broader scientific community. Proper documentation allows researchers to provide a detailed description of the modeling process, while publishing findings provides significant insights into the field.

8.2.9.1 Results Documentation

From feature selection and data preparation to model training, evaluation, and interpretation, each step of the QSAR modeling process needs to be well documented. This means recording the specific techniques used, such as feature engineering tactics, data cleansing techniques, and algorithm choices, and providing explanations for each choice. If results are well recorded, including performance metrics and error analysis, other researchers can review, repeat, and assess the process (Goodman et al., 2016). Researchers support best practices in QSAR modeling and future research aiming to expand on these findings by offering comprehensive documentation.

8.2.9.2 Publishing Results

In order to communicate discoveries and progress to the scientific community, reports or publications must be prepared. The novel aspects of the modeling methodology, such as the use of hybridized feature selection and advanced feature learning techniques (e.g., transfer learning, deep learning models), are regularly highlighted in publications on QSAR research. By spotting complex patterns in the data, these state-of-the-art techniques can significantly boost prediction power, making them a valuable contribution to the QSAR sector (Hansen et al., 2009). By publishing their findings, researchers promote information exchange, spur further developments in QSAR methodologies, and provide empirical evidence for the effectiveness of different modeling approaches. Documentation and publication not only increase the credibility and importance of QSAR studies but also support the ongoing advancement of computational models in chemistry, toxicology, and pharmacology by offering a foundation for replication and expansion by other researchers.

8.3 CONCLUSION

The importance of a multi-layered method to develop analytical models in chemical informatics is emphasized by the defined QSAR method. Researchers can generate QSAR models that more precisely represent the complicated networks between chemical structure and biological function by blending hybridized feature choice and feature learning methods.

Data gathering and preparation are the primary stages in this procedure, which promises that the dataset is ample and of brilliant quality. The most pertinent chemical descriptors are then found with the aid of sophisticated feature selection algorithms, which lower noise and improve model *interpretability*. More accurate estimates are made possible by the model's ability to extract intricate patterns from high-dimensional data over the use of feature learning methods like deep learning and transfer learning. When these methods are clubbed, models are produced that are consistent and generally applicable, which is indispensable for applications in toxicology, materials science, and drug development (Cherkasov et al., 2014).

This methodological approach addresses the data diversity and non-linear connections of the intrinsic constraints of QSAR modeling. The methodology can be continuously upgraded when the new data and computational techniques become available because of its flexibility. Hence it influences experimental sciences by enhancing the development of reliable QSAR models that can successfully predict biological activities across a wide range of biochemical substances because of the developments in computational chemistry (Tropsha, 2010).

REFERENCES

Bento, A. P., Hersey, A., Félix, E., Landrum, G., Gaulton, A., Atkinson, F., Bellis, L. J., De Veij, M., & Leach, A. R. (2020). An open source chemical structure curation pipeline using RDKit. *Journal of Cheminformatics*, *12*(1), 51. https://doi.org/10.1186/s13321-020-00456-1

Bergstra, J., & Bengio, Y. (2012). Random search for hyper-parameter optimization. *Journal of Machine Learning Research*, *13*, 281–305.

Bray, F., Jemal, A., Grey, N., Ferlay, J., & Forman, D. (2012). Global cancer transitions according to the Human Development Index (2008–2030): A population-based study. *The Lancet Oncology*, *13*(8), 790–801. https://doi.org/10.1016/S1470–2045(12)70211–5

Breiman, L. (2001). Random forests. *Machine Learning*, *45*(1), 5–32. https://doi.org/10.1023/A:1010933404324

Chandrashekar, G., & Sahin, F. (2014). A survey on feature selection methods. *Computers & Electrical Engineering*, *40*(1), 16–28. https://doi.org/10.1016/j.compeleceng.2013.11.024

Cherkasov, A., Muratov, E. N., Fourches, D., Varnek, A., Baskin, I. I., Cronin, M., Dearden, J., Gramatica, P., Martin, Y. C., Todeschini, R., Consonni, V., Kuz'min, V. E., Cramer, R., Benigni, R., Yang, C., Rathman, J., Terfloth, L., Gasteiger, J., Richard, A., & Tropsha, A. (2014). QSAR modeling: Where have you been? Where are you going to? *Journal of Medicinal Chemistry*, *57*(12), 4977–5010. https://doi.org/10.1021/jm4004285

Cortes, C., & Vapnik, V. (1995). Support-vector networks. *Machine Learning*, *20*(3), 273–297. https://doi.org/10.1007/BF00994018

Dara, S., Dhamercherla, S., Jadav, S. S., Babu, C. M., & Ahsan, M. J. (2022). Machine learning in drug discovery: A review. *Artificial Intelligence Review*, *55*(3), 1947–1999. https://doi.org/10.1007/s10462-021-10058-4

Draper, N. R., & Smith, H. (1998). *Applied regression analysis* (1st ed.). Wiley. https://doi.org/10.1002/9781118625590

Fourches, D., Muratov, E., & Tropsha, A. (2010). Trust, but verify: On the importance of chemical structure curation in cheminformatics and QSAR modeling research. *Journal of Chemical Information and Modeling*, *50*(7), 1189–1204. https://doi.org/10.1021/ci100176x

Friedman, J. H. (2001). Greedy function approximation: A gradient boosting machine. *The Annals of Statistics*, *29*(5). https://doi.org/10.1214/aos/1013203451

Goodfellow, I., Bengio, Y., & Courville, A. (2016). *Deep learning*. The MIT Press.

Goodman, S. N., Fanelli, D., & Ioannidis, J. P. A. (2016). What does research reproducibility mean? *Science Translational Medicine*, *8*(341). https://doi.org/10.1126/scitranslmed.aaf5027

Guyon, I., & Elisseeff, A. (2003). An introduction to variable and feature selection. *Journal of Machine Learning Research*, *3*, 1157–1182.

Hansen, K., Mika, S., Schroeter, T., Sutter, A., Ter Laak, A., Steger-Hartmann, T., Heinrich, N., & Müller, K.-R. (2009). Benchmark data set for in silico prediction of ames mutagenicity. *Journal of Chemical Information and Modeling*, *49*(9), 2077–2081. https://doi.org/10.1021/ci900161g

Hastie, T., Tibshirani, R., & Friedman, J. (2009). *The elements of statistical learning*. New York: Springer. https://doi.org/10.1007/978-0-387-84858-7

Hotamisligil, G. S. (2006). Inflammation and metabolic disorders. *Nature*, *444*(7121), 860–867. https://doi.org/10.1038/nature05485

Hyndman, R. J., & Koehler, A. B. (2006). Another look at measures of forecast accuracy. *International Journal of Forecasting*, *22*(4), 679–688. https://doi.org/10.1016/j.ijforecast.2006.03.001

Kim, S., Chen, J., Cheng, T., Gindulyte, A., He, J., He, S., Li, Q., Shoemaker, B. A., Thiessen, P. A., Yu, B., Zaslavsky, L., Zhang, J., & Bolton, E. E. (2021). PubChem in 2021: New data content and improved web interfaces. *Nucleic Acids Research*, *49*(D1), D1388–D1395. https://doi.org/10.1093/nar/gkaa971

Kuhn, M., & Johnson, K. (2013). *Applied predictive modeling*. New York: Springer. https://doi.org/10.1007/978-1-4614-6849-3

LeCun, Y., Bengio, Y., & Hinton, G. (2015). Deep learning. *Nature*, *521*(7553), 436–444. https://doi.org/10.1038/nature14539

Little, R., & Rubin, D. (2019). *Statistical analysis with missing data, third edition* (1st ed.). Wiley. https://doi.org/10.1002/9781119482260

Liu, H., & Yu, L. (2005). Toward integrating feature selection algorithms for classification and clustering. *IEEE Transactions on Knowledge and Data Engineering*, *17*(4), 491–502. https://doi.org/10.1109/TKDE.2005.66

Lundberg, S., & Lee, S.-I. (2017). *A unified approach to interpreting model predictions (Version 2)*. arXiv. https://doi.org/10.48550/ARXIV.1705.07874

Mendez, D., Gaulton, A., Bento, A. P., Chambers, J., De Veij, M., Félix, E., Magariños, M. P., Mosquera, J. F., Mutowo, P., Nowotka, M., Gordillo-Marañón, M., Hunter, F., Junco, L., Mugumbate, G., Rodriguez-Lopez, M., Atkinson, F., Bosc, N., Radoux, C. J., Segura-Cabrera, A., . . . Leach, A. R. (2019). ChEMBL: Towards direct deposition of bioassay data. *Nucleic Acids Research*, *47*(D1), D930–D940. https://doi.org/10.1093/nar/gky1075

Pan, S. J., & Yang, Q. (2010). A survey on transfer learning. *IEEE Transactions on Knowledge and Data Engineering*, *22*(10), 1345–1359. https://doi.org/10.1109/TKDE.2009.191

Powers, D. M. W. (2020). *Evaluation: From precision, recall and F-measure to ROC, informedness, markedness and correlation*. https://doi.org/10.48550/ARXIV.2010.16061

Ribeiro, M. T., Singh, S., & Guestrin, C. (2016). "Why should i trust you?": Explaining the predictions of any classifier. *Proceedings of the 22nd ACM SIGKDD international conference on knowledge discovery and data mining* (pp. 1135–1144). https://doi.org/10.1145/2939672.2939778

Ron Kohavi, C. S. (Ed.). (1995). *A study of cross-validation and bootstrap for accuracy estimation and model selection* (Vol. 2). IJCAI, San Mateo, CA: Morgan Kaufmann. https://dl.acm.org/doi/proceedings/10.5555/1643031

Saeys, Y., Inza, I., & Larrañaga, P. (2007). A review of feature selection techniques in bioinformatics. *Bioinformatics*, *23*(19), 2507–2517. https://doi.org/10.1093/bioinformatics/btm344

Spelmen, V. S., & Porkodi, R. (2018). A review on handling imbalanced data. In *2018 international conference on current trends towards converging technologies (ICCTCT)* (pp. 1–11). https://doi.org/10.1109/ICCTCT.2018.8551020

Tibshirani, R. (1996). Regression shrinkage and selection via the lasso. *Journal of the Royal Statistical Society Series B: Statistical Methodology*, *58*(1), 267–288. https://doi.org/10.1111/j.2517–6161.1996.tb02080.x

Tropsha, A. (2010). Best practices for QSAR model development, validation, and exploitation. *Molecular Informatics*, *29*(6–7), 476–488. https://doi.org/10.1002/minf.201000061

Vaishya, R., Misra, A., Vaish, A., & Singh, S. K. (2024). Diabetes and tuberculosis syndemic in India: A narrative review of facts, gaps in care and challenges. *Journal of Diabetes*, *16*(5), e13427. https://doi.org/10.1111/1753–0407.13427

van der Maaten, L., & Hinton, G. (2008). Visualizing data using t-SNE. *Journal of Machine Learning Research*, *9*(86), 2579–2605.

Vilar, S., Cozza, G., & Moro, S. (2008). Medicinal chemistry and the molecular operating environment (MOE): Application of QSAR and molecular docking to drug discovery. *Current Topics in Medicinal Chemistry*, *8*(18), 1555–1572. https://doi.org/10.2174/156802608786786624

Vos, T., Lim, S. S., Abbafati, C., Abbas, K. M., Abbasi, M., Abbasifard, M., Abbasi-Kangevari, M., Abbastabar, H., Abd-Allah, F., Abdelalim, A., Abdollahi, M., Abdollahpour, I., Abolhassani, H., Aboyans, V., Abrams, E. M., Abreu, L. G., Abrigo, M. R. M., Abu-Raddad, L. J., Abushouk, A. I., . . . Murray, C. J. L. (2020). Global burden of 369 diseases and injuries in 204 countries and territories, 1990–2019: A systematic analysis for the Global Burden of Disease Study 2019. *The Lancet*, *396*(10258), 1204–1222. https://doi.org/10.1016/S0140–6736(20)30925–9

Willmott, C., & Matsuura, K. (2005). Advantages of the mean absolute error (MAE) over the root mean square error (RMSE) in assessing average model performance. *Climate Research*, *30*, 79–82. https://doi.org/10.3354/cr030079

Wyss-Coray, T. (2016). Ageing, neurodegeneration and brain rejuvenation. *Nature*, *539*(7628), 180–186. https://doi.org/10.1038/nature20411

Yap, C. W. (2011). PaDEL descriptor: An open source software to calculate molecular descriptors and fingerprints. *Journal of Computational Chemistry*, *32*(7), 1466–1474. https://doi.org/10.1002/jcc.21707

9 Stability Analysis of Recurrent Shunting On-Center Off-Surround Neural Networks with Nonlinear Transfer Functions

An Energy Function Approach

Rakesh Sengupta and Usha Desai

9.1 INTRODUCTION

Previous researchers (Sengupta, Bapiraju, and Pattanayak, 2024) developed a stability analysis method, which can be applied to recurrent shunting on-center off-surround neural networks with less than linear transfer function. This method can be used to analyze the stability of the network under various parameters, as demonstrated by Raijmakers, Van Der Maas, and Molenaar (1996) in a distance-dependent on-center off-surround shunting neural network. The method can also be extended to stochastic discrete-time recurrent neural networks with time-varying delays, as shown by Hou et al. (2013), and to switched neutral recurrent neural networks, as demonstrated by Jie, Yanli, and Kai (2012). These studies collectively highlight the versatility and applicability of the stability analysis method in different types of neural networks.

In this chapter, we present a novel application of a stability analysis method developed in previous work to investigate the dynamics of a recurrent shunting on-center off-surround neural network characterized by a less than linear transfer function (Grossberg, 1968). The network architecture under scrutiny exhibits dynamics important for understanding various cognitive processes, making it a subject of interest for computational neuroscience and artificial intelligence research (Sengupta, Surampudi, and Melcher, 2014; Verma and Sengupta, 2023). By employing our

DOI: 10.1201/9781003473442-9

stability analysis method, we aim to provide insights into the behavior of such networks, shedding light on their stability properties and potential implications for information processing in biological and artificial systems. This investigation holds promise for elucidating fundamental principles underlying neural computation and may inform the design and optimization of neural-inspired algorithms for diverse applications ranging from pattern recognition to short-term memory (Sengupta et al., 2024; Vindhya et al., 2024).

While previous studies have focused on various applications of stability analysis methods to different forms of recurrent neural networks (Cohen and Grossberg, 1983), there remains a gap in the application of such methods to networks with sigmoid-like activation functions, particularly in the context of shunting models. Shunting recurrent networks, with their inherent balance between excitatory and inhibitory interactions, present a unique challenge for stability analysis, especially under complex input conditions like sequential and transient inputs. These networks are crucial for simulating cognitive functions such as working memory and attention, where dynamic responses to stimuli over time play a key role. Our work aims to address this gap by integrating both classical analytical stability conditions and Lyapunov-based approaches to provide a more robust understanding of the network's stability. This is especially important in scenarios where large input sets may drive networks toward instability, as in the case of additive models prone to catastrophic inhibition. The findings from this study will contribute to a deeper understanding of the dynamic behavior of shunting networks and their relevance to modeling biological memory and cognitive systems.

9.2 METHODS

A recurrent on-center off-surround shunting neural network with N nodes can be described by the following dynamical equation:

$$\dot{x} = \frac{dx_i}{dt} = -Ax_i + (B - x_i)\left(\sum_{k=1}^{N} C_{ki} f(x_k) + I_i\right) - (D + x_i)\sum_{k \neq i}^{N} E_{ki} f(x_k) \quad (9.1)$$

- x_i : Represents the membrane potential or activation level of the i -th neuron in the network. It is a function of time t .
- A: Represents the decay rate of the membrane potential of neuron i. It influences how fast the membrane potential of neuron i returns to its resting state in the absence of external input. It is generally kept at 1 to simulate biological neurons (Usher and Cohen, 1999).
- B : Represents the baseline or resting level of activation potential that neuron i tends to approach in the absence of external input.
- C_{ki} : Represents the weight of the excitatory connection from neuron k to neuron i. It influences how much the activation level of neuron i is influenced by the activation levels of other neurons in the network.
- $f(x_k)$: Represents the activation function of neuron k, which is applied to its membrane potential x_k . This function typically introduces nonlinearity into the network dynamics.

- I_i: Represents the external input or input bias to neuron i. It can represent sensory inputs, feedback signals, or any other external influences on the activation level of neuron i.
- D: Represents the leakage or inhibition rate of neuron i. It influences how much the activation level of neuron i is suppressed by activity.
- E_{ki}: Represents the weight of the inhibitory connection from neuron k to neuron i. It influences how much the activation level of neuron i is suppressed by the activation levels of other neurons in the network.

Taking the case of a fully connected network where all neurons influence each other with at equal distance we can simplify Equation 9.1 with $\{C_{ii}\}=1$, and $\{C_{ii}\}=0$, when $i \neq j$ and $\{E_{jj}\}=1, \forall i, j$ as

$$\frac{dx_i}{dt} = -x_i + (B - x_i) f(x_i) - (D + x_i) \sum_{k \neq i}^{N} f(x_k) + I_i \tag{9.2}$$

In the current work we are interested in the application of the shunting network to biological phenomena of enumeration, thus we intend to confine the scope of the dynamics to positive values of activation. Moreover, we intend to compare the shunting version to the additive version explored in Sengupta et al. (2014).

Thus we choose the less than linear activation function:

$$f(x) = \begin{cases} 0 & \text{for } x \leq 0 \\ \dfrac{x}{1+x} & \text{for } x > 0 \end{cases} \tag{9.3}$$

9.2.1 Stability Analysis: Steady-State

Considering the restrictions on the model we chose to focus on the steady-state activity of the network, where in absence of external input $\frac{dx_i}{dt} = 0$. Given Equation 9.3, we are going to use the following identity in the next part of the work:

$$f(x) - x = -xf(x) \tag{9.4}$$

If we define total excitatory input as $E\left(E = f(x_i)\right)$ and H as total inhibitory input $\left(H = \sum_{k \neq i}^{N} f(x_k)\right)$. Now, at steady-state the activity should be independent of the permutations of node indices i, we can denote the steady-state activity for the nodes as $x[n]$ (n is the no. of nodes active at steady-state).

$$0 = -x[n] + (B - x[n])E - (D - x[n])H \tag{9.5}$$

Using Equations 9.4 and 9.5, we have

$$x[n] = \frac{BE - DH}{1 + E + H} \tag{9.6}$$

Now considering that $H = (n-1)E$, and $E = f(x[n]) = \dfrac{x[n]}{1 + x[n]}$, we can write

$$x[n] = \frac{(B - (n-1)D) f(x[n])}{1 + nf(x[n])} \tag{9.7}$$

Using Equation 9.4, we can write

$$(1+n)x[n] = (B - (n-1)D + n) f(x[n]) \tag{9.8}$$

Using Equation 9.3 allows us to calculate steady-state activation as

$$x[n] = \frac{(B - 1 - (n-1)D)}{1 + n} \tag{9.9}$$

9.2.2 Stability Analysis: Non-Divergence

In order for stable steady-state activity, we must also have a non-divergence condition added to our stability analysis. If x_i and x_j are activities of i -th and j -th node respectively, then the non-divergence condition becomes $\dfrac{d(\Delta x)}{dt}$ and needs to have a negative slope, where $\Delta x = x_i - x_j$.

Following Equation 9.2 we have (using Equation 9.4)

$$\begin{aligned} \frac{d(\Delta x)}{dt} &= -\Delta x - \Delta x \sum_k^N f(x_k) + (B + D)\left(f(x_i) - f(x_j)\right) \\ &= -\Delta x - (B + D)\Delta x \left(\frac{f(x_i)}{x_i} \frac{f(x_j)}{x_j} \right) - \Delta x \sum_k^N f(x_k) \end{aligned} \tag{9.10}$$

This can simplified using Equation 9.4. Moreover, we take advantage of the fact that near steady-state $f(x_i) \to f(x[n])$. Thus we have

$$\frac{d(\Delta x)}{dt} = \Delta x \left[-1 - nf(x[n]) - (B + D)\left(\frac{f(x[n])}{x[n]} \right)^2 \right] \tag{9.11}$$

With a substitution $a = B + D\text{-}nD$, and considering that non-divergence requires that the coefficient of Δx to be less than 0, we can write using Equations 9.7 and 9.8 (as $1 + nf(x[n]) = a\dfrac{f(x[n]}{x[n]}$ and $\dfrac{f(x[n]}{x[n]} = \dfrac{1+n}{a+n}$)

$$(B+D)(1+n)+a(a+n)\geq 0 \tag{9.12}$$

9.2.3 Stability: Energy Function

Sengupta et al. (2024) have explored an energy function formulation to investigate stability of different varieties of neural networks. We use the same formalism here to explore the stability of the network proposed here. The energy function (H) is constructed as

$$H=\sum^{N}\int dH_i \propto \sum^{N}\int \dot{x}_i d\dot{x}_i \tag{9.13}$$

Using Equations 9.2 and 9.7, we can write (upon substituting $a=B+D-nD$):

$$\begin{aligned} d\dot{x}_i &= -dx_i\left(1+nf\left(x_i\right)\right)-\left(B-x_i\right)\left(\frac{f\left(x_i\right)}{x_i}\right)^2 dx_i \\ &= -dx_i\left[a\left(\frac{f(x_i}{x_i}\right)+\left(B-x_i\right)\left(\frac{f\left(x_i\right)}{x_i}\right)^2\right] \end{aligned} \tag{9.14}$$

Now using Equations 9.13 and 9.14, we can write after substituting $B-x_i=a'$ at steady-state following Equation 9.9,

$$dH_i=\dot{x}_i d\dot{x}_i=-\left[a\left(\frac{f\left(x_i\right)}{x_i}\right)+a'\left(\frac{f\left(x_i\right)}{x_i}\right)^2\right]\dot{x}_i^{\,2}dt \tag{9.15}$$

The Lyapunov function thus constructed will be on a decreasing slope if the following condition holds

$$a'\left(1+n\right)+a\left(a+n\right)\geq 0 \tag{9.16}$$

By similarity of the form for both stability conditions we can ascertain that the differences between Equations 9.12 and 9.15 are due to the fact that the later also accounts for winner-take-all (WTA) dynamics that are excluded from the former. In fact, it is self-evident that if Equation 9.15 is satisfied it also ensures the non-divergence criterion given in Equation 9.12.

9.2.4 Comparing Stability Conditions

The non-divergence condition is given by the inequality

$$(B+D)(1+n)+a(a+n)\geq 0$$

where $a=B+D-nD$ and n represents the number of neurons with positive activations. For the condition to be violated, the inequality must be reversed, i.e.,

$$(B+D)(1+n)+a(a+n)<0$$

Substituting $a = B+D-nD$, the inequality becomes

$$(B+D)(1+n)+(B+D-nD)(B+D-nD+n)<0$$

This inequality provides the threshold where the network becomes unstable. If this inequality is violated, the network will not maintain stable activations, leading to divergence.

The Lyapunov stability condition is derived from the energy function and can be expressed as

$$a'(1+n)+a(a+n)\geq 0$$

where $a' = B-x[n]$, and $x[n]$ is the steady-state activation of neurons with positive activations. For instability to occur, this condition is violated when

$$a'(1+n)+a(a+n)<0$$

Expanding $a' = B-x[n]$, the inequality becomes

$$(B-x[n])(1+n)+(B+D-nD)(B+D-nD+n)<0$$

This provides the threshold where the system fails to satisfy Lyapunov stability. If this inequality holds, the system will become unstable and diverge from its equilibrium state.

Both the non-divergence and Lyapunov stability criteria are necessary for ensuring the stability of the shunting network. However, the Lyapunov condition is more stringent, as it takes into account the network's energy function and can fail under more restrictive scenarios compared to the non-divergence condition. By comparing these two inequalities, we can identify parameter regimes where the network might diverge or fail to maintain stability. In particular, certain combinations of *B*, *D*, and *n* may satisfy one condition but not the other, providing insight into the network's robustness under varying input conditions.

The non-divergence condition (Equation 9.12) is more stringent and depends primarily on global network parameters *B*, *D*, and the number of active neurons n. The Lyapunov stability condition (Equation 9.15) introduces an additional local factor $a' = B-x[n]$, which depends on the actual activation level $x[n]$ of the neurons. This adds more nuance and can lead to cases where the system seems stable in the Lyapunov sense but does not satisfy the global non-divergence condition.

For the Lyapunov condition to be satisfied while the non-divergence condition is not:

- **Lyapunov condition** depends on the local activation $x[n]$ and can be satisfied even if the network's global inhibitory effects are significant.
- **Non-divergence condition** depends on global network parameters *B* and *D* and becomes stringent with a large number of active neurons *n*.

So we can conclude the following:

- In the case where B is large enough to overpower the effects of inhibition D, both stability conditions are satisfied.
- The Lyapunov condition tends to be more forgiving than the non-divergence condition. It allows for local neuron activity levels to compensate for global inhibitory effects, especially when individual neuron activity $x[n]$ is low relative to B.
- However, if D is large and B is relatively small, or if the number of active neurons n grows large, the non-divergence condition is violated before the Lyapunov condition fails.

The fact that the Lyapunov stability condition can be satisfied while the non-divergence condition is not indicates the following:

- **Local Stability**: The Lyapunov condition reflects local stability based on the current state of neuron activities, while the non-divergence condition requires global stability that accounts for the entire network's dynamics.
- **Potential for Transient Stability**: When the Lyapunov condition is satisfied but the non-divergence condition is not, the system may exhibit transient stability or short-term convergence to an equilibrium before eventually diverging.
- **Network Resilience to Noise**: The Lyapunov condition could suggest that the network can tolerate small disturbances or noise, as it reflects the system's capacity to return to stability under certain circumstances.

The Lyapunov stability condition is more sensitive to the current state of neuron activities and can allow the network to remain stable in some situations where the non-divergence condition might indicate global instability. However, when the non-divergence condition is violated, the network is more likely to exhibit long-term instability, even if local stability conditions hold temporarily.

9.3 RESULTS

In this section, we present the algorithm used to simulate the dynamics of a shunting recurrent network. The pseudocode provided next outlines the steps for updating neuron activities, applying external inputs, and checking stability conditions over time.

9.3.1 Simulation for Simultaneous Inputs to the Network

Algorithm 1 Shunting Recurrent Neural Network Simulation

1: **Input:** Number of neurons N, number of inputs *num_inputs*, parameters B, D, time step *dt*, simulation duration *t_end*

2: **Output:** Stability condition statuses

3: Initialize neuron activities x with random values

4: Initialize external inputs I as zeros

Set transient input duration *transient_duration* and value *transient_value*

Set noise mean *noise_mean* and standard deviation *noise_stddev*

Compute number of simulation steps *num_steps* as *t end/dt*

for $t = 1$ to *num_steps* **do**

if $t \leq transient\_duration$ **then**

Apply transient input: $I[1:num\_inputs] = transient\_value$

else

Set input to zero: $I[1:num\_inputs] = 0$

end if

Initialize rate of change *dx_dt* to zeros

for $i = 1$ to N **do**

Compute self-excitatory term: $self\_excitation = (B - x[i]) \cdot f(x[i])$

Compute inhibitory term: $inhibition = (D + x[i]) \cdot \sum_{k \neq i} f(x[k])$

Compute external input term: *input_term* = $I[i]$

Update rate of change: $dx\_dt[i] = -x[i] + self\_excitation - inhibition + input\_term$

end for

Add Gaussian noise to rate of change: *noise* = *noise_mean+noise_stddev·randn* $(N,1)$

Update neuron activities with noise: $x = x + dt \cdot (dx\_dt + noise)$

end for

The following parameters were used in the simulation of the shunting network (Table 9.1). In addition to simulating the network, we assess its stability using two criteria given Equations 9.12 and 9.15.

The non-divergence condition ensures that the network's activity does not grow unbounded, indicating stability or poor network behavior. The Lyapunov stability condition assesses stability by examining whether small perturbations will lead to divergence or remain bounded. By evaluating these conditions, we can determine if the network operates within a stable regime or if its dynamics might lead to instability. Comparing these criteria helps in understanding the impact of different parameters and input values on the network's stability.

Simulation results for the network are shown in Figures 9.1 and 9.2, which show the dynamics of the network as well as compare the analytical steady-state prediction with the ones obtained from simulation, respectively.

9.3.2 Sequential Presentation

The simulation results, shown in Figure 9.3, highlight the network's dynamics under sequential input presentation with parameters $B = 2.2$ and $D = 0.1$, and with eight sequential inputs. The figure demonstrates how the neuron activations evolve over time, reflecting the network's ability to process and retain information. Notably, the network

TABLE 9.1
Simulation Parameters for Shunting Network

Parameter	Value	Description
Number of Neurons (N)	10	Total number of neurons in the network
Number of Inputs (num_inputs)	4	Number of neurons receiving external inputs
Parameter B (B)	5	Self-excitatory influence parameter
Parameter D (D)	0.1	Inhibitory influence parameter
Time Step (dt)	0.01	Time increment for simulation
Simulation Duration (t_end)	10	Total time for simulation
Number of Steps (num_steps)	1000	Total discrete time steps
Transient Input Duration (transient_duration)	100	Duration for which inputs are clamped
Transient Input Value (transient_value)	0.33	Magnitude of external input during transient period
Noise Mean (noise_mean)	0	Mean of Gaussian noise
Noise Standard Deviation (noise_stddev)	0.03	Standard deviation of Gaussian noise

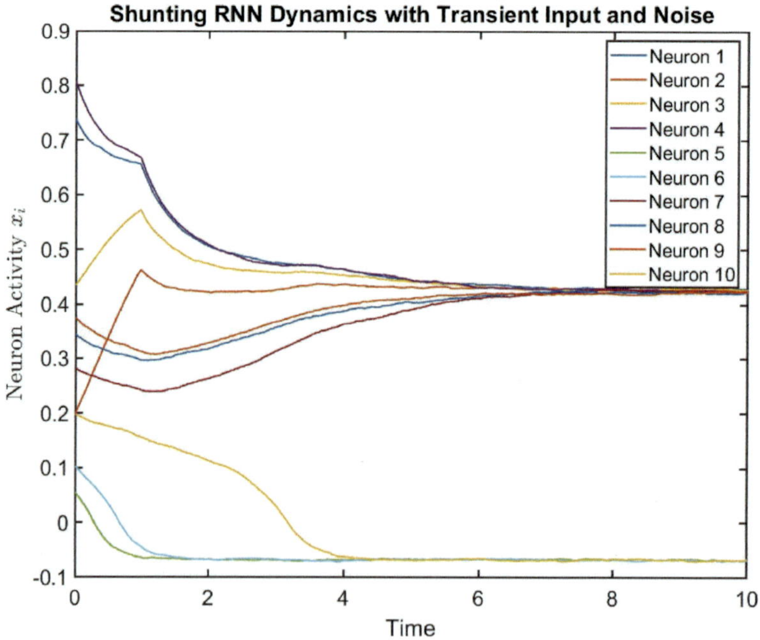

FIGURE 9.1 Dynamics of neuron activations over time. This figure shows the time evolution of the activation levels of all 10 neurons in the network. The plot illustrates how the activations of the neurons change as the network responds to transient inputs and noise. The initial transient period is evident, followed by the stabilization of activations. The different colored lines represent individual neurons, and the plot demonstrates the overall behavior of the network as it approaches a steady-state.

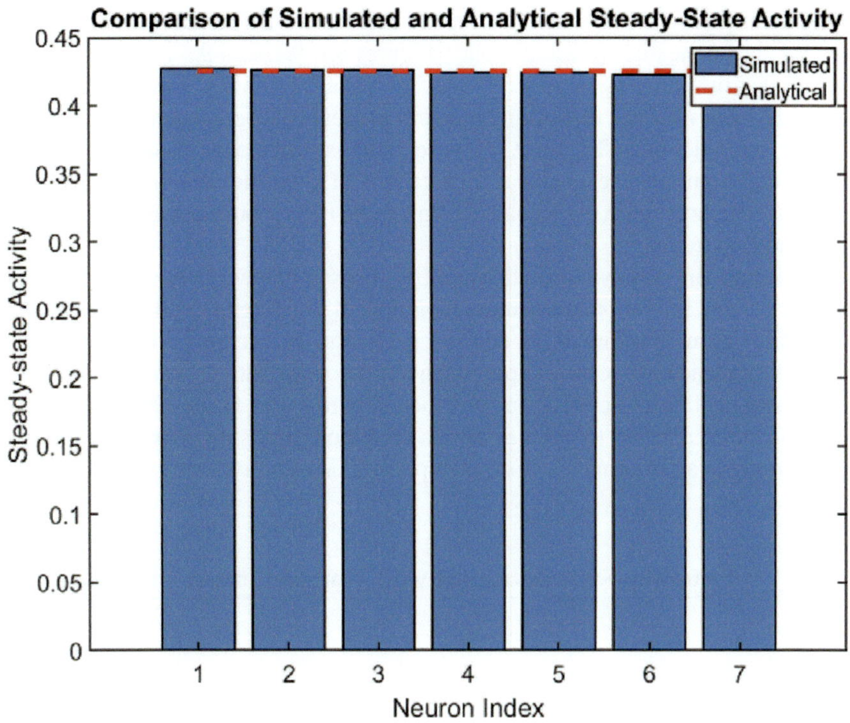

FIGURE 9.2 Comparison of analytical and simulated neuron activations. The bar plot compares the analytical steady-state values of neuron activations, $x[n]$, with the simulated values at the end of the simulation. The analytical values are calculated using the formula $x[n] = \frac{(B-1-(n-1)D)}{1+n}$, where n is the number of neurons with activation greater than zero. The simulated values are obtained from the final state of the network after applying transient inputs. This comparison helps validate the accuracy of the simulation against the theoretical predictions.

exhibits behavior akin to working memory dynamics, where neurons representing more recent inputs maintain higher activation levels compared to those associated with older inputs. This tendency to favor recent inputs is characteristic of working memory, where more recent information is more accessible and retained more effectively than older information. The observed pattern underscores the network's capability to prioritize recent data, mimicking the temporal aspects of human memory processes.

9.4 DISCUSSION

This chapter provides a comprehensive examination of stability criteria for shunting recurrent networks, integrating both analytical and Lyapunov function approaches. We derived and compared stability conditions from multiple perspectives, including the classical analytical criteria (see Equation 9.12) and the energy-based Lyapunov stability method (see Equation 9.15). Our analysis was complemented by simulations (parameters given in Table 9.1) that explored the network's response to both simultaneous and sequential transient inputs (Figures 9.1, 9.2, and 9.3). The simulations showed that the shunting network effectively manages transient inputs and demonstrates dynamics similar to working memory processes, where recent inputs are prioritized over older ones (Figure 9.3). These findings validate the theoretical stability criteria and highlight the practical implications of shunting networks in modeling short-term memory, offering valuable insights into their robustness and applicability in cognitive systems.

One significant observation is that additive recurrent networks are prone to reaching catastrophic inhibition levels more rapidly than shunting networks when dealing with a large number of inputs. In additive networks, the accumulation of inhibitory feedback can lead to excessive suppression of neuron activations, causing instability and a rapid decline in network performance (Endress and Szabó, 2017). This phenomenon, often referred to as catastrophic inhibition, limits the network's ability to maintain stable activations over extended periods or with numerous inputs.

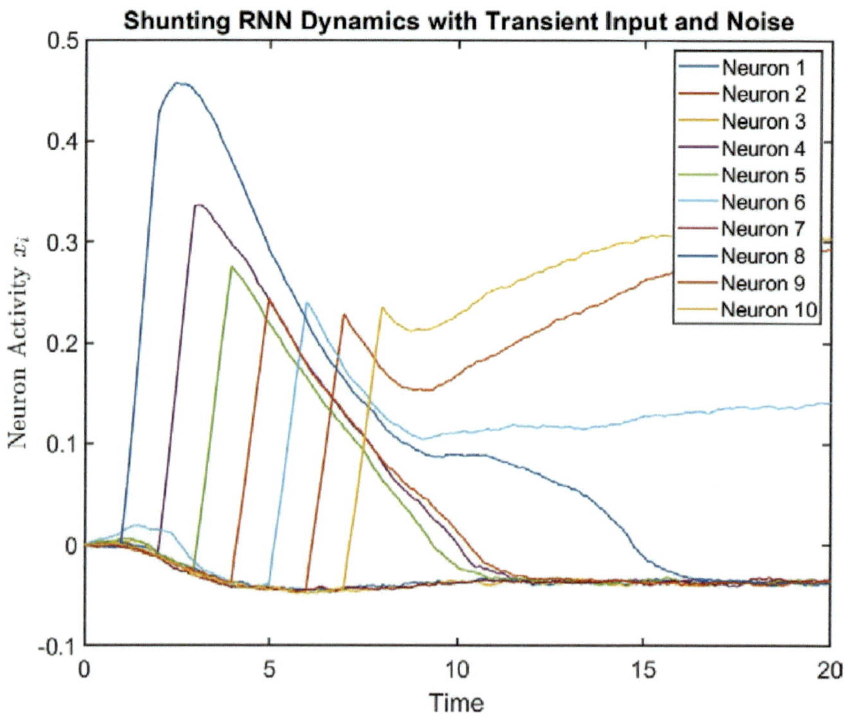

FIGURE 9.3 Dynamics of neuron activations with sequential input presentation. The plot shows the activation levels of neurons in the network over time using the parameters $B = 2.2$, $D = 0.1$, and eight sequential inputs. The figure illustrates the similarity to working memory dynamics, where recent inputs are more prominently remembered compared to older ones. This behavior is evident in the activation patterns, where neurons activated by more recent inputs maintain higher activation levels than those associated with earlier inputs.

In contrast, the shunting recurrent network, with its combination of shunting inhibition and excitatory feedback, manages to mitigate this issue more effectively. The shunting mechanism helps to balance excitation and inhibition, preventing the excessive suppression of neuron activations and allowing the network to handle a larger number of inputs without succumbing to instability. This balance results in more stable and robust activation dynamics, even as the number of inputs increases.

The shunting recurrent network's ability to model working memory processes has significant implications for short-term memory architectures. Its dynamics, where recent inputs are prioritized, closely mimic the behavior of biological short-term memory systems (Vindhya et al., 2024). This makes it a promising candidate for developing models that require effective handling of temporally sequential information. The observed similarity to working memory dynamics suggests that shunting networks could be leveraged to create more biologically plausible models of short-term memory, potentially enhancing our understanding of memory processes and informing the design of artificial systems with similar capabilities.

9.5 CONCLUSION

The current work presents a thorough analysis of stability criteria for shunting recurrent networks, integrating both analytical and Lyapunov function approaches. Our study validates theoretical stability conditions and demonstrates that shunting networks effectively manage transient inputs, exhibiting dynamics akin to working memory processes. Unlike additive networks, which are prone to catastrophic inhibition with a high number of inputs, shunting networks maintain stability and robustness due to their balanced excitation and inhibition. This capability not only underscores their practical advantages but also positions shunting networks as promising models for biological short-term memory systems, offering insights into their potential applications in cognitive and artificial systems.

BIBLIOGRAPHY

Cohen, M. A., and S. Grossberg (1983). Absolute stability of global pattern formation and parallel memory storage by competitive neural networks. *IEEE Transactions on Systems, Man, and Cybernetics* 5, 815–826.

Endress, A. D., and S. Szab´o (2017). Interference and memory capacity limitations. *Psychological Review* 124(5), 551.

Grossberg, S. (1968). Some physiological and biochemical consequences of psychological postulates. *Proceedings of the National Academy of Sciences* 60(3), 758–765.

Hou, L., H. Zhu, S. Zhong, Y. Zhang, and Y. Zeng (2013). Less conservative stability criteria for stochastic discrete-time recurrent neural networks with the time-varying delay. *Neurocomputing* 115, 72–80.

Jie, L., G. Yanli, and Z. Kai (2012). Stability and l 2-gain analysis for switched neutral recurrent neural networks. In *Proceedings of the 31st Chinese control conference*, pp. 2100–2105. IEEE.

Raijmakers, M. E., H. L. Van Der Maas, and P. C. Molenaar (1996). Numerical bifurcation analysis of distance-dependent on-center off-surround shunting neural networks. *Biological Cybernetics* 75(6), 495–507.

Sengupta, R., S. Bapiraju, and A. Pattanayak (2024a). Exploring emergent properties of recurrent neural networks using a novel energy function formalism. In *International conference on machine learning, optimization, and data science*, pp. 303–317. Springer.

Sengupta, R., A. Shukla, R. Janapati, and B. Verma (2024b). Comparative temporal dynamics of individuation and perceptual averaging using a biological neural network model. *International Journal of Hybrid Intelligent Systems* 20(2), 145–158.

Sengupta, R., B. R. Surampudi, and D. Melcher (2014). A visual sense of number emerges from the dynamics of a recurrent on-center off-surround neural network. *Brain Research* 1582, 114–124.

Usher, M., and J. D. Cohen (1999). Short term memory and selection processes in a frontal-lobe model. In *Connectionist models in cognitive neuroscience: The 5th neural computation and psychology workshop*, Birmingham, 8–10 September 1998, pp. 78–91. Springer.

Verma, B. K., and R. Sengupta (2023). Emergence of behavioral phenomena and adaptation effects in human numerosity decoder using recurrent neural networks. *Scientific Reports* 13(1), 19571.

Vindhya, L. S., R. Gnana Prasanna, R. Sengupta, and A. Shukla (2024). Modeling primacy, recency, and cued recall in serial memory task using on-center off-surround recurrent neural network. In *International conference on machine learning, optimization, and data science*, pp. 405–414. Springer.

10 ChatGPT
A Critical Analysis of Its Performance and Virtue Exploration

Nirmit Pratap Singh, Mahendra Dani, Eishani Bhattarcharya, Saee Joshi, Akash Saxena, Sanjeev Kumar Mathur, and Usha Desai

10.1 INTRODUCTION

In the recent past, the world was introduced to a large language model software that had the capability to generate texts on its own based on some prompts conveyed to it. The world was taken aback when it touched a magical figure of 1 million users in the first week of its launch. The reason: it had an extraordinary capability to produce texts like a human. However, the concept of an AI chatbot like ChatGPT is not new. In fact, history indicates that the first chatbot ELIZA, by Joseph Weizenbaum in the 1960s [1], came long before the behemoths like Google or Facebook (now Meta) were started. The history of AI goes back to the mid 20th-century at a Dartmouth summer research project that was based on AI [2, 3] and later paved way to the development of different machine learning algorithms for decision-making [4]. The subsequent years saw the creation of different machine learning technologies like neural network, genetic algorithms, etc. [3, 5]. What ChatGPT does is that it generates human like text responses as it goes through extensive training through large-scale datasets enabling it to learn different syntaxes, grammar and much more [6].

ChatGPT got huge attention in its first week of introduction due to the ability to generate texts like biased responses regarding the liberals and conservatives [7]. Large Language Models (LLMs), like ChatGPT, BERT (bidirectional encoder representations from transformers), ELMO (embeddings from language models) and Transformer-XL use different cases like text summarization, sentiment analysis, language translation, etc., because of their accuracy and performance in these natural language processing tasks [8], but the surprising feature the "accuracy".

ChatGPT has passed many examinations like United States Medical Licensing Examination, Psychology Today Verbal-Linguistic Intelligence IQ Test and the Operations Management exam [9], which are humongous milestones for a chatbot like ChatGPT; but its success lose the sheen in the failure in many examinations like

DOI: 10.1201/9781003473442-10

the Joint Entrance Examination (Mains and Advance) from India. There are many more examples like JEE where ChatGPT's responses were unsatisfactory.

Interesting research has been published [10] related to public health. The research contributes to the domain of public health and implications of inference drawn from the ChatGPT. Further, the research of [11] addressed a very critical issue of global warming and the role of the framework for understanding this issue, while suggesting feasible solutions for combating such deadly threats. For solving programming bugs, very interesting research on inference drawing was discussed with special reference to ChatGPT [12]. Further, in various references, researchers showed a serious concern about the misuse of the framework, and, at the same time, they discussed how this framework can be a boon for higher studies and research [13].

In [14] the authors argue about the replacement of classroom teacher with the framework as it is based on language processing models, and it can interact with humans very diligently [14]. The authors of [15] also discusses the issue of banning ChatGPT due to misuse of the framework.

Based on the discussion, throughout this research chapter, we will delve into the analysis of the responses given by ChatGPT in different domains like science, technology, business and social issues, and the objectives of the study are listed next:

1. To understand and analyze the framework of the ChatGPT interface.
2. To identify areas of potential problem domains for the evaluation of the ChatGPT interface.
3. To analyze the response obtained from the interface and deduce meaningful conclusions.
4. To give recommendations and provide sense of direction to the research based on the investigation and results analysis.

Section 10.2 describes the basic details of ChatGPT framework, Section 10.3 elucidates the benchmark details and the results of the application of these benchmarks on ChatGPT platform. Finally, Section 10.4 presents major conclusions derived from the analysis. ChatGPT is a big revolution in the field of artificial intelligence as it is claimed that this framework provides answers to all critical queries raised by human users. A mixed response has been obtained from the community for using this framework for solving engineering design, language processing, information sharing, documentation and policymaking, and many other applications have benefitted from this framework. In this chapter, we evaluate the performance of ChatGPT on certain benchmarks. These benchmarks are devised based on mathematical ability, critical thinking, algorithm design, socio-economic prompts and health science and medicines. Evaluation of the framework has been carried out and analyzed in order to furnish the final recommendation. We observed that the framework is poor while dealing with certain mathematical problems. However, we find that algorithm design, critical thinking and other policy-based documentation is well handled by the framework. We observe that, overall, a 76.92% success rate has been achieved by the framework on the proposed benchmarks.

10.2 WHAT IS CHATGPT?

ChatGPT, evolved by Open AI, is a modern-age chatbot and highly advanced tool that is based on language learning models. Its launch date was 30th November 2022 as a prototype. It has gained attention the world over. It has been incessantly mesmerizing social media users, students, teachers, engineers, authors, businessmen, etc. With machine learning principles and algorithms, with ChatGPT at its core; it has been able to address any question from various fields. However, its ledge is out of bounds, and it has broken all the shackles to cross over into education, management, marketing, literature, science, arts, etc. [16]. The beauty of ChatGPT is its ability to generate answers that are based on the user's prompt. The most pivotal feature of ChatGPT is that it comprehends and generates answers to the user's needs. Its capabilities include providing answers to descriptive questions, handling questions related to emotional and social issues, providing information on almost any topic, etc. ChatGPT also possesses the capability to adapt to any role as required based on the user's need. Engineers can use ChatGPT as their full-time assistant, capable of answering their queries related to a problem-solving aspect, or as a technical writer to help in documentation or as a pair programmer to help enhance writing and implementing algorithmic logic into fully functional programs. Students can use ChatGPT as their teaching aid, which can help them in solving subject-related doubts and questions, or as a writing assistant [17, 18]. Teachers too can use ChatGPT as their full-time assistant, which can help gather teaching material or as a problem setter to set questions and assignments for their subject. Market analysts can use ChatGPT to keep records of changes happening in the market [19, 20]. Businessmen and innovators can also use ChatGPT to innovate a new product and come up with a new idea that helps solve a real-world problem [21].

10.2.1 Workflow and Algorithm of ChatGPT

In ChatGPT, 'G' represents 'generative', showing its capability to generate text based on the user's prompt. Due to generative text formation, ChatGPT falls under the generative AI category. 'P' represents 'pre-training', which reflects that ChatGPT is a pre-trained machine learning model, and 'T' represents 'Transformer', which is the architecture of ChatGPT. In the following subsections, both the workflow and algorithm of ChatGPT are discussed briefly.

10.2.2 Algorithm of ChatGPT

ChatGPT follows a 10-staged algorithm. The first stage is pre-training followed by (in sequence), transformer architecture, tokenization, context window, fine tuning, prompt encoding, iterative decoding, probability distribution, sampling strategy and response generation, which has been depicted in Figure 10.1 as a pictorial representation.

10.2.2.1 Pre-Training

Pre-training is the initial stage in which the model is pre-trained with a large corpus of datasets. The datasets are derived from books, articles and websites. Large

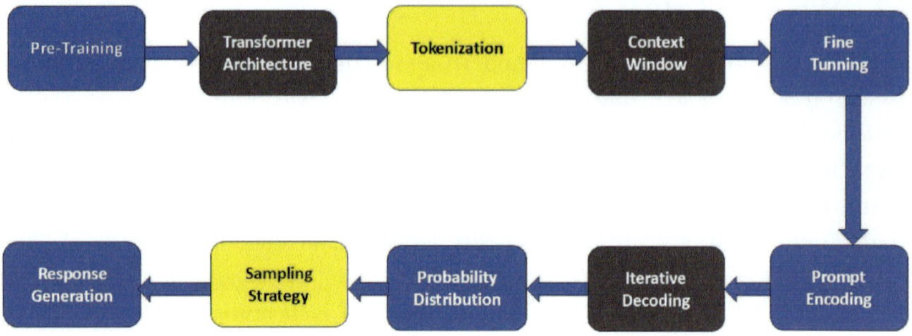

FIGURE 10.1 ChatGPT algorithm.

amounts of text data are also used from the internet to train the model. Both supervised and unsupervised machine learning techniques are used to train the model with the derived datasets. Being a language-based model, natural language processing methods are also used in this stage.

10.2.2.2 Transformer Architecture

Transformer architecture is a type of neural network architecture commonly used in machine learning, more so in natural language processing (NLP) tasks [14]. Transformer architecture is used for self-attention mechanisms, which allows the model to capture dependencies between different positions within a sequence of data. The components of transformer architecture are encoder and decoder, self-attention, multi-head attention, positional encoding and feed-forward networks as shown in Figure 10.2.

A tree graph of rounded rectangles with one central node and 5 child nodes
Figure 10.2 Components of transformer architecture.

- The encoder processes the input sequence, while the decoder generates the output sequence. Both the encoder and decoder are composed of multiple layers.
- Self-attention allows the model to give importance to different elements within a sequence while making predictions. It assigns a weight to each element based on its relevance to other elements in the sequence. By considering all elements simultaneously, the model can capture dependencies between different positions efficiently.
- Multi-head attention means using the self-attention mechanism parallelly for different inputs and layers. Each head attends to different subspaces of the input, allowing the model to capture different types of information simultaneously. This helps to improve the model's capability to learn complex patterns.
- Positional encoding is a technique being used to inject positional information into the input embeddings. It provides the model with a sense of relative or absolute position of elements within the sequence.

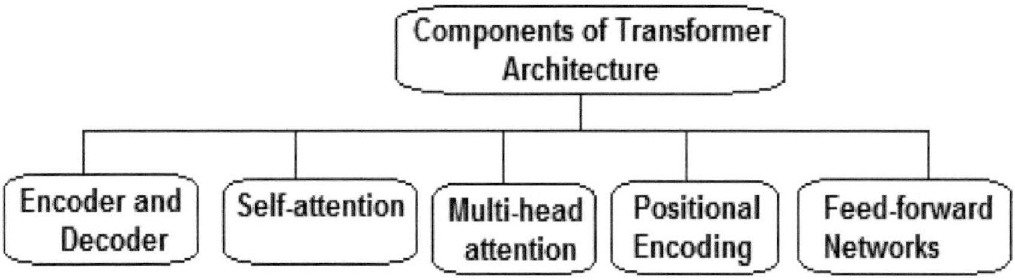

FIGURE 10.2 Components of transformer architecture.

- Each layer in the transformer architecture also includes feed-forward neural networks. These networks process the outputs of the self-attention mechanism, allowing the model to learn complex relationships and capture higher-level features.

10.2.2.3 Tokenization

Tokenization is one of the most important processes. When ChatGPT is provided with an input, these inputs are divided into smaller inputs called tokens. These tokens can be characters, sub-words or words of a sentence. For example, the input "Sky is blue" might be tokenized as ["Sky", "is", "blue"]. The role of tokenization in decoding the input is text segmentation, vocabulary creation, input encoding, handling out-of-vocabulary words, sequence length management and efficient computation as shown in Figure 10.3.

- **Text Segmentation**: Tokenization is the process of breaking down the input into smaller tokens. These tokens can be characters, sub-words or words. Tokenization provides a structured representation of the input, enabling the model to process it systematically.
- **Vocabulary Creation:** The large text data processing is not efficient. Tokenization creates a dictionary or vocabulary of tokens for the model. Each token is assigned a numerical value that is used in training and inference to process the input. Using numerical values instead of text-based tokens improves the computational efficiency of the model.
- **Input Encoding:** After tokenization, the input text is encoded by mapping each token to its corresponding numerical representation from the vocabulary. This encoding allows the model to interpret the input as a sequence of numbers, which can be efficiently processed by the neural network. The encoded tokens serve as input to the model's layers and operations.
- **Handling Out-of-Vocabulary Words:** Tokenization helps deal with out-of-vocabulary (OOV) words, which are words not present in the model's vocabulary. When encountering an OOV word, the tokenization process typically breaks it down into sub-words or characters that are part of the

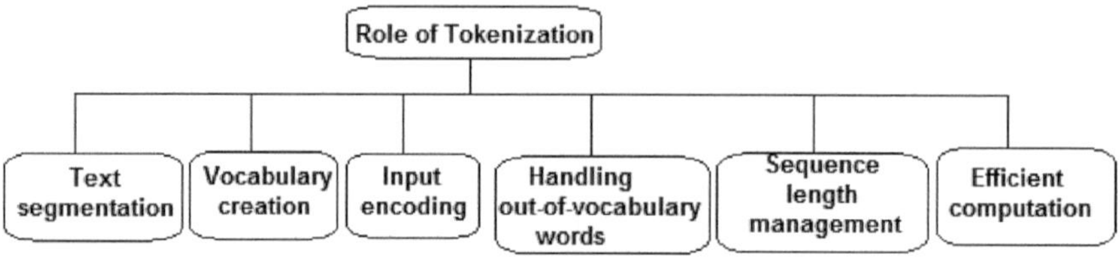

FIGURE 10.3 Role of tokenization.

vocabulary. This way, even if the model hasn't seen a particular word during training, it can still comprehend and generate responses based on the sub-words or characters it is familiar with.

- **Sequence Length Management:** Tokenization assists in managing the sequence length, especially in models with limited memory or computational constraints. If the input exceeds the maximum sequence length that the model can handle, tokenization allows it to be divided into smaller chunks or blocks. This enables the model to process the input in a sliding window fashion and consider a limited context while generating responses.
- **Efficient Computation:** By representing text as numerical tokens, tokenization enables efficient computations within the neural network. Vector operations can be performed on the token representations, leveraging hardware acceleration and parallel processing capabilities. This speeds up the training and inference processes, making it more feasible to train large-scale language models like ChatGPT.

10.2.2.4 Context Window

Handling the sequence length limitations are important. ChatGPT processes input text in blocks of tokens, typically 2048 at a time. This helps the model to consider limited context, and the prediction of response is improved.

10.2.2.5 Fine Tuning

After pre-training, the model is further fine-tuned on specific tasks using supervised machine learning methods. Custom datasets created by OpenAI are used for fine tuning. Fine tuning is important because it can be tailored for specific tasks. During pre-training it is trained on vast database, which helps its understanding of language. But fine tuning is done with narrow task specific datasets with the help of human reviewers which. Other advantages of fine tuning are human oversight and guidance, bias reduction, improving safety and responsiveness of the model.

10.2.2.6 Prompt Encoding

Prompt encoding is the process of encoding text-based tokens in numerical representations. As discussed in Section 10.2.2.3, this process is used to increase the efficiency of the model.

10.2.2.7 Iterative Decoding

Being a generative AI model, ChatGPT generates responses iteratively. It begins from the start token and predicts the next token based on the context and previous tokens. It continuously iterates until it reaches the end token. When the end token is reached, it stops iterations, and the response is complete.

10.2.2.8 Probability Distribution

At each decoding step, the model assigns a probability distribution over the vocabulary for the next token. This distribution is derived from the output of the final layer of the transformer model. Prediction of the next token is based on probability distribution. For example, the model may assign a higher probability to the word water "carbon dioxide" when it is prompted by respiration in humans.

10.2.2.9 Sampling Strategy

ChatGPT uses greedy sampling, nucleus sampling and temperature sampling methods to decode during decoding. In greedy sampling, the model selects the token with highest probability. This strategy favors high-confidence predictions but can lead to repetitive or overly deterministic responses. Top-k sampling limits the selection of tokens to a predefined subset, where k represents a cumulative probability threshold. The model samples from the smallest set of tokens that together account for at least the threshold probability. This technique introduces diversity and reduces the chance of repeating the same response. Temperature scaling is another strategy used during decoding. It introduces a temperature parameter that controls the randomness of the sampling process. Higher temperatures (above 1.0) encourage the model to explore a wider range of tokens, leading to more diverse and creative responses. Lower temperatures (below 1.0) make the sampling process more focused and deterministic, generating more conservative and precise responses. Adjusting the temperature can impact the balance between exploration and exploitation in the model's response generation.

10.2.2.10 Response Generation

This is the final stage of the algorithm. ChatGPT generates responses based on probability distribution and the chosen sampling strategy. The model selects the next token and continues generating the response. This process repeats until an end token is generated or maximum response length is reached.

10.2.2.10.1 Workflow of ChatGPT

The workflow of ChatGPT can be categorized into six process, namely, user' prompt, model response, user follow-up, model response, iterative conversation and interactive back and forth as depicted in Figure 10.4.

10.2.2.11 User Prompt

The conversation between a user and ChatGPT begins with the user's prompt or query. The prompt or query is a text-based input for the model. For example, "What are the effects of global warming?"

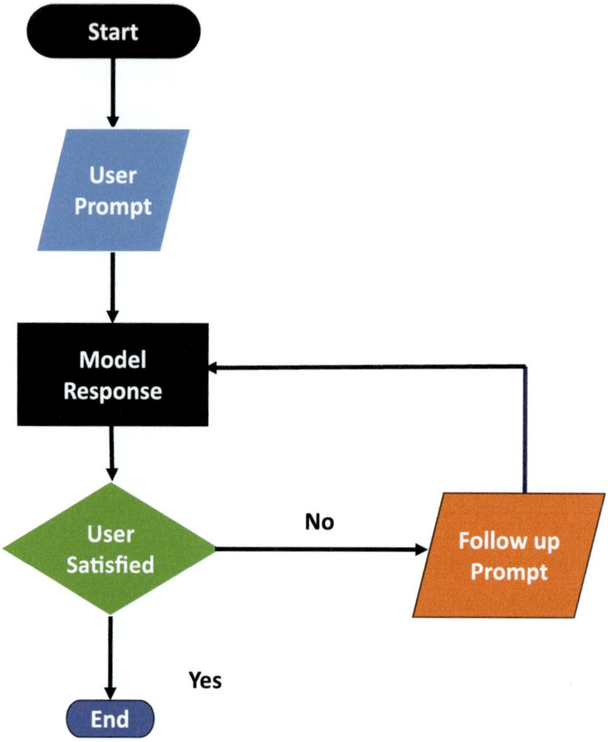

FIGURE 10.4 Workflow of ChatGPT.

10.2.2.12 Model Response

As discussed in Section 10.2.2, the input prompt is decoded by the model and a response is generated. The response is based on probability distribution, contextual background and sampling strategy.

10.2.2.13 User Follow-Up

There are two possible states for the users. Either the user is satisfied with the response or the user is unsatisfied. If the user is satisfied, then the conversation might end or else a new conversation can be started by giving a different input. If the user is unsatisfied with the response, then by giving follow-up prompts the conversation might proceed.

10.3 EVALUATION OF THE PERFORMANCE OF CHATGPT

In this section, the authors have presented a comprehensive analysis of the performance of ChatGPT. Table 10.1 and Table 10.2 exhibit the nature of problems asked from the interface and the analysis of the response is presented in detail along with the success rate analysis. By inspecting Tables 10.1 and 10.2, it is concluded that a

TABLE 10.1
Benchmarks Functions for Evaluation of ChatGPT Framework

Category		Problem	Frequency	Details
Mathematics	M-1	Geometry	1	If in a parallelogram ABDC, the coordinates of A B, and C are respectively (1, 2), (3, 4) and (2, 5), then the equation of the diagonal AD is
	M-2	Permutation and combination	3	In how many of the distinct permutations of the letters in MISSISSIPPI do the four Is not come together?
	M-3	Complex number theory	1	Finding out the complex conjugate of a given complex number
	M-4	Number theory-from Lowell Putnam Mathematical Competition	2	A grasshopper starts at the origin in the coordinate plane and makes a sequence of hops. Each hop has length 5, and after each hop the grasshopper is at a point whose coordinates are both integers; thus, there are 12 possible locations for the grasshopper after the first hop. What is the smallest number of hops needed for the grasshopper to reach the point (2021, 2021)?
	M-5	Calculus	1	Integration
	M-6	Millennium prize problem (unsolved)	2	The question is whether or not, for all problems for which an algorithm can verify a given solution quickly (that is, in polynomial time), an algorithm can also find that solution quickly. Since the former describes the class of problems termed NP, while the latter describes P, the question is equivalent to asking whether all problems in NP are also in P.
	M-7	Permutation and combination	2	A committee of 3 persons is to be constituted from a group of 2 men and 3 women. In how many ways can this be done? How many of these committees would consist of 1 man and 2 women?
	M-8	Permutation and combination	4	In a small village, there are 87 families, of which 52 families have at most 2 children. In a rural development program, 20 families are to be chosen for assistance, of which at least 18 families must have at most 2 children. In how many ways can the choice be made?
	M-9	Permutation and combination	2	How many 5-digit telephone numbers can be constructed using the digits 0 to 9, if each number starts with 67 and no digit appears more than once?

(Continued)

TABLE 10.1 (Continued)
Benchmarks Functions for Evaluation of ChatGPT Framework

Category	Problem	Frequency	Details
M-10	(Permutation and Combination)	3	Find n if $2^nC_3:^nC_3 = 11: 1$
M-11	Geometry	1	Two sides of a parallelogram are along the lines x + y = 3 and x - y + 3 = 0. If its diagonals intersect at (2,4) the one of its vertex is-
M-12	Geometry	1	The shortest distance between the points (3/2, 0) and the curve $y = \sqrt{x}$, x > 0
M-13	Geometry	1	If the line 3x + 4y - 24 = 0 intersects the x-axis at the point A and the Y-axis at the point B then the incentre of the triangle OAB is where O is origin
M-14	Geometry	1	Orthocenter of the triangle with vertices (0,0), (3,4) and (4,0) is

TABLE 10.2
Benchmarks Functions for Evaluation of ChatGPT Framework

Category	Problem	f	Details
Algorithm Design	Genetic algorithm and Operators G-1	1	Which algorithm is good: Gradient Descent or Genetic algorithm?
	G-2	1	What are the factors in which we can say that an algorithm is stable?
	G-3	1	What are the basic encoding steps of genetic algorithms? What are the evolutionary operators in genetic engineering?
Travel	Planning a travel through AI-based system T-1	1	My budget is 2000 USD, which are the best destinations in Germany?
	T-2	1	List of households required in Germany.
	T-3	1	Effective budget plan for an international student to do the masters in an expensive city like Zürich (Switzerland). (Zürich being the second most expensive city on the planet)
	T-4	1	Tell me some off-the-beaten destinations in Indonesia.
Marketing	E-1	1	Risks of ChatGPT in Marketing
	E-2	1	Risk assessment in ensuring ethical ChatGPT marketing
Event Organization	Event organization (EM-1)	1	Suppose you were to organize the IPL and give an entire management plan to conduct smoothly.
	(EM-2)	1	Make a plan to organize an event for a tech company so that it attracts maximum people.
	(EM-3)	1	What are points to be kept in mind when organizing a cultural event in a country like India?
Finance	Investment and financial planning (F-1)	1	How important is financial planning and at what age is it advisable to start gaining knowledge about it?

(Continued)

TABLE 10.2 (Continued)
Benchmarks Functions for Evaluation of ChatGPT Framework

Category	Problem	f	Details
	Demonetization in India (F-2)	1	Express your views on demonetization in 2016 and the latest demonetization of Rs.2000 in India.
Socio-Economic Issues Addiction	Behavioral addiction (SC-1)	1	Give some ways to combat social media addiction.
Education	Efficient learning process	1	What are the required changes in the Indian educational system to make the process of learning and gaining knowledge more efficient?
Research	Guidance to conduct research	1	How to conduct research in the AI domain?
Environmental	Air Pollution (En-1)	1	Explain how to prevent air pollution.
	Noise Pollution (En-2)	1	Implication of Noise Pollution and Critical level of Noise for Humans.
	Water Pollution (E-3)	1	What are the basic sources of water pollution?
Health	Covid-19 (H-1)	1	What are the main causes of Covid-19?
	Covid-19 (H-2)	1	How can developed countries prevent the spread of Covid-19?
	Obesity (H-3)	1	Explain the gravity of obesity and suggest ways to prevent and cure it.
	Cancer (H-4)	1	Suggest some ways to spread awareness about cancer and the importance of early detection.
	AI and Health Care (H-5)	1	What are the recent advances in healthcare augmented with AI?

diverse number of problems pertaining to the domain of mathematics, algorithm design, social analysis, policy framing and many other generic domains are incorporated for evaluation.

A basic mathematical calculation has been put to test from the framework. This was related to geometry. It is found that with a single prompt, the framework gives an erroneous answer. Hence, the success of this framework in this problem is minimal (M-1). A basic problem from permutation and combination was subjected to test. It did reach the answer when prompted, but there was a repetition of response (M-2). In a basic problem of complex numbers (M-3) where the simple core concept of conjugate must be applied; ChatGPT did very well and gave the correct answer, confirming that ChatGPT is aware of even basic concepts of mathematics. A very tough problem from the Lowell William Putnam Mathematical competition was also put to test that required a very high order thinking skill (M-4). ChatGPT initially gave the wrong answer, but when it was prompted again it finally reached the solution. A simple integration problem was asked, and ChatGPT failed to get the correct answer (M-5). ChatGPT lags behind when it comes to solving problems involving concepts from different fields of mathematics, even solving a simple problem like this. As in this question, it tried very long methods instead of using the concepts of algebra to reduce the function by which it would have got the answers correctly and in less time.

A research question was interrogated that was not yet solved. When it was given to ChatGPT it simply refused to attempt the question stating that it is a research topic and scientists and mathematicians are still working on it (M-6). Another set of permutation and combination problems were asked to make a group of a certain number of people in which ChatGPT succeeded. One another permutation and combination problem were asked, and ChatGPT failed to solve it. A noteworthy point here is that it solved a few questions of the same topic but failed abjectly when the question was altered. The reason for this may be the kind of data (here questions) it is trained on [6].

Again, a permutation and combination question of creating phone numbers was raised which ChatGPT solved correctly. A simple equation was given to be solved involving combinations, but ChatGPT again failed to apply multiple concepts together. It happened three times repeatedly. The details of these permutation and combination-based questions are designated (M-7 to M-10). A geometry related to parallelogram was questioned, and ChatGPT failed to give the correct response. It applied the correct concepts but failed to do the calculations correctly. Again, another geometry-based problem was asked to which it even applied the wrong concepts as well as the wrong calculations, unlike the previous one where only calculation mistakes were there. One more geometry problem was asked, and here also it applied the wrong concept. This question can be solved using the direct formula or by the long method to which ChatGPT went for the long basic method. It applied all concepts correctly, but, by the end, it applied a few wrong concepts and failed miserably. The moot question: Which of the two algorithms either gradient descent or genetic algorithm is good? ChatGPT was asked to respond to this. It stated that all the conditions where each has its own importance and advantage. It was asked to mention the factors in which we can say that an algorithm is stable to which it stated different factors like robustness, convergence, precision, scalability, validation and sensitivity analysis. What are the basic encoding steps of genetic algorithms? What are the evolutionary operators in genetic engineering? ChatGPT answered this very accurately by stating encoding methods like binary encoding, real valued encoding and permutation encoding and evolutionary operators like selection, crossover, mutation, elitism and adaption.

ChatGPT was asked for the best destinations in Germany under a 2000 USD budget to which it gave satisfactory responses with the top five cities in Germany. It stated the different costs like food, accommodation, traveling and many other activities including where to cut the costs. ChatGPT was asked about the households in Germany to which gave an appropriate response that includes day-to-day necessities like furniture, bedding, lightings, etc. Zürich is one of the most expensive cities in the world. For students studying in Zürich, an effective budget is a necessity to survive in this city. ChatGPT was asked the same. It gave the correct response stating all important aspects like traveling cost, accommodation, etc. and even suggested doing a part-time job offered by many universities. ChatGPT gave the top five places in the response like Belitung Island, Derawan Islands, Morotai Island, Wakatobi and Tana Toraja, just like we searched on a search engine (T-1 to T-4). ChatGPT provides all the major risks and also ways to mitigate these risks. The response of ChatGPT highlights the importance of risk assessment and gives the major frameworks to consider. ChatGPT answered this query in a way that is easy to understand, clear and concise (E-1 and E-2). It covers all the possible aspects to include while organizing the IPL. This suggests that ChatGPT has good organization and management skills. ChatGPT answered very cleverly about keeping all points like venue, timing, duration, security arrangements, etc. and even promotional activities to increase the strength of the event. It gave satisfactory response covering all points like knowing the culture, tradition, security, venue, etc., but one problem was that it was not able to think of how not to hurt the feelings of other religions and cultures in a country like India with diverse culture religions and languages (EM-1 to EM-3). This is where it failed not once but twice. ChatGPT provides in-depth knowledge about financial planning as a financial advisor would have provided for a beginner. It provides a comprehensive answer to the query (F-1).

ChatGPT provides a quick overview of the objectives of demonetization. Also, it simplifies the demonetization process by providing the pros and cons for the same to ensure better understanding for common people (F-2). Although ChatGPT's knowledge is limited to September 2021, it tackles the question of current (2023) demonetization (Rs. 2000 notes) by considering it as a hypothetical situation and provides a comprehensive response. ChatGPT effectively responds to the question by providing a clear and concise answer. It suggests all the major ways to combat social media addiction, be it of any level whether mild or severe (SC-1). ChatGPT provides an answer that is to the point and relevant. However, the New Education Policy (NEP) in India covers most of these points. Since the knowledge of ChatGPT is limited to September 2021, it doesn't have any information regarding NEP. ChatGPT gives steps to conduct research. It acts as a mentor to a beginner in the field of research. The answer given by ChatGPT covers all the necessary major aspects.

ChatGPT's answer is comprehensive and to the point. It covers all the necessary points. It answers the question without deviating from the main topic. ChatGPT's response includes all the necessary points: effects, measures, etc. The response of ChatGPT is comprehensive and gives information about all the sources of pollution. ChatGPT provides the cause of COVID-19 with proper explanation. ChatGPT provides a satisfactory response including maximum suggestions. ChatGPT does a pretty good job in answering these prompts. It includes all the major points giving a satisfactory response to the user's question. It provides effects and ways to prevent and address diseases. ChatGPT includes all the major points giving a satisfactory response to the user's question. It provides ways to promote awareness, and ways to address diseases. The response by ChatGPT highlights the recent advances in health care augmented with AI (H-1 to H-5).

10.3.1 Discussion

From the evaluation, authors came to the conclusion that theoretical concepts, design algorithms, and fundamental knowledge of the processes are well received by the framework. It is pertinent to mention here that while evaluating the performance of the ChatGPT framework on mathematical and precise numerical problems, the framework response is unsteady. As on prompting, the response is edited. The evaluation of the framework shall be done on bigger benchmark datasets to seek fruitful suggestions on designs that involve public health, revenue and other critical issues. It is a big yes to the framework, as it can provide an edge to critical thinking besides being useful.

10.4 CONCLUSION

In the area of artificial intelligence, NLP has prominent importance. The research related to ChatGPT is in spotlight due to its capability of solving many problems in an efficient and effective manner. In this chapter, we defined a set of 39 benchmarks of diverse quality and nature. Then, we evaluated the response of this framework. We find that for certain mathematical problems answers given by the framework are not accurate. It will be apt to say that continuous prompting can yield better results. However, while evaluating the framework on algorithm design and other knowledge-based questions, the performance was found satisfactory. While evaluating the framework for questions related to general behavior, social and health related problems, the response provided by the framework was found satisfactory. In our next work, we shall design algorithms and evaluate the performance of ChatGPT and statistical tools with each other.

REFERENCES

[1] Okuda, Takuma, and Sanae Shoda. "AI-based chatbot service for financial industry." *Fujitsu Scientific and Technical Journal* 54.2 (2018): 4–8.

[2] McCarthy, John, Marvin L. Minsky, Nathaniel Rochester, and Claude E. Shannon. "A proposal for the dartmouth summer research project on artificial intelligence, August 31, 1955." *AI Magazine* 27.4 (2006): 12.

[3] Jordan, Michael I., and Tom M. Mitchell. "Machine learning: Trends, perspectives, and prospects." *Science* 349.6245 (2015): 255–260.

[4] Domingos, Pedro. *The master algorithm: How the quest for the ultimate learning machine will remake our world.* Basic Books, 2015.

[5] Sallam, Malik. "ChatGPT utility in healthcare education, research, and practice: Systematic review on the promising perspectives and valid concerns." *Healthcare* 11.6 (2023). MDPI.

[6] Brown, Tom, B. Mann, N. Ryder, M. Subbiah , J. D. Kaplan, P. Dhariwal , A. Neelakantan , P. Shyam , G. Sastry, A. Askell, and S. Agarwal . "Language models are few-shot learners." *Advances in Neural Information Processing Systems* 33 (2020): 1877–1901.

[7] McGee, Robert W. "Is chat GPT biased against conservatives? An empirical study." *An Empirical Study (February 15, 2023)* (2023).

[8] Elkassem, Asser Abou, and Andrew D. Smith. "Potential use cases for ChatGPT in radiology reporting." *American Journal of Roentgenology* 221 (2023): 373–376.

[9] Frieder, Simon, Luca Pinchetti, Ryan-Rhys Griffiths, Tommaso Salvatori, Thomas Lukasiewicz, Philipp Petersen, and Julius Berner. "Mathematical capabilities of chatgpt." *arXiv preprint arXiv:2301.13867* (2023).

[10] Biswas, Som S. "Role of chat gpt in public health." *Annals of Biomedical Engineering* 51.5 (2023): 868–869.

[11] Biswas, Som S. "Potential use of chat gpt in global warming." *Annals of Biomedical Engineering* 51.6 (2023): 1126–1127.

[12] Surameery, Nigar M. Shafiq, and Mohammed Y. Shakor. "Use chat gpt to solve programming bugs." *International Journal of Information Technology & Computer Engineering (IJITC)* 3.1 (2023): 17–22.

[13] Fuchs, Kevin. "Exploring the opportunities and challenges of NLP models in higher education: Is Chat GPT a blessing or a curse?" *Frontiers in Education* 8 (2023).

[14] Ausat, Abu Muna Almaududi, Berdinata Massang, Mukhtar Efendi, Nofirman Nofirman, and Yasir Riady. "Can chat GPT replace the role of the teacher in the classroom: A fundamental analysis." *Journal on Education* 5.4 (2023): 16100–16106.

[15] Yu, Hao. "Reflection on whether Chat GPT should be banned by academia from the perspective of education and teaching." *Frontiers in Psychology* 14 (2023): 1181712.

[16] Mhlanga, David. "Open AI in education, the responsible and ethical use of ChatGPT towards lifelong learning." *Education, the Responsible and Ethical Use of ChatGPT Towards Lifelong Learning* (February 11, 2023) (2023).

[17] Chen, Tzeng-Ji. "ChatGPT and other artificial intelligence applications speed up scientific writing." *Journal of the Chinese Medical Association* 86.4 (2023): 351–353.

[18] Aydın, Ömer, and EnisKaraarslan. "OpenAI ChatGPT generated literature review: Digital twin in healthcare." Available at SSRN 4308687 (2022).

[19] Street, Daniel, and Joseph Wilck. "'Let's have a chat': Principles for the effective application of ChatGPT and large language models in the practice of forensic accounting." Available at SSRN 4351817 (2023).

[20] Vaswani, A. "Attention is all you need." *Advances in Neural Information Processing Systems* 30 (2017).

[21] Shetty, S. S., C. Singh, S. B. Rao, U. Desai, and P. M. Srinivas. "Prediction on illegal drug consumption promotion from Twitter data." In *International Conference on Emergent Converging Technologies and Biomedical Systems*, September 23, 2022 (pp. 647–657). Singapore: Springer Nature.

11 Fundus Image Restoration and Enhancement Using Multi Resolution CNN Framework

Laya Tojo, Manju Devi, and Annie Sujith

11.1 INTRODUCTION

Examination of medical images plays a major role in the identification of diseases. It focuses on the examination and evaluation of digital images. Various image processing methods and computer tools are used in the identification of diseases. Recent studies have shown that quick advancements in biomedical image processing are essential because they reduce the necessity for intrusive diagnostic procedures. Various techniques to detect and diagnose various diseases like heart defects, tumors, Alzheimer's, cancers, bone defects, edemas, etc., are improved with the help of computed assisted diagnosis techniques. The observation of fundus images helps to analyze critical retinal diseases such as glaucoma, diabetic retinopathy, retinal tear, macular degeneration related with age, retinitis pigmentosa, etc. The images taken with the normal fundus camera are of low image quality. The images are mostly degraded mainly due to noise, blur, low contrast features and irregular illumination. Hence it is very essential that the fundus image must therefore be effectively removed from noise in order to apply disease detection techniques, as well as to detect and evaluate minute variations in the retinal vasculature. The increase in blood pressure and increase in blood glucose level are primary reasons for recognized eye diseases like glaucoma and hypertensive retinopathy. These diseases can develop in the next stages without major symptoms, whereas general symptoms include intra-retinal micro vascular abnormalities and leakages. In order to diagnose and treat ophthalmologic conditions including age-related macular degeneration (AMD) and diabetes mellitus, fundus photography is essential. The human eye's refractive errors, incorrect camera calibration and high flash are the primary causes in the deterioration of retinal image in the quality. Retinal images are regarded as low light images. They do not have full illumination due to sensor quality and eyes range. In retinal images, low light conditions and noise are mainly due to poor camera focus, eye motion, iris reflection and quality of lens. As retina is a very sensitive

DOI: 10.1201/9781003473442-11

portion of the eye, high flash can result in migraine health issues. Hence enhancement and denoising of retinal images are necessary. Retinal images are susceptible to various blur effects due to improper image acquisition conditions and settings. Retinal pictures are typically used by ophthalmologists to diagnose specific conditions. Because of unreliable diagnosis, poor camera settings, movement of eye, inconsistent illumination and pupil dilation, fundus cameras usually fail to acquire better-quality retinal images. There are many medical image noises like photon noise, periodic noise, Gaussian noise, impulse, speckle noise, Gaussian noise etc. These noises can degrade the image quality to a great extent. We have taken additive white Gaussian noise (AWGN) as it is easy to model mathematically. In order to restore blurred retinal image and also to enhance the retinal image clarity, multi-resolution dual CNN algorithm is used in the work.

11.2 RELATED WORK

One well-known issue that researchers are attempting to address is denoising. In recent years, deep learning algorithms have substituted denoising approaches such as non-linear filters, chroma and luminous noise separation, linear smoothing filters, block matching algorithms, wavelet transform filters, random field machine learning algorithm and others. There have been very few works regarding the image denoising of medical images. Medical images are images that contain visual and meaningful information. But it will be corrupted with different noises like speckle noise, Gaussian noise, quantization noise etc. In [1] a classification of medical images task is performed on X-ray images using DenseNet-121 convolutional neural network. Fine-tuned models are more affected by denoising techniques than randomly initialized models. There is no significance between PSNR and SSIM. With the help of two datasets, the efficiency of AlexNet CNN mode is analyzed. It proved that group of images that noise harmoniously cover area of disease symptoms have better effect with respect to CNN. The multi-scale dilated convolution of CNN [2] by implementing dilated convolution conserves contextual information and expands receptive field. Residual learning helps to speed up learning procedure. The total variational (TV) method [3] removes the noise and preserves edges when compared to traditional denoising techniques like linear smoothing, median filtering, transform domain methods using FFT and DCT. The undesirable artifacts generated have been minimized using second (higher-order) regularization methods, and [4] proposes an effective deep convolutional neural network model for medical picture denoising using a limited training dataset by incorporating batch normalization and residual learning; training process is sped up and performance is improved. The limitation was artifacts resulted due to the compression of medical images.

By adding non sparsity penalty function, the mixed noise reduction is achieved thereby improving better visual quality of dark images [5]. The neural network, which consists of convolution operation, batch normalization and ReLU layers, and convolution operation maps noisy image patches to clean version and thereby solves low light denoising problem. The low light image denoising based on Poisson noise model [6] preserves image details without compromising noise reduction. The artifacts, blurring and enhancement issues, are eliminated in the work [7] by utilizing super pixel based adaptive denoising and luminance adaptive contrast enhancement. The technique based on adaptive sigmoid function [8] effectively eliminated noise and improved the contrast of fundus images. The method proved to be efficient for preprocessing color retinal images that are used in computer-aided clinical diagnosis. The method adaptive histogram equalization tuned with non-similar grouping curvelet [9] adopts a joint enhancement denoising method by including curvelet features to preserve better edges. Halo ringing artifacts are prevented by adaptive histogram enhancement method. The drawback was it could not address luminosity related issues. Out of the three methods, contrast stretching (CS), histogram equalization (HE) and contrast limited adaptive histogram equalization (CLAHE) methods prove that poor quality images are corrected and image denoising is performed well on fundus images [10]. There are many works carried out in classification of retinal images based on CNN [11–13]. The CNN classification framework helps to classify images without the help of any preprocessing edge detection stages. The VGG19 model is fine-tuned with retinal database, and the transfer learning approach is employed [14]. Fundus image enhancement technique fusing original retinal image and the image background information is presented in [15]. Deep CNN is developed [16] and helps to analyze fundus images, and it has 18 convolution layers and 3 fully connected layers. It proved to be accurate in diagnosing and grading diabetic retinopathy. The technology helped ophthalmologists in early diagnosis and tracking retinal diseases to some extent [17]. The restored and enhanced image after applying the MR-DCNN algorithm gave good results in the case of retinal images from the STARE dataset [18], and the comparison of our results with existing retinal image enhancement techniques is clearly mentioned in this work.

11.3 PROPOSED METHOD

Noisy input is fed to our MR-DCNN model (Figure 11.1). The image with noise is represented by the equation $y = n + x$, where x denotes a clean input, n is AWGN with a standard deviation of σ and y is the corrupted data. There are mainly four blocks that serve as basic building blocks of the proposed method.

(1) FEB_CNN, 2 Feature extraction blocks
(2) EB_CNN, an Enhancement block
(3) CB_CNN, a Compression block
(4) RB_CNN, a Reconstruction block.

Sparse features are combined in FEBs; thereby diverse features can be extracted. By incorporating sparsity, local and global features can be extracted. This helps to handle corrupted noisy information efficiently.

EB_CNN combines the features of the two sub-networks, and by doing so it increases the retrieved features. CB CNN lowers the computational cost. The reconstruction block RB CNN recreates a clear quality image. Figure 11.1 displays the proposed multi-resolution dual CNN for image denoising. This consists of 2, 16-layer structures with 4 main blocks. Sparse blocks are beneficial as they enhance the effectiveness and performance. FEB_CNN consists of two sub-networks: FEBnet1 and

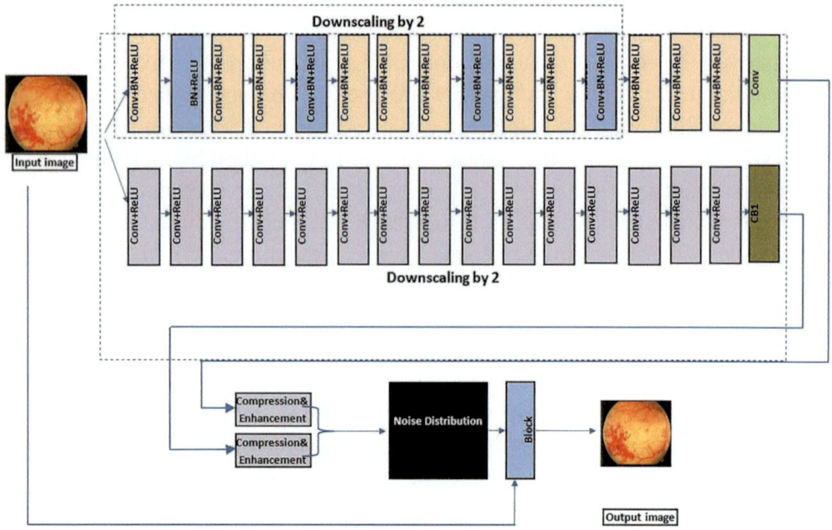

FIGURE 11.1 MR-DCNN architecture.

FEBnet2. By making use of sparsity in FEB blocks, dilated convolution is achieved. The network is assumed to have y as its input and x as its output. The function of the feature extraction block task is given as

$$FEBj = Fj(y), j = 1,2 \tag{11.1}$$

Feature extraction function is indicated by $F_j(y)$, and the extracted features of the jth network is denoted by FEB_j.

EB can be bifurcated into enhancement block1 (EB1) and enhancement block2 (EB2). Feature extraction block output is sent into the enhancement block.

$$OE1 = E(FEB1, FEB2) \tag{11.2}$$

where OE1 denotes enhancement EB1 output and E denotes enhancement block EB1 and EB2 functions.

Compression block (CB_CNN) consists of three compression blocks: CB1, CB2 and CB3. One compression block associated with FEBnet1 is CB1 as shown in Figure 11.1. The other compression block, CB2, situated among enhancement blocks, enhances the retrieved features as follows:

The output of compression block CB2 is

$$OCB2 = C1(OE1) \tag{11.3}$$

where C_1 denotes compression function.

The EB2 gathers additional data given as

$$OE2 = E(OCB2, y) \tag{11.4}$$

OE2 stands for enhancement block EB2 output.

The following is the output CB3:

$$OCB3 = C1(OE2) \tag{11.5}$$

Reconstructing the latent clean input *y* is the key goal. The residual operation yields the latent image *y*:

$$x = y - OCB \tag{11.6}$$

where '-' denotes the residual operation. We have achieved many benefits by incorporating these parameters in proposed multi-resolution dual CNN: (1) Using the help of double networks, numerous features and even minute details in complex images could be extracted. (2) Reduction in memory usage, computational cost and elimination of redundant information is achieved with the help of compression blocks. (3) Small filters helps to reduce the complexity of denoiser to a great extent. The dual networks FEBnetl and FEBnet2 implementation reduce the computational operations, thereby boosting the performance.

11.4 EXPERIMENTAL RESULTS

11.4.1 Effect of Downscaling the CNN Layers

CNN can be varied in three ways: width, height and depth wise (Figure 11.2). Width and height represent the size of layers whereas depth represents the number of blocks inside CNN. Inside the CNN layers we have different blocks of width × height. We have varied width and height from 32 × 32 to 16 ×16, thereby introducing multi-resolution CNN. By downscaling, the computational complexity has been reduced to a great extent. The 2-tier dual CNN architecture helps in feature extraction happening in a more detailed manner.

In the proposed work, the width and height of CNN, 32 × 32, after convolution with 64 filters of 3 × 3, the total number of operations is 9.4 million operations. After downscaling the CNN layers by 2, the number of operations has been drastically reduced to 2.3 million operations from 9.4 million operations.

We have developed a dual 16-layer network called multi-resolution dual CNN. The starting parameters and weights are as follows: There are a total of 128 batches. There are 30 epochs in the trained model. The optimization algorithm used was Adam. The MR-DCNN model in the research was trained and tested using Matlab 2020. All analysis is carried out on a computer with an Intel® CoreTM i5–8265U 1.60 GHz processor and 8 GB of RAM. Both standard datasets and custom datasets gathered from the SRM Medical College Hospital were

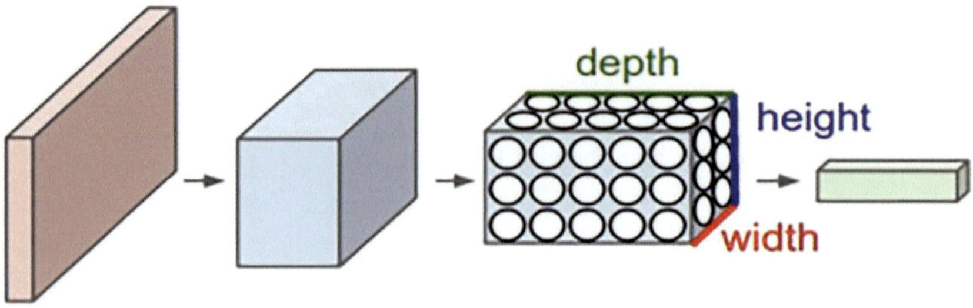

FIGURE 11.2 D view of CNN.

used to compare the outcomes with the current method. STARE database fundus images with resolution 700*605 were captured using TRV-50 Fundus camera. Gaussian noise with varying σ values were added to fundus images for testing MR-DCNN algorithm's efficiency and performance. In comparison to the present method, the suggested algorithm will denoise the fundus image and thereby improve visual clarity. In comparison to the original image, the vessel features are very clearly evident in the restored image. It can also be used for further picture analysis and illness diagnostics. Figure 11.3 shows the retinal images from the popular STARE dataset. Due to the introduction of a multi-resolution and dual CNN, the suggested MR-DCNN may obtain and maintain better crisp edge details, resulting in better PSNR, SSIM and MSE values and enhance visual quality as shown in Table 11.1.

11.4.2 Training and Testing Dataset

Training data includes 400 images (320 images from real noisy and synthetic images and 20 retinal images). Gray level and color images are part of the 256 × 256 synthetic noisy images. The real noisy images are collected from different digital devices like Canon, Nikon, Sony A5, etc. The retinal images are taken from STARE database [18], Kaggle database [19] and DRIVE database [20]. CNN learns these noisy images, trains on these data and generates a model file automatically. Based on the noise level intensity, it takes particular characteristics and stores in model file (feature extraction). The information about various noisy images, noise types and filters are fed to CNN during the training phase. The CNN takes the available information given during training and makes a model file automatically. Several iterations are done to develop a good training data in our experiment.

11.4.3 Retinal Image Database

The retinal picture can be obtained through direct image capture or from a publicly accessible database. The following are some databases that we have taken during our training phase.

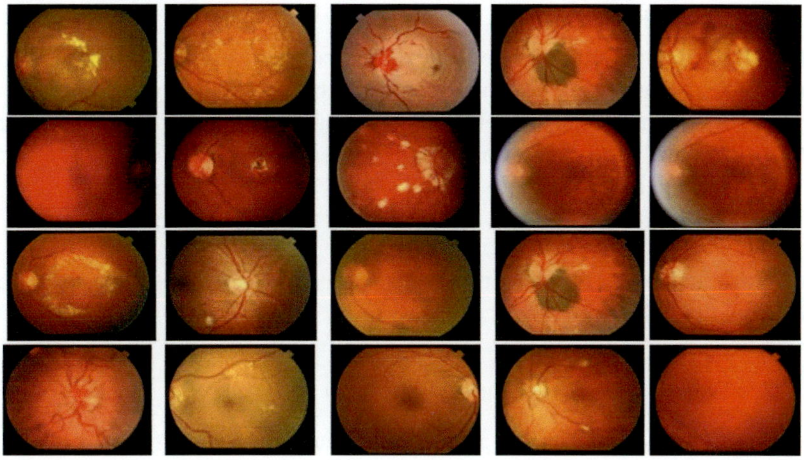

FIGURE 11.3 STARE dataset.

TABLE 11.1
PSNR, SSIM and MSE Values Obtained Using MR-DCNN Method on STARE Dataset

Images	PSNR	SSIM	MSE
Im001	39.31	0.929	0.0004
Im002	39.82	0.946	0.0017
Im003	38.12	0.917	0.0018
Im004	41.31	0.953	0.0013
Im005	38.32	0.934	0.0006
Im006	40.64	0.956	0.0014
Im007	40.65	0.964	0.0058
Im008	39.81	0.949	0.0044
Im009	44.44	0.955	0.0012
Im010	38.27	0.958	0.0451
Im011	38.44	0.981	0.0027
Im012	39.56	0.943	0.004
Im013	36.84	0.946	0.0028
Im014	39.15	0.912	0.0008
Im015	37.17	0.923	0.0021
Im016	39.25	0.984	0.0009

11.4.3.1 STARE Database

Scanning and digitizing retinal imaging photographs produced the STARE database [18], as structured analysis of retina. They were taken using a 700 × 605 pixel camera with an 8-bit color channel and 35 degree narrow field of view.

11.4.3.2 DRIVE Database

The DRIVE (digital retinal image for vessel extraction) [20] fundus image database is accessible to everyone. The fundus photos of this collection were taken from 453 participants in a group diabetic retinopathy screening program, ranging in age from 31 to 86 year old. This database contains 40 fundus images, 20 of which are for training and 20 for testing.

11.4.3.3 Kaggle Database

The Kaggle database [19] contains of 3200 retinal images. These images are captured from three different fundus cameras.

11.4.4 Training and Denoising Workflow

In training phase, the local and global features are extracted. As the convergence error is large initially, iterations are performed in an optimized manner. The optimum value is set in the algorithm. The iterations are performed until the convergence error decreases and reaches the optimum value. After 100 iterations, a model file is generated. We use this model file during the testing phase. The proposed MR-DCNN is tested on 100 retinal images from STARE database [18]. CNN uses the test image and does classification and feature extraction here. The model file given to CNN during testing code has data available in enhancement, feature extraction, compression and reconstruction blocks. CNN converts the input data into similar blocks and does comparison with these blocks. If it matches, it uses particular filter and does denoising and gives output.

11.4.5 Quantitative Analysis

Retinal images were taken from STARE dataset. We have worked with this dataset in order to analyze the performance. Gaussian noise with noise levels σ=15, 25, 30, 50 is added to the image for testing MR-DCNN algorithm performance. Table 11.2 shows the performance comparison of the proposed MR-DCNN method on Gaussian noise affected retinal images with similar existing denoising and enhancement methods for retinal images, and our PSNR results outperforms the existing methods.

Table 11.2 shows performance comparison of MR-DCNN method on Gaussian noise affected retinal images with various existing technologies like CLAHE-HPF-GF, Morphology-CLAHE-Wiener and CLAHE-Median-Order filter. As seen in Table 11.2, the multi-resolution dual CNN method produces best results for the given retinal images.

Table 11.3 depicts the comparison of performance of the MR-DCNN method on Gaussian noise prone retinal images with similar prevailing denoising and enhancement methods, and our SSIM results outperforms the existing methods as shown in Figure 11.4.

Testing time also considered as a major factor in evaluating denoising methods. The running time of 20 retinal images with respect to CPU and GPU is tabulated in Table 11.4. The left side of the table is the running time of CPU, while right is the GPU run time.

TABLE 11.2
Performance Comparison of the Gaussian Noise Affected Retinal Images

Images	MR-DCNN	CLAHE + HPF + GF	Morphology filter + CLAHE + Wiener Filter	CLAHE + Median + Order Filter
	PSNR	PSNR	PSNR	PSNR
IM001	39.31	35.34	35.337	28.87
IM002	39.82	36.04	38.067	28.83
IM003	38.12	32.96	32.079	28.76
IM004	41.31	40.39	39.118	28.82
IM005	38.32	33.38	31.455	28.82
IM006	40.64	39.29	39.333	28.88
IM007	40.65	37.18	36.888	28.82
IM008	39.81	36.48	37.081	28.82
IM009	44.44	43.59	50.723	28.82
IM010	38.27	38.65	44.657	28.88
IM011	38.44	35.48	35.374	28.78
IM012	39.56	38.69	41.729	29.95
IM013	36.84	33.00	32.210	28.88
IM014	39.15	29.10	26.073	26.83
IM015	37.17	30.35	28.716	28.76
IM016	39.25	33.72	32.476	28.91

TABLE 11.3
Performance Comparison of the Contrast Stretching-Median Filter, Histogram Equalization-Median Filter, and Contrast Limited Adaptive Histogram Equalization Filter with the MR-DCNN Method on Retinal Pictures that Have Been Altered by Gaussian Noise

Images	CS+ Median filter	HE+ Median Filter	CLAHE + Filter	MR-DCNN
	SSIM	SSIM	SSIM	SSIM
IM001	0.93	0.81	0.86	0.9915
IM002	0.9	0.84	0.86	0.987
IM003	0.89	0.77	0.82	0.9908
IM004	0.88	0.84	0.88	0.9891
IM005	0.91	0.78	0.79	0.996
IM006	0.89	0.86	0.89	0.9908
IM007	0.85	0.79	0.89	0.9877
IM008	0.93	0.82	0.83	0.9628

(Continued)

TABLE 11.3 (Continued)
Performance Comparison of the Contrast Stretching-Median Filter, Histogram Equalization-Median Filter, and Contrast Limited Adaptive Histogram Equalization Filter with the MR-DCNN Method on Retinal Pictures that Have Been Altered by Gaussian Noise

Images	CS+ Median filter	HE+ Median Filter	CLAHE + Filter	MR-DCNN
IM009	0.83	0.71	0.86	0.9861
IM010	0.88	0.74	0.88	0.989
IM011	0.84	0.67	0.87	0.9858
IM012	0.93	0.83	0.87	0.9857
IM013	0.78	0.72	0.9	0.9649
IM014	0.87	0.78	0.86	0.992
IM015	0.87	0.77	0.86	0.9862
IM016	0.86	0.71	0.85	0.9706
IM017	0.88	0.76	0.86	0.9915
IM018	0.87	0.77	0.85	0.9968
IM019	0.86	0.71	0.78	0.9955

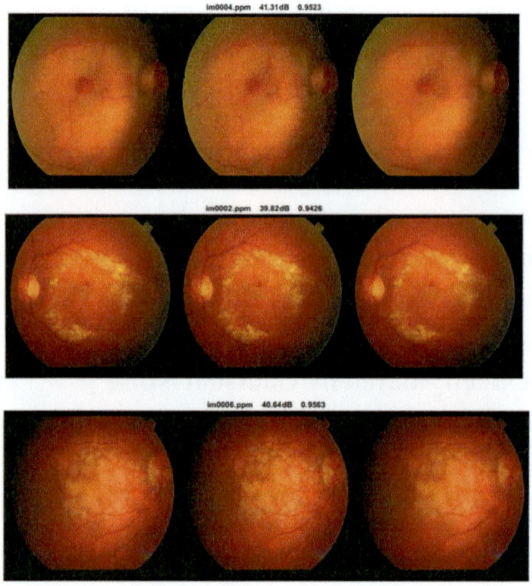

FIGURE 11.4 Denoised retinal images from STARE database.

The algorithm gave good results when it is tried with real-time patients fundus images. Figure 11.5 shows original image, noisy image and enhance image with better PSNR and SSIM values of [39.82,.9635], [39.46,0.9592], [38.25,.9494] and [39.74,.9625]. The results prove that our algorithm worked well in removing noise from a patient's fundus image.

TABLE 11.4
Results of Running Time of Retinal Images with Respect to CPU and GPU.

Run Time Comparison for the Noisy Images of Size 256 x 256

	CPU	GPU
Images	**(Intel®Core (TM)-i5–8265U-8) GB RAM**	**(Intel®Core (TM)-i7–10750H-16) GB RAM, Nvidia graphics card**
IM001	48.6299 s	14.5316s
IM002	47.7581s	15.8592s
IM003	50.9669s	14.8875s
IM004	47.5364s	14.6168s
IM005	50.3911s	14.4957s
IM006	51.6053s	14.5612s
IM007	48.3878s	15.5624s
IM008	49.8061s	14.6321s
IM009	48.2659s	15.7894s
IM010	48.0096s	14.6257s
IM011	52.4495s	15.5416s
IM012	46.5275s	14.8592s
IM013	50.3584s	14.8675s
IM014	51.9647s	15.6268s
IM015	48.7629s	14.9557s
IM016	49.3895s	14.1252s

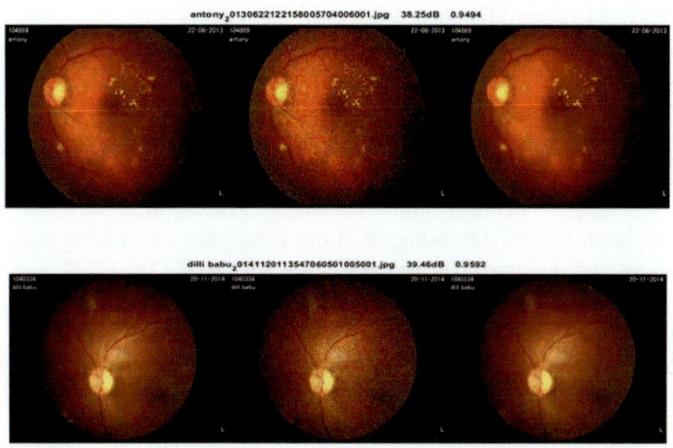

FIGURE 11.5 Denoised retinal images from patients' retinal dataset.

11.5 CONCLUSION

We presented the development of the MR-DCNN algorithm to enhance the natural images in visual perception and clarity by removing noise effects. By incorporating sparse mechanism in dual networks and by downscaling the width and height of CNN layers, we could reduce the computational complexity and achieve better performance and speed. According to the experimental findings, the suggested MR-DCNN method can improve visual quality without even sacrificing PSNR, SSIM or MSE values. MR-DCNN helps to recover the sharp edge, boundaries and visibility of retinal images. In our work, the reinforcement is little partial; even though we have trained with most of the dataset for natural images. The reinforcement part of the algorithm makes it work for fundus images also. In the training phase the algorithm will train itself on training data and generate model file automatically.

11.6 FUTURE SCOPE

Medical image denoising is comparatively very useful area, and there are still many works in that domain. In this work, we have used image restoration to remove blur and image enhancement to enhance image. In future work, we need to explore hardware. Fundus lens itself has to modify and get a clear image.

REFERENCES

[1] Yamashita, R., Nishio, M., Do, R.K.G. Convolutional neural networks: An overview and application in radiology. *Insights Imaging* 9, 611–629 (2018). https://doi.org/10.1007/s13244-018-0639-9

[2] Wang, Y., Wang, G., Chen, C. Multi-scale dilated convolution of convolutional neural network for image denoising. *Multimedia Tools Applications* 78, 19945–19960 (2019). https://doi.org/10.1007/s11042-019-7377-y

[3] Thanh, L.T., Thanh, D.N.H. Medical images denoising method based on total variation regularization and anscombe transform. In *2019 19th international symposium on communications and information technologies (ISCIT)*, 2019, pp. 26–30. https://doi.org/10.1109/ISCIT.2019.8905207

[4] Jifara, W., Jiang, F., Rho, S. Medical image denoising using convolutional neural network: A residual learning approach. *The Journal of Supercomputing* 75, 704–718 (2019). https://doi.org/10.1007/s11227-017-2080-0

[5] Zhang, L., Zhao, D., Xu, D., Lu, D. A neural network based low-light image denoising method. In *2017 3rd IEEE international conference on computer and communications (ICCC)*, 2017, pp. 1868–1872. https://doi.org/10.1109/CompComm.2017.8322862

[6] Yang, Q., Jung, C., Fu, Q., Song, H. Low light image denoising based on Poisson noise model and weighted TV regularization. In *2018 25th IEEE international conference on image processing (ICIP)*, 2018, pp. 3199–3203. https://doi.org/10.1109/ICIP.2018.8451840

[7] Li, L., Wang, R., Wang, W., Gao, W. A low-light image enhancement method for both denoising and contrast enlarging. In *2015 IEEE international conference on image processing (ICIP)*, 2015, pp. 3730–3734. https://doi.org/10.1109/ICIP.2015.7351501

[8] Anilet Bala, A., Aruna Priya, P., Maik, V. Retinal image enhancement using curvelet based sigmoid mapping of histogram equalization. *Journal of Physics: Conference Series* (1964). Advances in Computational Electronics and Communication Engineering.

[9] Erwin, E. Improved image quality retinal fundus with contrast limited adaptive histogram equalization and filter variation. In *2019 international conference on informatics, multimedia, cyber and information system (ICIMCIS)*, October 24–25, 2019, Jakarta.

[10] Ervin, E. Improving retinal image quality using the contrast stretching, histogram equalization and CLAHE methods with median filters. *International Journal of Image, Graphics and Signal Processing*, April 2020.

[11] El-Hag, N.A., Sedik, A., El-Shafai, W., El-Hoseny, H., Khalaf, A.A.M., El-Fishawy, A.S., Al-Nuaimy, W., Abd El-Samie, F.E., El-Banby, G.M. Classification of retinal images based on convolutional neural network. *Microscopy Research and Technique* 84(3), 394–414 (2021). https://doi.org/10.1002/jemt.23596. Epub December 22, 2020.

[12] Das, A., Giri, R., Chourasia , G., Bala, A.A. Classification of retinal diseases using transfer learning approach. In *2019 international conference on communication and electronics systems (ICCES)*, 2019, pp. 2080–2084. https://doi.org/10.1109/ICCES45898.2019.9002415

[13] Gayathri, S., Ponnusami, P., Gopi, V.P. Alightweight CNN for diabetic retinopathy classification from fundus images. *Biomedical Signal Processing and Control* 6(7), 102115 (2020). https://doi.org/10.1016/j.bspc.2020.102115

[14] Chen, C., Chuah , J.H., Ali, R. Retinal vessel segmentation in fundus images using convolutional neural network. In *2021 international conference on high performance big data and intelligent systems (HPBD&IS)*, 2021, pp. 261–265. https://doi.org/10.1109/HPBDIS53214.2021.9658459

[15] Shaban, M., Oğur, Z., Mahmoud, A., Switala, A.E. A convolutional neural network for the screening and staging of diabetic retinopathy, June 2020.

[16] Shrestha, S. Image denoising using new adaptive based median filters. *Signal Image Process* 5(4), 1–13 (2014).

[17] Hegde, N., Krishna, S., Manvi, S.S. Diabetic retinopathy diagnosis system based on artificial intelligence. In *Human-machine interface technology advancements and applications*, 2023, pp. 213–230. CRC Press.

[18] Fundus Image Database. http://cecas.clemson.edu/?ahoover/stare/

[19] Fundus Image Dataset. https://www.kaggle.com/datasets/iamachal/fundus-image-dataset

[20] DRIVE Training Set. https://datasets.activeloop.ai/docs/ml/datasets/drive-dataset/

12 An Application of Improved Support Vector Machine Classifier for the Study of Breast Cancer Detection

Jayapandian Natarajan, Ann Marry, Huda Yasmin, Jessica Eldo, Sivaraman Eswaran, Nilima Zade, and Krishna Kumar P R

12.1 INTRODUCTION

Cancer is known to be one of the most challenging diseases to treat, identify, or detect. Advancements in artificial intelligence (AI) and machine learning (ML) have the potential to significantly enhance cancer diagnosis and detection [1]. These techniques can greatly improve predictive accuracy in medical applications [2]. This makes the study of AI and ML a vast field open to discoveries and research. Breast cancer involves irregular growth in breast tissue and remains one of the most common diseases impacting women [3]. It is known to be a leading cause of the large number of cancer-related deaths among women. According to the World Health Organisation, in the year 2020 alone, breast cancer caused approximately 658,000 deaths globally [4]. When breast cells undergo mutation there are chances where the cell growth becomes uncontrollable, which might lead to the formation of tumours, which is breast cancer [5]. There is the possibility of uncontrollably growing breast cells resulting in mutations, which could cause tumours to form and lead to breast cancer. Figure 12.1 illustrates a foundational classification model for breast cancer detection using machine learning algorithms. According to the figure, the image database is fed as input. The image undergoes processing that leads to feature extraction. Depending on the provided features, the classifier is trained to detect if the cells are malignant or benign. If the cells turn out to be benign, they are classified as non-cancerous cells, else they are cancerous cells. These are the malignant cells that also invade the nearby cells and spread rapidly, which can be life threatening. The existing breast cancer detection methods include mammography, ultrasound, MRI, biopsy, and fine needle aspiration [6]. Success rates of predicting the correct results using mammography are 87%, 85%–100% for biopsy, and 60%–96% for fine

DOI: 10.1201/9781003473442-12

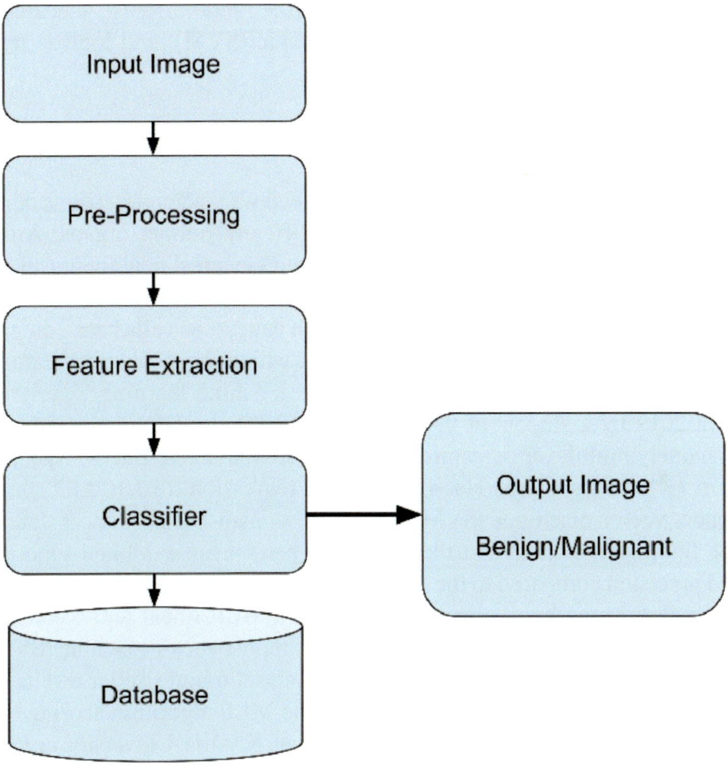

FIGURE 12.1 Classification model for cancer detection.

needle aspiration. Each method is overly complex in its own way. Biopsy is a costly technique, though effective, and fine needle aspiration includes extracting cells from the lumps for further diagnosis.

This allows learning with or without the assistance of human beings. Machine learning methods are applicable for diagnosing and detecting cancer [7]. This could help predict malignant and benign cells effectively. Each component in Figure 12.1 is vital for the proper functioning of the algorithm. The model includes the input, preprocessing, feature extraction, classifier, and then the output. The input segment includes the breast cancer dataset, which are images that undergo diagnosis. For example, the Breast Cancer Wisconsin dataset is a widely used dataset for breast cancer-related research purposes [8]. The same is being used for this research chapter. The dataset images are processed, which involves cleaning the data to eliminate the noise, and the attributes of the image are extracted, which are used to train the classifiers. A classifier is constructed, which plays a key role in detecting the cancerous cell. These include various machine learning algorithms, which includes support vector machine, k-nearest neighbors, naïve Bayes, decision tree, random forest, and others commonly used for these purposes. They are responsible for automatically ordering or categorising the data into one or more sets of classes. This chapter aims to compare five distinct ML algorithms like random forest, k-nearest neighbor (KNN), decision tree, support vector machine (SVM), and logistic regression applied to the Wisconsin Breast Cancer dataset.

12.2 LITERATURE REVIEW

Several researchers have undertaken analyses, reviews, and comparisons of machine learning algorithms for detecting cancer in different human organs. Among the widely studied algorithms for this purpose are the k-nearest neighbours and support vector machine. A study conducted by researchers at MIT, Chennai in 2009 found that SVMs could efficiently classify images with cancerous cells based on grey level information of images after enhancement, after which morphological features were extracted. The comparative study of nonlinear machine learning algorithms conducted in 2019 by a student at the University of Toledo, US, compared five algorithms, namely multilayer perceptron (MLP), Gaussian naïve Bayes (NB), k-nearest neighbors (KNN) algorithm, classification and regression trees (CART), as well as the support vector machines (SVM) on the Wisconsin Breast Cancer dataset. The research findings indicated that the multilayer perceptron exhibited superior accuracy and precision compared to the other algorithms studied [9]. Yet another comparison of six algorithms, consisting of GRU-SVM 4, MLP, linear regression, SoftMax regression, nearest neighbor (NN) search, and support vector machine (SVM), also based on Wisconsin Diagnostic Breast Cancer dataset found similar results, with all algorithms showing above 90% accuracy and the MLP algorithm scoring a 99.04% accuracy rate. Studies conducted by professors at Khalifa University in UAE, and MIT in the United States, comparing SVMs, random forests, and Bayesian networks showed that SVMs had a higher accuracy among the three, but RFs had the highest probability of correct tumour classification. Similar tests were conducted on the detection of lung cancer using genetic optimisation, SVM, and KNN algorithms using preprocessed CT scan images as well as MRI and ultrasound images. The studies used pixel segmentation on the images and extracted features from them to identify cancerous growth. The SVM algorithm managed to significantly reduce false positives and classify the cancerous cells correctly by training models based on the data [10]. A study conducted at a university in Ethiopia employed a grid search to observe the optimal hyperparameter concerning the KNN for cancer detection [11]. The research concluded that the performance of the KNN algorithm improved from 90.1% to 94.35% depending on the hyperparameter or K value chosen for grid search. A similar report conducted and used the genetic algorithm to improve the classification performance of KNN and succeeded in reducing its computation time. Overall, SVMs and MLPs showed the most accurate results and successfully classified and segmented images with high accuracy [12–13].

12.3 PROBLEM STATEMENT

There exist two main types of breast cancers: benign and malignant. Benign tumours generally do not proliferate to other parts of the body and rarely ever invade nearby cells and tissues [14]. They mostly do not grow back and can be removed through suitable chemotherapy procedures or surgery. Conversely, malignant tumours are considered life threatening because they often invade nearby cells and tissues [15], spreading to other parts of the body and potentially leading to chronic cancer and even death. Breast cancer comprises a diverse group of diseases, each with unique subtypes and specific molecular characteristics [16]. This complexity has resulted in challenges in developing effective treatments for each subtype. Other factors that contribute to the difficulty in treating breast cancer include drug resistance, patient requirements, and retention. Despite ongoing research, there is still a lack of predictive biomarkers that can accurately predict the progression of the disease, making it difficult to provide targeted treatments for individual patients. Millions of people are affected by breast cancer. It is a dreadful issue that has been the subject of countless research and discussions on how to spread awareness among women about its risks and effects. Research in this area is crucial for improving early detection methods, understanding risk factors, and developing effective treatment options. Early diagnosis increases the chances of successful treatment and reduces the need for aggressive interventions [17], while prevention strategies developed through research can help reduce the incidence of the disease. The importance of research in this field extends beyond its immediate implications for patients and has wider implications for society and scientific progress [18]. By alleviating human suffering, enhancing healthcare efficiency, and contributing to the broader body of scientific knowledge, research on breast cancer can benefit both the scientific community and society at large [19]. Breast cancer is regarded as the most common type of cancer among women in urban areas and the second most common in rural regions [20]. Unfortunately, most cases are detected at an advanced stage because of the lack of awareness about the disease and limited access to breast cancer screening programs [21]. Therefore, it is essential to create new methods for early detection of breast cancer. Our goal is to implement innovative methods that can help detect breast cancer in its preliminary stages. Our experiment aims to identify a reliable algorithm for detecting breast cancer. To accomplish this, we have used five machine learning algorithms and assessed and compared the results to identify the model with the highest accuracy. The discoveries of this study may have practical indications for clinical practices and public health policies and improve cancer detection technology [22]. It is crucial to further investigate these algorithms and how they can be used to identify breast cancer early to improve results for affected individuals.

12.4 PROPOSED BREAST CANCER DETECTION

Detecting the presence of malignant or benign cells in a provided dataset using machine learning algorithms. The research chapter utilises the Wisconsin Breast Cancer Diagnostic (WBCD) dataset as its sample data. Dr. Wolberg and colleagues gathered this dataset at the University of Wisconsin hospitals. Over a three-year period, data was gathered on a regular basis. The dataset is available on the Kaggle website. There are 699 cases in all. It has several characteristics that aid in differentiating between benign and malignant cells. For each cell nucleus, 10 real valued features are calculated.

1. The average distance from the centre of the nucleus to its boundary, the radius.
2. The variability of pixel intensity within the nucleus, the texture.
3. The total length around the boundary of the nucleus, the perimeter.
4. The total space enclosed within the nucleus boundary, the area.
5. The measure of how smooth or irregular the nucleus boundaries, smoothness.
6. A ratio calculated as (perimeter squared divided by the area minus 1.0), known as compactness.
7. The extent to which the nucleus boundary curves inward, concavity.
8. The concave points are the count of inward curving segments along the nucleus boundary.

The data was split into two classes: benign (458 instances) and malignant (241 instances) based on the commonalities between the occurrences. Subsequently, the raw data undergoes processing to remove noise and enhance the precision of manufacturing. Additionally, this lessens data inconsistency and redundancy. Classification is applied to the data following preprocessing. Various machine learning methods could be applied to this. Machine learning algorithms can be categorised into supervised and unsupervised learning approaches. Whereas unsupervised data has no preset objectives or datasets, supervised learning uses a collection of data to train the machine. Supervised learning is the most recommended strategy for the categorisation process. Through training with a specific dataset, the computer acquires knowledge and generates predictions based on the models derived from this data. Machine learning has shown to be significant in a few real-world applications. For instance, in the domains of social networks, speech recognition, medical expert systems, agriculture, finance, etc. Classification is a branch of machine learning; as previously said, supervised learning gains knowledge from the examples given to it and from its historical observations. As the name suggests, the method's main focus is categorising the incoming data into certain, preexisting classes. Three distinct machine learning algorithms used to classify the Wisconsin cancer dataset are the KNN, the DT, and the SVM.

12.4.1 Support Vector Machine (SVM)

A support vector machine is a machine learning algorithm used to address challenges connected to regression and classification by using supervised max margins together with related learning. Often shortened to SVMs, these models find use in numerous fields including signal processing, picture and speech recognition, and natural language processing. Using a kernel approach, SVMs efficiently carry out regression analysis and classification. The SVM algorithm's main objective is to identify the best hyperplane in any dimensional space such as 1D and 2D, which allows data points to be significantly divided into distinct object classes. The hyperplane is configured in such a way that there is as much space as feasible on either side of the hyperplane, while considered with the closest points of various classes. The number of features being focused on determines the dimension. For example, the hyperplane would only be a line for two features. The hyperplane would be a 2D plane for three features and so on. Hard margins and soft margins are the two types of margins that are used for hyperplanes. A hard margin or maximum margin hyperplane is a hyperplane that is nearly midway between two classes that are as far apart as feasible. The requirement that the data be easily distinct and linearly separable applies represented using Equation 12.1. For all training samples (x_i, y_i), this can be asserted as minimizing weight $\|w\|$ with respect to

$$y_i\left(w^T \ x_i + b\right) \geq 1 \tag{12.1}$$

where, w^T is the weight vector, x_i is a data point, and b is the bias.

A soft margin is applied to lessen the severity of the margin requirement when outliers make it difficult for the data to be separated.

This permits some misclassification, which is offset by a penalty term that represents the expense of permitting data points to be on the incorrect side of the boundary. Minimising weight as given in Equation 12.2

$$\|w\| + C\sum \xi_i \tag{12.2}$$

where ξ_i is the degree of misclassification for each data point and C is the misclassification rate A parameter for regularisation margin maximisation and penalty for misclassification are balanced by C.

Larger values of C will cause it to act like a hard margin SVM; lesser values result in softer margin SVMs, which are more flexible and allow for more misclassifications. SVM employs a kernel trick when the data cannot be separated linearly. To make it easier to locate the hyperplane, it implicitly divides the initial input data points into high-dimensional feature spaces. It stays away from explicit mapping for decision boundaries or nonlinear functions. Sigmoid, linear, polynomial, and radial basis functions are examples of frequently used kernel functions. Computation is simpler when the kernel is written as a feature map which satisfies the function as in Equation 12.3.

$$k\left(x, x'\right) = \langle \varphi\left(x\right), \varphi\left(x'\right)\rangle \upsilon. \tag{12.3}$$

SVMs are widely used in many different applications, including geosounding, seismic liquefaction potential, general data classification, facial recognition and biometrics, handwriting recognition, surface texture classification, speech recognition, steganography detection, and the topic of this chapter, cancer detection. This is because SVMs can classify unknown data into distinct categories based on unique features. SVMs can be trained to detect and discriminate between malignant and normal cells using a variety of imaging techniques using supervised learning approaches. Machine learning techniques could be used by AI models to eliminate false positives, classify benign or malignant cancer growth, and forecast the level of harm from cancerous growth. This could assist an early diagnosis of cancer and aid doctors to diagnose the appropriate cancer type and course of treatment. Figure 12.2 represents the block diagram of SVM overall classification process, and the respective algorithm steps are given in Figure 12.3.

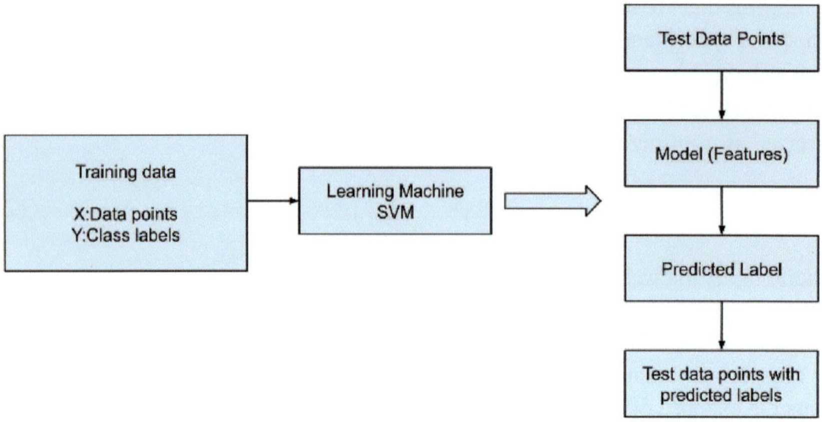

FIGURE 12.2 SVM label prediction and classification process.

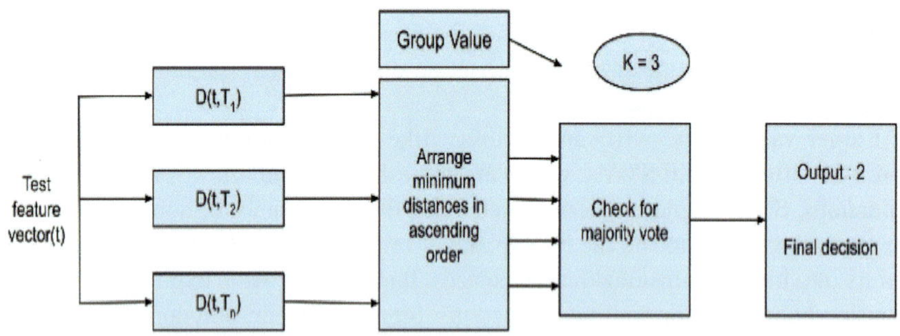

FIGURE 12.3 Algorithm steps for SVM classification, considered in proposed study.

12.4.2 K-Nearest Neighbours Algorithm (KNN)

This is a supervised learning technique that classifies input according to the categorisation of its neighbours. Since the KNN algorithm uses distance as its basis for classification, two points are more similar the closer they are to one another. The Euclidean and Manhattan methods are two distinct ways to find the distance between two places. A new point's properties are labelled according to the points that are adjacent to it, or its neighbours. The KNN algorithm is one of the popular machine learning algorithm, and the algorithm steps are given in Table 12.1.

Prior to classification, the new element is placed in the category where the majority of the shared features occur by comparing its similarity measure to that of the neighbouring K elements. K, the total number of neighbours in this algorithm, is a positive integer. This number is calculated using the formula for Euclidean distance.

$$d=\sqrt{\left[(x2-x1)^2+(y2-y1)^2\right]} \tag{12.4}$$

TABLE 12.1
KNN classification algorithm steps applied in proposed study

Proposed Algorithm Steps: K-Nearest Neighbours

Step 1: Start

Step 2:

1. Determine the value of 'K': Choose the number of nearest neighbours (K) to consider._
2. Calculate distances: Calculate the distance between the new data point and all other data points in the dataset using a chosen distance metric (e.g., Euclidean distance).
3. Select the K-Nearest Neighbours: Identify the 'K' data points that are closest to the new data point based on the calculated distances.
4. Assign the new data point to the class that is most frequent among its 'K' nearest neighbours (majority voting).

Step 3: Stop.

KNN algorithm is a non-parameterised algorithm, it does not make assumptions based on existing data.

12.4.3 Decision Tree Learning

This algorithm constitutes a supervised learning machine learning method suitable for both classification and regression tasks that constructs a tree structured model. It is capable of handling complex data, serving as the foundation for ensemble methods in machine learning. It accommodates both numerical and categorical data, making decisions based on features or attributes to arrive at predictions or outcomes. Known for their intuitive nature and interpretability, these models are highly favoured across diverse fields like data mining, pattern recognition, and decision support systems. In addition, it can be applied to cancer detection, leveraging their ability to make decisions based on features or attributes. They can be integrated into a more comprehensive approach to cancer detection and combined with other machine learning techniques or clinical assessments for greater accuracy. In our binary class classification problem, we applied the ID3 algorithm to develop a decision tree. The decision tree algorithm follows the algorithm here:

1. Select the most informative feature among the input attributes and designate it as the root node of the tree.
2. Divide the training dataset into smaller groups according to the values of the selected attribute.
3. Continue through each subset iteratively, repeating steps 1 and 2 recursively until leaf nodes are formed at the terminal ends of each branch within the tree structure.

When employing the decision tree algorithm for classification, the entire input training dataset serves as the starting point. The depth of the decision tree algorithm is crucial in classification tasks; higher depths may lead to overfitting issues. The size of tree corresponds to the number of nodes it contains, and each node plays a role in binary classification.

12.4.4 Random Forest Algorithm

This is a supervised learning technique capable of being applicable to both classification and regression tasks. It follows the concept of ensemble learning, which enhances detection accuracy by giving it access to a variety of classifier samples. It contains several decision trees of different subtrees of a given dataset, which takes the average of all the results, thus improving prediction. Instead of utilising a single decision tree, it incorporates multiple decision trees to enhance decision-making accuracy, leading to more robust outcomes. Since the feature selection is based on randomness, it minimises the correlation between data obtained from different decision trees. Using the random forest algorithm has a lot of advantages, such as requiring less training time than other ML algorithms, predicting highly accurate outputs, and working well with large datasets. Accuracy in results is not affected much in cases of missing data. This algorithm is used to eliminate overfitting and biassing and ensure overall variance for precise prediction.

12.4.5 Logistic Regression

This statistical approach employs a logistic function to represent a binary dependent variable. By estimating the probability of an observation belonging to a particular class, it transforms linear regression into a classifier. Regularisation techniques like Ridge and LASSO are frequently used to prevent overfitting, with L2 regularisation applied in classification models. The regularisation term controls the growth of parameters, and the hyper parameter value "lambda" is discovered over cross-validation. If lambda is too high, it can cause underfitting, and if it is equal to 0, it results in no regularisation effect. Therefore, when choosing lambda, it is essential to balance the bias vs variance trade-off. Input data outlining features of tumour cells is fed into the model and then converted into a NumPy array. The trained model is assessed for its accuracy score on training and test datasets. The model is then used to predict the malignancy of a tumour. The logistic regression model can provide informed clinical decisions and precise predictions.

12.5 RESULTS AND DISCUSSION

After applying machine learning algorithms to the WBCD dataset, a comparison study is conducted based on each algorithm's accuracy, precision, recall, along with F-measure. Table 12.2 presents details of materials and methodology considered in prosed study. Accuracy is crucial to measure the correctness to foretell the prediction which is initially calculated by the proportion of properly classified samples (accurate positives and negatives) to the sum of instances. Precision measures the correctness of predictions by indicating the ratio of the true positives to the number of actual positives. Recall aims to assess how accurately the model can detect pertinent events. Lastly, the F-measure, a performance metric used to gauge model performance, merge precision, and recall yielding an assessment for the considered algorithms' effectiveness. Table 12.3 gives results of performance measure using DT, SVM, KNN, LR, and RFA. In which LR achieves highest precision of 99.4% and using SVM with 98.26% of recall rate, F-measure of 98.2% and accuracy of 98.27%.

TABLE 12.2
Experimental Setup for Classification Breast Cancer Images

Component	Details
Dataset	WBCD Dataset
Dataset Source	Kaggle
Total Instances	699
Classes	Benign (458 instances), Malignant (241 instances)
Algorithms Compared	SVM, KNN, DT, RFA, LR
Training/Testing Split	70% training, 30% testing
Evaluation Metrics	Accuracy, Precision, Recall, F-measure
Preprocessing Steps	Data cleaning, noise reduction, feature extraction

TABLE 12.3
Results of Performance Measure (%)

Classifier	Precision	Recall	F-Measure	Accuracy
Decision Tree	95.07	95.23	95.15	94.28
Support Vector Machine	98.15	98.26	98.2	98.27
K-Nearest Neighbour	97.16	97.34	97.25	97.25
Logistic Regression	99.4	96.4	92.98	97.63
Random Forest Algorithm	96.9	94	95	96.5

Figure 12.4 shows the accuracy level of proposed and existing methodologies where x label 1, 2, 3, 4 and 5 signifies DT, RFA, LR, SVM and KNN, respectively. Figure 12.4 is plotted to analyse various datasets and also comparing the accuracy level. The experimental result demonstrates DT with 94.28% at the same time RFA with 96.5% overall accuracy. Next highest agrees level using KNN and LR algorithms with 97%. Finally, using the proposed SVM algorithm achieves 98.27% of overall accuracy.

Figure 12.5 deliberates the precision level of different machine learning algorithms, where the x label 1, 2, 3, 4, and 5 indicates DT, SVM, KNN, LR, and RFA, respectively. This experiment using DT and RFA is providing almost similar value of precision that is 95% and 96%, respectively. In this case SVM provides 98.15% and KNN with 97%. In this study the precision level of LR is 99.4%. Figure 12.6 deliberates the recall level of different machine learning algorithms, where the x label 1,2,3,4, and 5 indicates DT, SVM, KNN, LR, and RFA, respectively. This experiment using the decision tree (DT) and random forest algorithm (RFA) provides almost similar value that is 95% and 96%. In this case support vector machine (SVM) achieves 98.26% and the k-nearest neighbour (KNN) algorithm provides 97% result and logistic regression (LR) with 96.4% of recall rate.

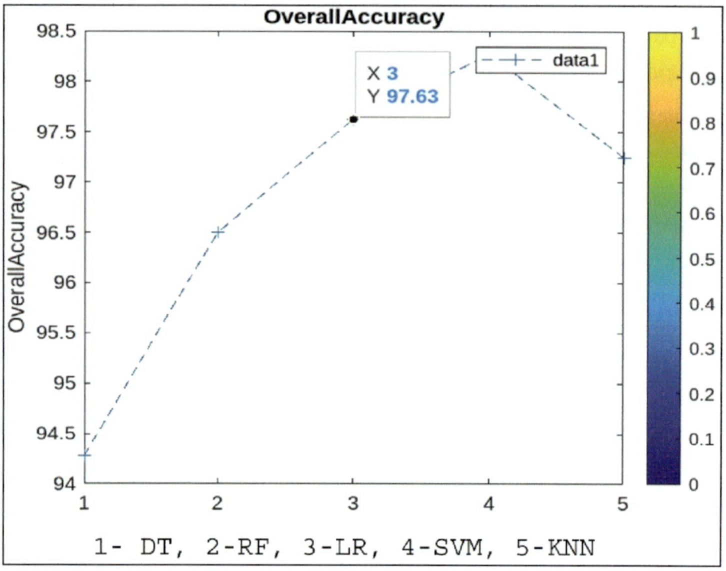

FIGURE 12.4 Accuracy level comparison.

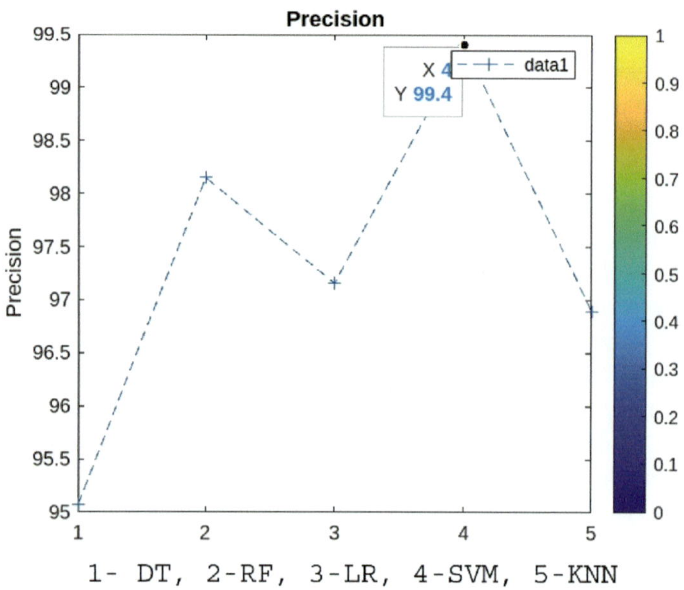

FIGURE 12.5 Precision level comparison.

Figure 12.7 shows the F-measure of different machine learning algorithms, where the x label 1,2,3,4, and 5 indicates DT, SVM, KNN, LR, and RFA, respectively. In this experiment DT and RFA provide an almost similar value that is 95% and SVM with 98.2% and the KNN algorithm provides 97.25%. In this F-measure of LR, the classifier is 92%.

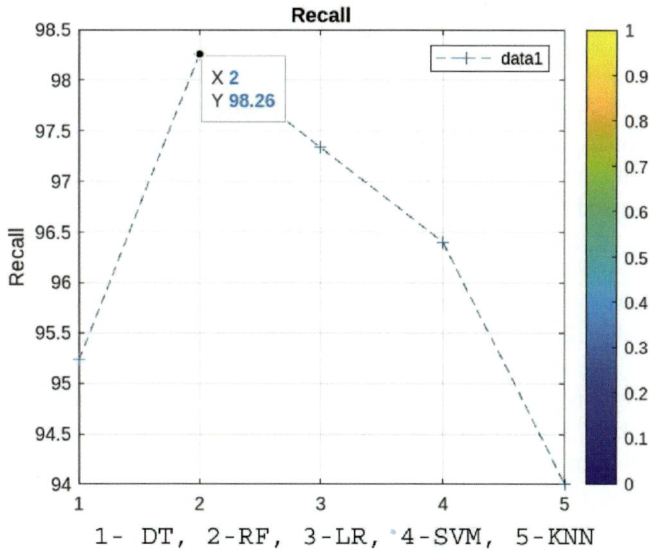

FIGURE 12.6 Recall level comparison.

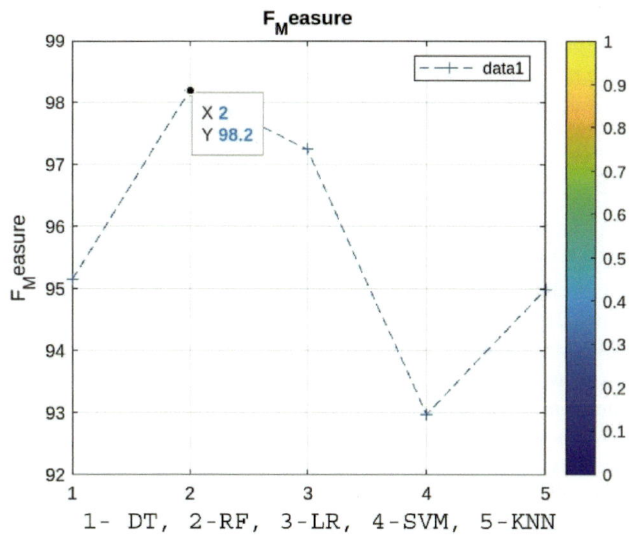

FIGURE 12.7 F-measure comparison.

12.6 CONCLUSION

The proposed study provides valuable insights for efficient detection of breast cancer using the WBCD dataset and ML algorithms. The findings of our study reveal that SVM achieved the highest overall accuracy at 98.27%, surpassing the other algorithms in predictive performance. KNN also demonstrated strong performance, achieving an accuracy of 97.25%. The simplicity and effectiveness of KNN in classifying tumours based on their nearest neighbours make it a practical tool for initial diagnostic screenings. Logistic regression (LR), with the accuracy of 97.63%, shows its strength in handling binary classification problems, providing clear and interpretable results that are crucial in a clinical setting. The RFA, with the accuracy of 96.50%, is proved to provide effective due to its ensemble learning approach, which mitigates the risks of overfitting and bias. Decision trees, while achieving a lower accuracy of 94.28%, still offer significant interpretability and ease of implementation, making them useful for decision support systems in health care. Our comparative analysis highlights the importance of selecting the most applicable and most effective machine learning algorithms particularly for the requirements of diagnosing tasks. While SVM emerged as the most accurate algorithm in this study, other algorithms like KNN and RFA also showed promising results, indicating that they can be valuable in different diagnostic scenarios. Future research should focus on further refining these algorithms and exploring their applicability to other types of cancer and medical conditions. Additionally, combining multiple algorithms and leveraging ensemble learning techniques could potentially yield even higher accuracy and robustness in diagnostic applications. In conclusion, the utilisation of machine learning algorithms for detecting breast cancer holds immense promise. Superior achievement of SVM, along with strengths of KNN, LR, RFA, and DT, demonstrates the potential of these technologies to enhance diagnostic accuracy and rapid detection of breast cancer. Continued advancements in machine learning and their application in medical diagnostics will undoubtedly contribute to better healthcare outcomes and improved quality of life for patients worldwide.

REFERENCES

[1] Iqbal, M. J., Javed, Z., Sadia, H., Qureshi, I. A., Irshad, A., Ahmed, R., Malik, K., Raza, S., Abbas, A., Pezzani, R., & Sharifi-Rad, J. Clinical applications of artificial intelligence and machine learning in cancer diagnosis: Looking into the future. Cancer Cell International, 21(1), 270. (2021)

[2] Shehab, M., Abualigah, L., Shambour, Q., Abu Hashem, M. A., Shambour, M. K. Y., Alsalibi, A. I., & Gandomi, A. H. Machine learning in medical applications: A review of state of the art methods. Computers in Biology and Medicine, 145, 105458. (2022)

[3] Feng, Y., Spezia, M., Huang, S., Yuan, C., Zeng, Z., Zhang, L., Ji, X., Liu, W., Huang, B., Luo, W., Liu, B., & Ren, G. Breast cancer development and progression: Risk factors, cancer stem cells, signaling pathways, genomics, and molecular pathogenesis. Genes & Diseases, 5(2), 77–106. (2018)

[4] Osouli Tabrizi, S., Mehdizadeh, A., Naghdi, M., Sanaat, Z., Vahed, N., & Farshbaf Khalili, A. The effectiveness of omega 3 fatty acids on health outcomes in women with breast cancer: A systematic review. Food Science & Nutrition, 11(8), 4355–4371. (2023)

[5] Kabel, A. M. Tumor markers of breast cancer: New prospectives. Journal of Oncological Sciences, 3(1), 5–11. (2017)

[6] Singh, R., Deo, S. V. S., Dhamija, E., Mathur, S., & Thulkar, S. To evaluate the accuracy of axillary staging using ultrasound and ultrasound guided fine needle aspiration cytology (USG-FNAC) in early breast cancer patients—A prospective study. Indian Journal of Surgical Oncology, 11, 726–734. (2020)

[7] Vicini, S., Bortolotto, C., Rengo, M., Ballerini, D., Bellini, D., Carbone, I., Preda, L., Laghi, A., Coppola, F., & Faggioni, L. A narrative review on current imaging applications of artificial intelligence and radiomics in oncology: Focus on the three most common cancers. La radiologia medica, 127(8), 819–836. (2022)

[8] Yedjou, C. G., Tchounwou, S. S., Aló, R. A., Elhag, R., Mochona, B., & Latinwo, L. Application of machine learning algorithms in breast cancer diagnosis and classification. International Journal of Science Academic Research, 2(1), 3081. (2021)

[9] Shamshirband, S., Esmaeilbeiki, F., Zarehaghi, D., Neyshabouri, M., Samadianfard, S., Ghorbani, M. A., Mosavi, A., Nabipour, N., & Chau, K. W. Comparative analysis of hybrid models of firefly optimization algorithm with support vector machines and multilayer perceptron for predicting soil temperature at different depths. Engineering Applications of Computational Fluid Mechanics, 14(1), 939–953. (2020)

[10] Kaur, P., Singh, G., & Kaur, P. Intellectual detection and validation of automated mammogram breast cancer images by multiclass SVM using deep learning classification. Informatics in Medicine Unlocked, 16, 100151. (2019)

[11] Belete, D. M., & Huchaiah, M. D. Grid search in hyperparameter optimization of machine learning models for prediction of HIV/AIDS test results. International Journal of Computers and Applications, 44(9), 875–886. (2022)

[12] Rajasree, P. M., Jatti, A., Santosh, D., Desai, U., & Krishnappa, V. D. Breast masses detection and segmentation in full-field digital mammograms using unified convolution neural network. In *2022 44th annual international conference of the IEEE engineering in medicine & biology society (EMBC)*, Glasgow, Scotland, United Kingdom, 2022, pp. 1002–1007.

[13] Desai, U., Kola, K. S., Nikhitha, S., Nithin, G., Raj, G. P., & Karthik, G. Comparison of machine learning and quantum machine learning for breast cancer detection. In *2024 international conference on smart systems for applications in electrical sciences (ICSSES)*, Tumakuru, India, 2024, pp. 1–6.

[14] Compton, C., & Compton, C. The nature and origins of cancer. cancer: The enemy from within: A comprehensive textbook of cancer's causes, complexities and consequences, 2020, pp. 1–23.

[15] Kozłowski, M., & Tarlaci, S. *Cancerous tumor life: Biological and physical aspects.* Sultan Tarlaci. (2023)

[16] Begg, C. B., Orlow, I., Zabor, E. C., Arora, A., Sharma, A., Seshan, V. E., & Bernstein, J. L. Identifying etiologically distinct sub types of cancer: A demonstration project involving breast cancer. Cancer Medicine, 4(9), 1432–1439. (2015)

[17] Bruix, J., Reig, M., & Sherman, M. Evidence based diagnosis, staging, and treatment of patients with hepatocellular carcinoma. Gastroenterology, 150(4), 835–853. (2016)

[18] Chapman, A. R. Towards an understanding of the right to enjoy the benefits of scientific progress and its applications. In Manisuli Ssenyonjo (ed.), *Economic, social and cultural rights* (pp. 375–410). Routledge. (2017)

[19] Evans, R. G., & Stoddart, G. L. Producing health, consuming health care. In *Why are some people healthy and others not?* (pp. 27–64). Routledge. (2017)

[20] Malvia, S., Bagadi, S. A., Dubey, U. S., & Saxena, S. Epidemiology of breast cancer in Indian women. Asia Pacific Journal of Clinical Oncology, 13(4), 289–295. (2017)

[21] Ginsburg, O., Yip, C. H., Brooks, A., Cabanes, A., Caleffi, M., Dunstan Yataco, J. A., & Anderson, B. O. Breast cancer early detection: A phased approach to implementation. Cancer, 126, 2379–2393. (2020)

[22] Mateo, J., Steuten, L., Aftimos, P., André, F., Davies, M., Garralda, E., Geissler, J., Husereau, D., Martinez-Lopez, I., Normanno, N., Reis-Filho, J. S., & Voest, E. Delivering precision oncology to patients with cancer. Nature Medicine, 28(4), 658–665. (2022)

Index

O

P

Q

R

S

T

U

V

W